WHEN THE CHURCH WOKE

WHEN THE CHURCH WOKE

William B. Lawrence

CASCADE *Books* • Eugene, Oregon

WHEN THE CHURCH WOKE

Copyright © 2022 William B. Lawrence. All rights reserved. Except for brief quotations in critical publications or reviews, no part of this book may be reproduced in any manner without prior written permission from the publisher. Write: Permissions, Wipf and Stock Publishers, 199 W. 8th Ave., Suite 3, Eugene, OR 97401.

Cascade Books
An Imprint of Wipf and Stock Publishers
199 W. 8th Ave., Suite 3
Eugene, OR 97401

www.wipfandstock.com

PAPERBACK ISBN: 978-1-6667-3541-3
HARDCOVER ISBN: 978-1-6667-9246-1
EBOOK ISBN: 978-1-6667-9247-8

Cataloguing-in-Publication data:

Names: Lawrence, William B. (William Benjamin), 1946-, author.

Title: When the church woke / William B. Lawrence.

Description: Eugene, OR : Cascade Books, 2022 | Includes bibliographical references and index.

Identifiers: ISBN 978-1-6667-3541-3 (paperback) | ISBN 978-1-6667-9246-1 (hardcover) | ISBN 978-1-6667-9247-8 (ebook)

Subjects: LCSH: Anti-racism—Religious aspects—Christianity. | United Methodist Church (U.S.)—History. | Race relations—Religious aspects—Christianity. | Racism—Religious aspects—Christianity. | Race—Religious aspects—Christianity. | Church renewal—United Methodist Church (U.S.).

Classification: BT734.2 .L36 2022 (paperback) | BT734.2 .L36 (ebook)

Scripture taken from the Common English Bible®, CEB® Copyright © 2010, 2011 by Common English Bible.™ Used by permission. All rights reserved worldwide. The "CEB" and "Common English Bible" trademarks are registered in the United States Patent and Trademark Office by Common English Bible. Use of either trademark requires the permission of Common English Bible.

VERSION NUMBER 101922

... you know what time it is
... wake up from your sleep.

—Romans 13:11
Common English Bible

Contents

Acknowledgments | ix
Preface | xi

INTRODUCTION
  On Not Being Ashamed of the Gospel | 1

PART ONE: When the Church Stirred but Never Quite Woke

CHAPTER ONE
  A Cascade of Crises | 13

CHAPTER TWO
  Religion and Religious Freedom in America | 26

CHAPTER THREE
  The Founding Generation | 41

CHAPTER FOUR
  From Founding a Church to Forming Separated Methodism | 58

CHAPTER FIVE
  Divided in Church and Society | 75

CHAPTER SIX
  Beneath the Cross of Jesus | 87

PART TWO: When the Future Woke the Church

CHAPTER SEVEN
  A Matter of Mission | 105

CHAPTER EIGHT
  The 8:46 Lectionary | 121

CHAPTER NINE
Miraculous Gifts and Messianic Commissions
for a Messy World | 135

CHAPTER TEN
When the Future Builds the Church | 146

CHAPTER ELEVEN
Sacred Treasure | 160

CHAPTER TWELVE
Creating the Church of the Future | 173

POSTSCRIPT
Beyond Algernon's Flowers | 184

Bibliography | 187
Index | 195

Acknowledgments

Neither this book nor any other contribution of mine to the world would have occurred without the partnership, friendship, and love that my wife, Naomi, and I have shared for more than five decades. Since our wedding on May 24, 1969, we have moved a dozen times, experienced itinerant careers in tiny towns and huge cities, brought two children into the world, watched five grandchildren grow in the world, and rediscovered together many times that love is patient and kind, as the ancient hymn in the apostle's letter says. Her patience is essential to my life.

For this project, I acknowledge with profound gratitude a great number of individuals whose help and wisdom have come in many forms and who are too numerous to name. But they include Kathy Armistead (who first proposed the idea that eventually became this book), Evelyn Parker (whose conversations with me about the meaning of a church that "woke" encouraged my thinking), and S T Kimbrough (who offered recommendations about its publication). In addition, I am grateful to individuals who have assisted with locating resources: namely Jane Elder, Henry Stokes, Lauren Grego, and Emily Shank, in particular. And I appreciate immensely the work of my editor, Charlie Collier, copyeditor Caleb Shupe, and the team at Wipf & Stock.

Finally, I pause to give thanks for many in the community of saints, who no longer draw breath on the earth but who still inspire with their spirit. They include my parents, who sacrificed so much for the principles of democracy in the nation, for the practices of faith in the church, and for the possibilities of education beyond anything they ever personally experienced. And I honor the many mentors and teachers from whose guidance I have benefited through the years as they fulfilled their vocations in ministerial and scholarly endeavors, including Bard Thompson (the finest teacher among the many outstanding ones under whom I studied) and James K.

Mathews (the epitome of episcopal leadership among the many bishops with whom I have worked).

Preface

Anyone who casually observes Christianity, either from within it or outside of it, could think that the church is vexed by sex. Roman Catholics restrict their leaders' roles by gender, demand celibacy for clergy, and have tried to settle criminal and civil complaints about sexual assaults that they suppressed. Founders of successful religious institutions, like Bill Hybels and the late Ravi Zacharias, have had their reputations wrecked by independently verified allegations of sexual misconduct. Southern Baptist pastors and leaders of other independent congregations have evaded accountability for sexual abuse simply by relocating to other churches. Lutherans, Episcopalians, and Presbyterians have endured denominational division driven by differences over homosexuality. United Methodists, who have condemned and tried to ban sexual practices outside of monogamous heterosexual marriage, now seem on the verge of schism over sex.

Yet, if that is the topic hitting the headlines, it is not the most serious problem facing the church. There is an issue that has bedeviled Christianity almost as long as it has been present in America. Within Methodism specifically it runs deep, and it is inseparable from the American context in which United Methodism came to exist. It has been called "America's original sin."[1]

The problem is racist White superiority. Schisms will not settle it, though many have happened. Church laws cannot eradicate it, even if they try. Ritualized confessions cannot end it unless they are embodied in acts of repentance, reparation, and reconciliation.

This racist complex with its sense of White superiority has festered for four hundred years in America. It has lived for two hundred fifty years in American Methodism. It is so embedded in the structures and systems of the church that it seems ordinary.

---

1. Wallis, *America's Original Sin*.

It is insidious and subtle. It has been expressed in violence and in passive aggressiveness. It has been built into church practices. Its existence has been denied. Its demise has been falsely claimed. Its end has been dreamed, only to have the dream deferred. Its power has been shown to be politically effective. It infects religious circles and invades the soul of the American church.

When I was a district superintendent in the United Methodist Church, one of my roles was to facilitate the bishop's appointments of pastors to places of ministry. Methodist pastors are not called, contracted, or hired. They are sent by an appointing bishop after being approved by an annual conference. Appointment processes are complicated. One part of the process is a district superintendent's introduction of the bishop's intended appointee to members of the pastor-parish relations committee for a charge. Unless a pastoral objection to the appointment is raised by the pastor or the committee, the appointment is made.

On a spring evening thirty years ago, I met with the pastor-parish relations committee for two northeastern Pennsylvania congregations (a "two-point charge" in Methodist jargon). We reviewed the prospective pastor's resume, and I said she was ready to be introduced. There were no objections. The committee members, like members of both congregations, were unanimously White. I told them that the person to be appointed as their pastor was Black.

I invited her into the room. A deep silence filled the space.

One committee member said they had no problem with the pastor's race. Another said that having a Black pastor would not be an issue, adding, "When I was a child, we always had a Black maid." The pastor-to-be broke the tension with the truth. She said, as I recall, *I will be the one who takes your grandbabies and baptizes them. I will be the one who holds your hand as I pray with you in the hospital before your surgery. I will be the one who preaches to you on Sunday and represents you in the community on other days. Will you be comfortable with that?*

It was a confrontational question. And it was necessary to expose the racist undercurrent that controlled the room. Such questions and confrontations could lead to confession, correction, forgiveness, and reconciliation. But they require recognizing the truth and acting on it. Only if the church woke to the truth could the church be saved from the sin.

If, in the third decade of the twenty-first century, a schism over sexuality seems likely for American Methodists, it will be a tense and bitter business. But it will occur once and then it will be finished. Those who wish to banish homosexuality from the church will have a denomination with a polity to do so. Those who seek full inclusion of all persons, regardless of sexual identity, also will have a polity for doing so. It might end fifty years of fighting.

But the difficulties and divisions over race in American Methodism have been part of the church in America throughout its history. Those divisions have spawned multiple schisms, yet racism remains. Too little has been resolved about the problems of racial animosity and White supremacy. What endures is deeply rooted. It requires atonement.

Such things are hard to discuss and even harder to enact. But if the church woke, healing could happen by the power of the gospel.

William B. Lawrence
The First Sunday of Advent
November 28, 2021

INTRODUCTION

On Not Being Ashamed of the Gospel

The Gospel according to Romans

Many years ago, when someone asked me to cite my favorite passage in Scripture, I said, "Romans 1:16 . . . for I am not ashamed of the gospel." Sometime later, she sent me a gift. It was a framed needlepoint with the words from that text.

The apostle Paul wanted the church not to be ashamed of the gospel. However, is the gospel ashamed of the church? Examples from the modern era point to an unsettling answer.

In the sixteenth century, Martin Luther insisted that the gospel had been imprisoned by the sacramental system of the church, which was in the thrall of political and profitable priorities in Europe. He expressed his view in "The Babylonian Captivity of the Church."[1] Within a week after its publication, the church issued a decree condemning him. Within a year, he stood before the emperor and was judged to be a heretical outlaw. He fled into hiding as a fugitive.

The church woke. Its awakening became actions collectively called the Reformation that were a watershed for renewing Christian life. But it also caused church strife. It was five hundred years, in fact, before Protestants and Catholics reconciled differences over Luther's teaching on a fundamental theological principle that was the basis of his critique of church practices.[2]

---

1. Luther, "Babylonian Captivity of the Church."
2. The Lutheran World Federation (lutheranworld.org), the Roman Catholic

In the seventeenth century, women in colonial Massachusetts were accused of victimizing men with "horrid" deeds and of being "hellish" persons, as Puritan preacher Cotton Mather put it. One of those accused was Mary Webster. She was tried, convicted, and hanged, based on a church leader's allegation. But, after hanging from a rope on a tree overnight, she survived.[3]

The church woke. The epidemic of fear abated. By 1700, the executions stopped. Yet dozens of people died as the result of actions the church initiated or tolerated. And it took three hundred years for Massachusetts to exonerate the innocent victims.[4]

In the eighteenth century, with the Church of England at the center of political, cultural, and educational institutions in England, an Anglican priest and Lincoln College fellow at Oxford named John Wesley preached at St. Mary's Church in Oxford. He said that the leaders of the city and church failed their mission. Calling them "triflers with God," he cited Psalm 119:126, saying it is time for God to do something.[5] Wesley was never permitted in that pulpit again. The vice chancellor of the university, objecting to his August 1744 sermon, banned him.

But the church woke. Wesley's Methodist movement flourished as a force for renewal.

In the nineteenth century, Methodism grew in America, but only men were allowed to lead it. Women were excluded from pastoral ministries. Methodists, who split into northern and southern denominations over slavery, united to stop women from preaching in Methodist pulpits. In 1830, the church tried Sally Thompson of New York on charges that she was sowing discord and behaving immorally because she dared to preach. Although she was acquitted, her detractors appealed, and she was dismissed from membership in the Methodist Episcopal Church.[6]

The church woke. Women and men sounded alarms. Phoebe Palmer preached and taught the Bible. Frances Willard was a Methodist educator and force for social change. But it took over a hundred years for the

---

Church (ewtn.com), *Joint Declaration on the Doctrine of Justification*, 1999. In ensuing years, the document was also adopted by the World Methodist Council and others.

3. Martin, introduction to *The Handmaid's Tale*, vii–viii. Webster's family fled Massachusetts for Canada. One member of her extended family is Margaret Atwood, the author of *The Handmaid's Tale*.

4. See Sudborough, "Mass. Senate."

5. Wesley, "Scriptural Christianity," 1:179. Wesley's translation of the text from Psalm 119 is, "It is time for thee, O Lord, to lay to thine hand!" The *Common English Bible* translation is, "It is time for the Lord to do something!"

6. Richey et al., *Methodist Experience in America*, 2:218–24.

Methodist Church to grant women clergy equality. It took still longer for the United Methodist Church to elect women as bishops.

In the twentieth century, with Christian institutions as the dominant religious influences at mid-century and with the church at the center of segregated social and political systems in the nation, the long and violent history of racist practices in America reached a turning point. The Supreme Court in 1954 reversed a ruling issued in 1896 regarding school segregation. But the church, an exemplar of racial segregation, seemed ambivalent about addressing it.

In January 1963, eight White religious leaders in Alabama published "An Appeal for Law and Order and Common Sense." It was explicitly directed at "southerners" who were upset "that a series of court decisions will soon bring about desegregation of certain schools and colleges in Alabama." It implied, without condemning racial injustices or White supremacy, that segregated ways of life may be changing. It urged opponents of integration, including those in the church, "to pursue their convictions in the courts . . . and to abide by the decisions of those same courts."[7]

The signers of the statement—seven church bishops and pastors, and one rabbi—issued a second statement three months later. It expressed gratitude for the "forbearance" that responsible citizens of Alabama exhibited. But it also expressed dismay that "we are now confronted by a series of demonstrations by some of our Negro citizens directed and led in part by outsiders." It closed by urging "our own Negro community to withdraw support from these demonstrations."[8]

Among the eight who signed both documents were the two Methodist bishops assigned to annual conferences in the state of Alabama. Their appeals came in the context of developments in the civil rights movement and in reactions to them. In December 1955, the bus boycott began in Montgomery, Alabama. In 1956, "lay defenders of segregation were the most powerful group within Alabama Methodism."[9]

The church woke in response to the second statement. Written on Good Friday and then published in both Birmingham newspapers on Holy Saturday, it prompted an inmate housed in the Birmingham city jail to issue a "Letter from Birmingham Jail" two days after Easter. In his twenty-one-page letter, Dr. Martin Luther King Jr. called the signers of the statements "men of genuine good will" and said their criticisms were "sincerely set

---

7. See the "White Minister's Law," paras. 3, 12. The two Methodist bishops who signed were Nolan B. Harmon and Paul Hardin Jr.

8. See "The White Minister's Law," 2.

9. Nicholas, *Go and Be Reconciled*, 25.

forth."[10] But he added that he, too, was a southerner rather than an outsider, that he was "in Birmingham because injustice is here," and that he was doing what the eighth-century prophets and the apostle Paul did.[11] He wrote that the White religious authors of the statements, including the bishops, "have never felt the stinging darts of segregation" and yet are demanding that Black people wait for justice.[12] He expressed a hope that they "can understand our legitimate and unavoidable impatience."[13] He quoted another bishop of the church, Saint Augustine, saying, "An unjust law is no law at all."[14]

Dr. King started writing this prophecy with a pencil in the margins of a newspaper. He spoke with a voice that woke the church. Five years after he wrote from that jail and only a few weeks after he was murdered for saying such things, the United Methodist Church chose to end its constitutionally segregated church government. Yet, United Methodists have not desegregated their local churches or brought racial justice to the land. Nearly sixty years after Dr. King wrote to religious leaders, including Methodist bishops, the gospel is still ashamed of the church.

Of all the difficulties facing the church today, none has been as pervasive or enduring as the matters of racial division. Church practices defer confronting racism, White supremacy, and congregational segregation. They are evidence of a failure to address its sin. The apostle Paul, in his Letter to the Romans, implored the church not to be ashamed of the gospel. But the gospel is surely ashamed of the church to which it gave rise.

Paul's writings lack a narrative of Jesus' life but offer the substance of his gospel, which is a matter both of knowing and of acting. To know the faith and to live the faith are one single message. Paul says in Rom 13:8–9 that love is our entire obligation. He summarizes God's word by saying, "Love your neighbor as yourself." From his perspective, love is Christianity's ultimate doctrine and discipline, as his Corinthian correspondence shows.

His Letter to the Romans is a doctrinal textbook. Any list of the theological items it covers cites most of the deeply debated issues in the history of the church. Among the topics Romans discusses are the relationships between Jews and Christians, the meaning of baptism, the nature of prayer, Christianity's views of civil governments, the dangers of divisive teachings, and the power of Christ over death. Romans touches tough topics because the gospel confronts difficult matters. They are not just important. They are

---

10. King, "Letter from Birmingham Jail," 85.
11. King, "Letter from Birmingham Jail," 86.
12. King, "Letter from Birmingham Jail," 91.
13. King, "Letter from Birmingham Jail," 92.
14. King, "Letter from Birmingham Jail," 93.

On Not Being Ashamed of the Gospel

matters of death and life. Knowing and acting should not be delayed or deferred if the gospel is to be unashamed of the church.

Time for Waking from Sleep

Paul alarms the church by saying that it is "time to wake from sleep." In Rom 13:11, his summons comes through two distinctive Greek words.

He says now is the "time" using the word καιρόν (KAIRON). It refers not to a moment in history, or a sequence of events in chronological order, or a quantity measured by clocks and calendars. It refers to a quality that fills chronological time with opportunities because promises are present, hopes are poised to be put into practice, truth can be known, and love can be shared.

He tells us to wake from "sleep" using the word ὕπνου (HYPNO). In the very few New Testament passages where this word appears, it means more than a night's rest or a day's nap.[15] It offers a platform for an encounter with the sacred.

This rare word is used to describe what Joseph was doing when an angel visited him in Matt 1:24. It is the word used to proclaim life defeating death in Jesus' raising of Lazarus in John 11:13. It is the word used regarding spiritual revival in Acts 20:9, when Eutychus fell three floors to an apparent death. But rather than dying, Eutychus woke. And so did the church.

The word is the root of the English word "hypnosis," a form of focused concentration so intense it can appear that the hypnotized person is deeply asleep. But, instead of dozing, anyone undergoing hypnosis grows acutely aware of hidden things, like cloaked memories or clouded mysteries that hold otherwise inaccessible truths.

In biblical passages where the word appears, awakening from ὕπνου (HYPNO) means being free to act based on truth revealed. When Joseph woke from meeting an angel, he was free to act as a husband, to live with the pregnant Mary as his wife, and to parent her child. When Lazarus woke from four entombed days and was unbound, he was free to go.[16] When Eutychus woke where he fell, his awakening set the whole church—not only Eutychus—free for mission.[17] When the church woke, its actions are liberating and transformational.

Paul's concise summary of the gospel—to love a neighbor as oneself—is more than an ethic. It is an arousing alarm, demanding actions that show

---

15. Besides Rom 13:11, see Matt 1:24; John 11:13; and Acts 20:9.
16. John 11:44.
17. Acts 20:10–12.

the difference between death and life. As N. T. Wright noted, ὕπνου (HYP-NO) echoes the mystery of Easter.[18] To awaken in καιρόν (KAIRON) from ὕπνου (HYPNO) is to practice powerful, perfect love through resurrection.

The gospel, of which the church should be unashamed, is a matter of knowing and acting. Its gift of salvation is the substantive grace that empowers the church to know and to act. This is good news for the world, which is in crisis, and for the church, which is also in critical condition.

In the third decade of the twenty-first century, a cascade of crises has caused dangerous, debilitating difficulties for the devout. Churches quit assembling, and their empty buildings fell strangely silent. Their organizational systems seemed stymied by the challenges.

But "sleep" sets a stage for a new awakening. Voices from the street are heard saying, "Black Lives Matter." Media spread words and images that confuse truth with falsehood. It is time for the church to wake from sleep, to affirm the truth we know, and to take action.

On Being Awakened in America

This book seeks to address that urgency with a refreshed look at the role of religion in America, giving specific attention to the Methodist sectors of the Christian community. It is an effort to convey what the church must know about its purpose and history, about its waking and being set free for action. It is an attempt to affirm power that is available in the holy mysteries of love for healing and hope without being ashamed of the gospel. It endeavors to speak of things that Christians, and specifically American Methodists, either do not know or prefer not to know about the church. In addition, it is a qualitative look at religion in America with a deeper probe of American Methodism to see the crises of the present as the time to know the good news and to act upon it.

Whether we can find enough chronological time on clocks or calendars to be unashamed of the gospel is irrelevant. God's time has found us. The gospel is ashamed of the church. It is now time for us to wake from sleep.

This book is only one step in what will require long strides. But the situation is critical. Sacred power is present. Sacred promises are at hand, ready to be claimed. The message of the gospel is urgently needed now. The world and the church are caught in overlapping crises. It is time to demonstrate that we are not ashamed of the gospel. It is time the church woke.

---

18. Wright, "Letter to the Romans," 9:628.

A sense of awakening has been an important facet of America's religious history. During the eighteenth century, a "Great Awakening" featured itinerant evangelists who drew big crowds, spiritual disciplines that shaped small groups, and physical tics that affected worshipers' bodies. During the nineteenth century, a "Second Great Awakening" invented emotional techniques like a "mourner's bench" and altar calls to manipulate spirituality. New religions, like Seventh Day Adventists and Latter-Day Saints, formed. Others revived with expressions of holiness that had both individual and social dimensions. The church woke as a resource for abolishing slavery, and anti-slavery believers used the underground railroad or other abolitionist strategies for action.

The metaphor of awakening fit not only spiritual life but also cultural and political life in nineteenth-century America. During the 1860 presidential election campaign, young Republicans formed the "Wide Awakes" who yearned for an end to slavery and supported Abraham Lincoln's election to achieve it. Their rallies "created a circus atmosphere" with marches, fireworks, and wild cheers. In response, some supporters of Democratic nominee Stephen A. Douglas, calling themselves "Choloroformers [sic]," said they intended to put the "Wide Awakes" to sleep.[19]

In the twentieth and twenty-first centuries, the concept of awakening gained a new term, when African American musicians, novelists, playwrights, social activists, and others turned the expression of what happened when someone awoke into a single syllable "woke." A character in Barry Beckham's 1972 play *Garvey Lives!* says that after Marcus Garvey[20] woke him, he would "stay woke." Soul singer Erykah Badu popularized the word in "Master Teacher" in 2008 with its repetitive "I stay woke." In 2017, "woke" was added to the *Oxford English Dictionary*.[21]

The word "woke" became a lightning rod. As a term of art that emerged among Black Americans, its growing popularity acquired racialized overtones. Some advocates of "Black Lives Matter" celebrated being "woke," yet questioned its use by people outside of the Black community. Some adversaries of "Black Lives Matter" launched "woke wars." They tapped into racist stereotypes for political gain and offered a clear warning to Whites that being "woke" was contrary to their interests.[22] Thus, "woke" symbolized the depth of racism.

19. Goodwin, *Team of Rivals*, 268.

20. Marcus Garvey (1887–1940) established the Universal Negro Improvement Association (UNIA) in New York in 1914. Garvey believed that the systems of racial separation made racial conflicts inevitable.

21. See "New Words List June 2017."

22. See Tharoor, "U.S. and British Right."

The term became a dividing line in religious circles. As Southern Baptists prepared for their June 2021 Convention, leaders of one faction warned of the need to "wage war" against a "new moralism" and against "critical race theory," which "is one of these destructive heresies that have snuck in." An organizer said the convention needed "not an influx of the woke" but "an influx of the awakened to what the woke have been advancing."[23] For these mostly White Baptists, it was spiritually divine to be "awakened" but spiritually dangerous to be "woke."

On Being "Woke" Theologically

For a one-syllable, four-letter word, "woke" is well-traveled. It began as a simple verb in the past tense of the indicative mood and was used in such ordinary constructions as "My mother woke me in time to get to school" or "The sound of the fire alarm woke me in the middle of the night." A brief entry in one standard dictionary merely defined "woke" as the past tense and past participle of wake.

Grammatically, it was a verb. But usage transformed it dramatically. Under the influence of artists and creative writers, it morphed from a participle into an adjective and appeared as a predicate adjective.

When it was added in 2017 to the *Oxford English Dictionary*, it was labeled an adjective whose original meaning was "well-informed, up-to-date," and whose current form is "alert to racial or social discrimination and injustice."

What began as a verb has become a verbal modifier of particular significance for African American artists specifically and in the Black community generally as an expression of cultural, social, political, and personal identity. It became a feature of Black conversation and communal life. But this visibility opened an opportunity for critics of the "Black Lives Matter" movement and opponents of other justice initiatives to use "woke" for their purposes.

Soon, racists' references, such as characterizations of "woke politicians," became a code. The adjective was mocked. And the word "woke" gained a connotation that people who marched under a "Black Lives Matter" banner or who affirmed the marchers' message were a threat.

So, the word began as a verb with no racial implications. It morphed into an adjective of racial identity. Then it morphed into an adjective of attentiveness to racial injustice. Then it morphed into an adjective that became

---

23. Graham and Dias, "With Southern Baptists in Revolt, a Split Looms."

a tool, or a weapon, that carried racist connotations, bigoted implications, and political designations.

These transformations of usage for a single-syllable, four-letter word pose challenges for its use on the printed pages of a book. In this volume, "woke" has returned to its original form as a verb in the indicative mood. Sometimes it appears in the past tense, at other times it appears in the present tense, and occasionally it appears in the future tense. That is like the way a Greek word in the aorist tense expresses a point in time that may be in the past, the present, or even perhaps the future.

The reader may find this a bit unsettling, particularly in a sentence that states, "When the church woke, it will . . ." The subjunctive mood, "If the church woke, it would. . . ." has a level of familiarity and comfort. But that is unsatisfactory for theological reasons.

An important dimension of this volume is its eschatological emphasis. The eschaton is not merely a moral option but a theological fact. The future is moving into the present and is revealing itself in the present. The eschaton arrives with an opportunity for Christian disciples' choices, but its arrival does not mean their choices will prevail. The eschaton arrives, even if we do not find it comfortable or do not deem it something we would prefer.

The indicative mood, future tense, is the form that is most consistent with thinking about eschatology. It allows one to write and to use "woke" as a verb while making a theological point. When the church "woke," it will act eschatologically, for it will be oriented to the future that is intruding into the present from the margins of our time and experience. As a verb pointing to the future, it says what "will" occur. When the church "woke," it will act in the manner that the risen Lord has revealed, because that is how heaven manifests itself on earth

To be woke can have many forms and carry multiple cultural connotations. In the church, it is time we woke from sleep—not just because current crises compel it, but because the gospel commands it. There is truth to be known, and there are actions to be taken. The mystery of God's grace reveals it, the discipline of faith requires it, and the time is right for it.

PART ONE

When the Church Stirred but Never Quite Woke

CHAPTER ONE

A Cascade of Crises

The Dawn of a Critical Decade

As the year 2020 began, crises threatened every continent. Africans were coping with Somali pirates on the east coast, Boko Haram further west, economic difficulties in the south, and threats in the north so frightening that people risked their lives on little boats to cross the Mediterranean and seek safety in Europe. Europeans were facing a rise of extreme right-wing political forces and a separation of the United Kingdom from the European Union by Brexit, which endangered stability. Asians in Hong Kong swarmed in streets, huddled in universities, and resisted threats to seize their economic, cultural, religious, and political liberty. In North America, in a presidential election year, the United States Senate conducted a trial that could potentially remove the president from office. In South America and Australia, fires raged. In Antarctica, temperatures rose, and ice melted. And climate changes warmed the entire globe.[1]

On Friday, January 3, 2020, these crises became more acute. The president of the United States was informed in his daily intelligence briefing about the dangers of a new coronavirus. On that same day, many news media reported that the United States had assassinated the top military leader of Iran at an international airport in Iraq. And about the same time as the assassination was revealed, United Methodists announced that their church would split into two denominations.

---

1. By 2020, the number of "extremely hot days" had doubled since 1980 (Dale and Stylianou, "Climate Change").

The breaking news about the church involved a "protocol." Drafted by sixteen people as a way to end disputes over homosexuality that divided United Methodism for decades, it plans a schism. Initially, reports about the protocol did not include details of the division, although they signaled that the denomination's global legislative assembly—General Conference—might agree to institutional separation at its meeting in Minneapolis in May 2020.[2]

But the General Conference did not meet in May 2020. By the end of February, the virus mentioned in the presidential intelligence briefing threatened the world. A newly named disease SARS-CoV-2 (COVID-19) went viral internationally. Organizations, institutions, and businesses curtailed their operations or closed. Schools, libraries, theaters, and restaurants shut down. Travel diminished. People aboard cruise ships were stranded at sea or in port. Sports at all levels, from international professional elites to amateur clubs, came to abrupt halts.

Places of prayer discontinued public gatherings. However, a few religious bodies in the United States—claiming they were essential—defied public health rules, rejected government regulations, and even sought constitutional relief in the civil courts. Some of them admitted that they needed to assemble merely to collect offerings, or they would fail financially.

Hospitals and health care professionals faced prospects of being overwhelmed by the numbers of patients needing care. When human and material resources for treating seriously ill people were too scarce to meet everyone's needs, medical personnel had to make awful ethical choices and dreadful decisions. Health care options were stark: "*Who Lives? Who Dies?*"[3]

Individuals and institutions faced moral crises. Political, commercial, educational, and religious leaders faced administrative challenges. Nearly everyone felt inadequate for the tasks.

Then another event created yet another crisis. On May 25—Memorial Day in the United States—a Minnesota police officer subdued an African American man named George Floyd by kneeling on his neck for eight minutes and forty-six seconds, causing his death. A bystander had recorded the incident on video, which showed the amount of time that the officer's knee pressed into Mr. Floyd's neck. The video went viral. The incident offered

---

2. The reports about the assassination and the "Protocol of Reconciliation and Grace through Separation" appeared on January 3, 2020, in the *Washington Post* and the *New York Times*, as well as in broadcast reports on CNN and NPR. CNN cited the President's Daily Brief in a report by Vivian Salama on October 1, 2020.

3. These questions formed the cover of the *New York Times Magazine* on May 3, 2020.

a lens through which to view other occasions when Black people died in police custody or from police weaponry.

For some, it was merely a tragic result of an act by an officer who violated proper police procedure, ending in the sad death of Mr. Floyd. For others, it was just the most recent event of many, when Black persons were victims of White authorities. A long history of Black suffering from White mobs or vigilantes who terrorized Black people and property was reawakened. The truth—suppressed by those who prefer historical ignorance of Wilmington, Colfax, Tulsa, and other communities—is that Blacks in America have perennially been victims of public violence.

The death of George Floyd crystallized outrage around the nation and the world. People gathered, marched, protested, and published the names of other Black victims of such brutality. They demanded respect for the message that "Black Lives Matter."

Then, on June 1, another incident created another crisis. Amid a "Black Lives Matter" march in the nation's capital, on a street between the White House and St. John's Episcopal Church, clergy and members of the parish were offering water and first aid to marchers in need. Approximately thirty minutes before a curfew took effect to end such public assemblies, federal authorities used military maneuvers and chemical agents to remove marchers from the street. Shortly afterward, the president of the United States and several leaders of his administration walked across the newly cleared street, onto the grounds of St. John's Episcopal Church.

There, the president stood beside the church bulletin board. He held a Bible aloft and had his picture taken. It was an event that symbolized a critical turn for religion in America.

The response to it from church leaders was fast and furious. The Episcopal Bishop of the Washington Diocese expressed outrage that church property was used without permission for a political photo opportunity, noting that St. John's—where every president since James Monroe has worshiped—has procedures for presidential visits, but that they were ignored. Others insisted that the president did not come to worship or pray, but to pose for a campaign picture.

Ecumenical Christian leaders joined a chorus of complaints.[4] The president of the Southern Baptist Convention said, "The Bible is a book we should hold only with fear and trembling."[5] The president of the denomina-

---

4. Bailey and Boorstein, "I Find It Baffling and Reprehensible."
5. Bailey and Boorstein, "I Find It Baffling and Reprehensible," para. 17.

tion's Religious Liberty and Ethics Commission said, "The Bible is the Word of the living God, and should be treated with reverence and awe."[6] He added,

> The murder of African-American citizens, who bear the image of God, is morally wrong. . . . Violence against others and destruction of others' property is morally wrong. Pelting people with rubber bullets and spraying them with tear gas for peacefully protesting is morally wrong.[7]

The Roman Catholic Archbishop of Washington, noting that the president planned the next day to visit the National Shrine that honors Saint Pope John Paul II, said he found it

> baffling and reprehensible that any Catholic facility would allow itself to be so egregiously misused and manipulated in a fashion that violates our religious principles, which call us to defend the rights of all people, even those with whom we might disagree.[8]

The executive director of the Franciscan Action Network condemned the decision by the Knights of Columbus, the Roman Catholic men's organization that is responsible for the Saint Pope John Paul II Shrine, for arranging the presidential visit. He said he felt

> disgusted that the Knights would allow the Shrine to St. John Paul II to be used for what is transparently a Trump reelection campaign event.[9]

A few days after the presidential photographs were taken on the grounds of St. John's Episcopal Church and at the Roman Catholic Shrine to St. John Paul II, the United Methodist Bishop of the Washington Area and the Episcopal Bishop of the Washington Diocese assembled with others to pray for the deliverance of the nation. In their prayers, they decried the abuse of sacred symbols in partisan acts.

Religious voices were not the only ones raised. The chairman of the Joint Chiefs of Staff, the highest-ranking officer of the nation's military, had been in the presidential entourage that walked to the grounds of St. John's Church for the photo opportunity. He expressed his regret for having done so, and he publicly apologized for his action.[10]

---

6. Bailey and Boorstein, "I Find It Baffling and Reprehensible," para. 19.
7. Bailey and Boorstein, "I Find It Baffling and Reprehensible," para. 20.
8. Bailey and Boorstein, "I Find It Baffling and Reprehensible," para. 3.
9. Bailey and Boorstein, "I Find It Baffling and Reprehensible," para. 33.
10. See Greve and Borger, "Top US Military General." Similar reports appeared in print (*New York Times*, *Washington Post*), in broadcast and televised new reports (CNN,

The incident was a lot more than merely another event in an expanding number of crises in America. It showed how religious groups in general, and churches in particular, are entangled with national issues. The church, beset by parochial crises, also participates in public crises.

America's Distinctive Approach to Religion

Religion has a unique place in American society. Constitutionally, the United States has established a clear separation between the religious practices of Americans and the systems of government by which the people order the national political life. Article VI of the Constitution says that "no religious Test shall ever be required as a Qualification to any Office or public Trust under the United States." The first item in the Bill of Rights bars Congress from enacting any "law respecting an establishment of religion, or prohibiting the free exercise thereof."[11]

So, religions and their organizations have a separate status in America's constitutional system. Yet, religion was woven into America's social fabric and political systems before the nation was created. It was a key issue when the Constitution was crafted. It is a vital element in the nation's life. It is constitutionally distinguished from, but integral to, the nation's operations. This ambivalence appears in the nation's founding documents and in its formal rituals.

The Declaration of Independence affirms that human beings have basic rights, which are "unalienable" because the "Creator" granted those rights.[12] Most presidents and members of the Congress have taken their constitutionally required oaths of office[13] while placing a hand on a religious text, such as the Bible or the Qur'an. Political leaders often end speeches by asking God to bless America. Civil ceremonies usually include prayers of invocation and benediction offered by persons representing various religious

---

NPR), and on social media (*American Independent*) also on June 11, 2020. Because General Milley is a Princeton graduate, who had been a cadet in ROTC on campus, his apology also appeared in the *Daily Princetonian* on June 17, 2020.

11. To be precise, the prohibition is part of the First Amendment to the Constitution. Ten Amendments, after approval by Congress and ratified by three-fourths of the states, collectively became known as the Bill of Rights. The text of the Constitution is published by the American Civil Liberties Union in print and electronically and is available in the National Archives (see https://constitutioncenter.org/media/files/constitution.pdf).

12. National Archives (see https://www.archives.gov/founding-docs/declaration-transcript).

13. See Article VI of the Constitution of the United States of America (https://constitutioncenter.org/media/files/constitution.pdf).

traditions. Both the House of Representatives and the Senate in the United States Congress have chaplains, who begin daily sessions in their respective chambers with prayer. Most legislatures in the fifty states invite visiting clergy or other persons to pray at the opening of their assemblies. Many Christian houses of worship post the American flag inside their sanctuaries, and some also have the flag prominently displayed on the grounds outside their buildings.

Presidents and presidential candidates are expected to acknowledge their religious views and associations. When John F. Kennedy was a presidential candidate, he felt obliged to deliver a speech in Houston to explain how he (as a Roman Catholic) understood the relationship between his religious affiliation and his administration, should he be elected.[14] When Barack Obama was a candidate, he was so intensely pressured to justify the content of sermons by his Chicago pastor that he resigned from membership in the congregation.[15]

Americans link religion and the presidency. From Harry Truman to Barack Obama, every president met in the White House with Billy Graham, who was the most recognizable religious figure in the nation for sixty years.

Truman allowed Graham to pray for him in the White House. But he was so furious with Graham for discussing and demonstrating their prayer publicly that he declared Graham to be *persona non grata* in his administration.[16] Dwight Eisenhower decided to be a member of a Presbyterian church when he became president. But he was so angry when the congregation's pastor announced Eisenhower's plans to join that he advised the pastor to say nothing further about it or he would change his mind about joining.[17] Jimmy Carter, who taught Sunday School prior to his election and continued to do so while he was in the White House, distinguished such private religious activities from the public responsibilities of his office.

A justice of the Supreme Court may identify with a religion but not link a personal faith with public life. Harry Blackmun, who wrote the *Roe v. Wade* decision on abortion in 1973, was a United Methodist; but he did

---

14. On September 12, 1960, Kennedy addressed the Greater Houston Ministerial Association, which is an organization of Protestant clergy. Both the transcript and a recording of his speech were published by NPR on December 5, 2007 (see https://www.npr.org/templates/story/story.php?storyId=16920600).

15. See Powell, "Following Months of Criticism."

16. Raasch, "When Harry Met Billy."

17. Whitfield, *Culture of the Cold War*, 88. Eisenhower, who famously cussed like a soldier, used more colorful language—and characterized both the pastor and his congregation with more florid adjectives—when he ordered his staff to tell the clergyman to say nothing further about Eisenhower's religious beliefs or practices.

not write it based on his denominational position. Current justices are Catholic, Jewish, and Episcopalian but see their constitutional obligations as nonsectarian.

Members of Congress may cite their religious views and values in campaigns for office. Yet some are reticent about linking their personal religious beliefs as Jews, Mormons, Muslims, or Christians with their responsibilities in office, beyond citing some broad principles that might resonate with legislation. Still, others aggressively connect their spiritualities and their politics.

So, America's approach to religion is conflicted. The nation, with no established religion, functions politically as if it values religion. It has been a religious land with a "civil religion" that it adapted from Judeo-Christian traditions without doctrinal or disciplinary specificity.[18] America seems to combine being religious with simultaneously separating itself from religion.

American Religion as a Partisan Political Force

The photo taken at St. John's Church symbolized a shift in perspectives about religion in America. It demonstrated that religious matters have reached a point of crisis, at which a broadly balanced tolerance for religion is now being challenged by partisan piety. The politics of public policies on abortion have led to redefining "evangelical Christianity" as a voting bloc instead of as a Protestant theological perspective. The president, who used that bloc for his election, named an advisory panel of religious figures but limited the panel to those who favored him politically.

It crystallized what had been happening for a while. The president and the first lady had hosted a White House dinner in 2018 for a hundred religious leaders, who were invited because of their partisan support for him. Labeled "evangelicals" by secular news media, they tended to represent the political connotations of that term, not the theological ones.[19] Prior to the dinner, a select group of twelve met privately with the president. One said that rather than speaking "truth to power" they expressed "love to power."[20] Unlike Truman's attitude toward Billy Graham's public reenactment of their

---

18. See Bellah et al., *Good Society* and *Habits of the Heart*.

19. During and after the Reformation, the word "evangelical" was an ecclesiastical and theological term for Protestant Christians who emphasized the proclamation of the gospel or "good news," which translates the Greek word εὐαγγελίου (*evangel*) in Mark 1:1. During the late 1970s and continuing thereafter, at least in the American context, it became a term for an ideology that opposed abortion and homosexuality, while favoring certain laws and judicial appointments that represent such opposition.

20. Smith, "White House Hosts 100 Evangelicals," para. 11. See Thomas and Dobson, *Blinded by Might*.

prayer, the Trump administration publicly circulated photographs of religious leaders laying hands on him and praying for the president.[21] In a 2016 campaign event, Trump promised an audience of Christians in Iowa that, if he were elected, "Christianity will have power." Regarding the White House he said, "If I'm there, you're going to have plenty of power, you don't need anybody else."[22]

In his 2020 campaign, he said his opponent was a man who is "against God" and who will "hurt the Bible, hurt God."[23] Some religious leaders said Trump was chosen by God to be the agent of national deliverance, like the Persian leader Cyrus.[24] They felt his election to the presidency was an act of divine will, not a matter of his being personally devout.

Thus, the religious crisis in 2020 included a shift to considering religion as a partisan force, unlike anything seen since the temperance movement was a Protestant political wedge that culminated with the passage of Prohibition in 1919.[25] But vesting a president with divine favor and religious authority was a critical new element. It added to the cascading crises in 2020.

Religion in America was already a complex and conflicted matter by the time the events of 2020 entangled religious people and their institutions in broader crises. Photo opportunities at St. John's Church and at St. John Paul's Shrine added partisan political divisions to a church that was already divided by doctrine, discipline, denomination, and discrimination.

The events of 2020 created critical conditions with medical, moral, economic, spiritual, and educational dimensions. The crises for churches were not only that they had to close but also that they had to choose what to do and say amid the upheaval. Religious orders and institutions in America came to critical turning points. Christian leaders in the United Methodist Church had to decide what they could say to the world and how they could say it when their buildings were shuttered, their leaders were stymied, and

---

21. Jahi Chikwendiu, photo taken in September 2017, published in Bailey et al., "Trump Mocks."

22. Dias, "Christianity Will Have Power," para. 9.

23. Lemire, "Trump Claims Biden Opposes God," para. 3.

24. Block, "Is Trump Our Cyrus?" See Ezra 1:1–4.

25. The Eighteenth Amendment to the Constitution was ratified by the requisite number of states in January 1919, and it went into effect in January 1920. Among its religious ramifications was a distinction between "wets" and "drys" that took a sectarian turn in the 1928 presidential election between Al Smith (a Democrat and Roman Catholic characterized as a "wet") and Herbert Hoover (a Republican, who was the offspring of Quakers and was perceived to be a "dry"). Thirteen years later, in 1933, the Twenty-First Amendment to the Constitution was ratified and repealed Prohibition.

their members were struggling to stay safe. Sometimes the church seemed to say nothing.

Coping with Crises through Scripture and History

The Bible can help leaders know what to do or say. Its story of Esther tells of a woman who chose to aid her people in crisis by devising tactics to prevent their political destruction.[26] Its book of Amos says an upstart prophet, who was a shepherd and tree surgeon, rejected advice from a cleric named Amaziah, who told him to quit upsetting the king with criticisms. But Amos chose to speak the word of the Lord, whether the king wanted to hear it or not.[27]

The people who later assembled the books of the Bible knew the truth of history. So, they provided believers with the book of Amos, rather than a book by Amaziah. They included a story from the perspective of Esther, not from her antagonist Haman. Amid their crises, Amaziah and Haman never imagined that Amos or Esther could be causing godly trouble. The compilers of Scripture produced a Bible that celebrates prophetic courage to act as God's truth requires, not as worldly authority desires.

Christians have struggled with that. In the early history of the church, after centuries of periodic persecutions, Constantine made Christianity a legally tolerated religion in the Roman Empire by the Edict of Milan in 313. Decades later, a specific version of Christianity—the one expressed in the Nicene Creed—became the official religion of the empire by the collaborative political agreement known as the Edict of Thessalonica in 380. Thereby, Christians could count on the authority of the centralized state to enforce orthodoxy and punish heresy.

But, within fifteen years, the emperor who wrote the Edict of Thessalonica died. The centralized and dogmatically Christianized empire split apart. Advocates of alternative religious perspectives gained power. And the church faced living without the secure protections of civil authority.

Amid that crisis, the church woke. A bishop in North Africa named Augustine used his office to adjudicate claims for justice rather than force people to rely on the uncertainties of the corrupt civil courts.[28] He also wrote enduring theological works to teach the church how to fulfill its mission apart from the protections of worldly power.

---

26. Esth 5:6–8.
27. Amos 7:10–17.
28. See Brown, *Augustine of Hippo*.

In other crises, too, the church woke. Examples across centuries illustrate that.

In nineteenth-century America, a Black Methodist who had been enslaved in Maryland used his prodigious gifts for insight and for oratory to shape life after Emancipation. Frederick Douglass told stories of faith to help White people learn the truth about slavery and to help Black people discover the full meaning of freedom.[29]

In twentieth-century Africa, after nearly fifty years of a system called apartheid that had segregated races and brutalized Blacks, church leaders including a White Methodist named Peter Storey and a Black Anglican named Desmond Tutu recognized that the end of apartheid in South Africa was a moment of crisis requiring a religious response. A post-apartheid Commission on Truth and Reconciliation became a vital instrument not only for exposing truth about the horrors in the past but also for reconciling the races in new ways for the future.

Effective church leaders have vision to recognize a crisis, to see it as an occasion to tell truth, and to take awakened actions. Yet it is not always clear, when a moment of crisis comes, who the faithful leaders are, whose words should be heard, or whose ways should be heeded.

In eighteenth-century England, both the religious and political establishments felt stable and secure. But on Friday, August 24, 1744, on the Feast Day of St. Bartholomew, a forty-one-year-old Anglican priest used an Oxford pulpit (Great St. Mary's) to speak truth to power. John Wesley delivered a sermon titled "Scriptural Christianity."

Wesley took as his text Acts 4:31, "they were all filled with the Holy Ghost." He said that the church woke to life on the day of Pentecost and spread beyond that day. He imagined what it might mean to see "a Christian country upon the earth."[30] Then he turned his gaze upon the religious and civic leaders of the city and the university, whose seats of honor at the back of the nave were elevated. They were at his eye level when he asked from the pulpit:

> Is this a Christian city? Is Christianity, scriptural Christianity, found here? . . . Are all the thoughts of your hearts, all your temples and desires, suitable to your high calling? Are all your words like unto those which come out of the mouth of God? Is there in all your actions dignity and love?[31]

---

29. Blight, *Frederick Douglass*.
30. Wesley, "Scriptural Christianity," 1:173.
31. Wesley, "Scriptural Christianity," 1:174.

The founder of Methodism put his position in the university and his career in the ministry on the line as he challenged leaders of the academy, the community, and the church to recognize the nature of the crisis. He summoned city and university officials to be sensitive to the moment in which they were living. He delivered a word designed to awaken them from their institutional inertia and spiritual stupor. He challenged the authorities to assert their responsibilities for the Christian gospel of love.

After the service, the vice chancellor of the university demanded to see his sermon notes. It was clear that his message was unwelcome. Wesley was never invited or permitted to preach at St. Mary's again. But he woke a movement in the church.

The legacy of all Christians, including specifically Methodists, is to recognize in a crisis that an opportunity for renewal has come. Each critical turning point is a "time" to wake from "sleep," in the words of the apostle Paul. Viewing the cascading crises through such a lens is a way to hope that the church—when it wakes—will be unashamed of the gospel, and the gospel will be unashamed of the church.

A Method for Studying American Methodism

Such vision requires the methods of multiple disciplines to examine it carefully. That is certainly true for any focus on Methodism. The Wesleyan movement has distinctive theological emphases, and United Methodists use four sources and criteria for theological discernment. In "Our Theological Task," the church says a single authority or field of inquiry is insufficient for determining doctrine. "Wesley believed that the living core of the Christian faith was revealed in scripture, illumined by tradition, vivified in personal experience, and confirmed by reason."[32]

To examine Wesley's Methodist movement and the United Methodist Church within it, therefore, requires a comprehensive method. The methodology in this book includes Bible study, church history, systematic theology, and spiritual experience that has both individual and social dimensions. In addition, since Methodism in America is inseparable from the cultural, political, and economic developments that fashioned the church and the nation, one must see the church in its American context. The country and the connection[33] took shape in the same era. Each has had an impact upon

---

32. *The Book of Discipline of the United Methodist Church 2016*, ¶ 104 (80).

33. Wesley used the word "connection" (which he spelled "connexion") to define the polity of Methodism.

the other. For example, the schism of Methodism in 1844 over slavery was cited as part of the rationale for the secession of southern states.[34]

A multidisciplinary method more fully examines what happens when the church woke. There is evidence that the church woke in the past, stirred, yet failed to act. But when the church acts on what the gospel reveals, the church unashamedly fulfills its purpose as an eschatological agent of salvation. The mission on which the risen Christ sends the church to the world emerges in human life. Then the gospel lives, without being ashamed of the church.

A Matter of Knowing

Even simple things can become symbols to know the gospel's transforming power. The mysteries of heaven are revealed through ordinary events on earth, as the Bible bears witness.

In the Gospel of Luke, the Nativity narrative offers an example of such an awakening, and the church loves to tell it. In every Christmas pageant, as well as in every crèche on every lawn or mantel, is an image of a manger that was the crib for the Christ child. In displays and tableaux as well as in Christmas art—from classic to kitsch—the manger occupies a very special place.

As a physical object, of course, a manger was hardly a special thing. It was just a feeding trough for animals. It might be a niche in a wall, a plain place in a barn, or a pallet in a field.

But in some of the earliest words in the prophecy of Isaiah, it serves as a sign of spiritual ignorance. A donkey can find a manger that its owner provides, the prophet said, but the people of God cannot find the one who provides for them. Lacking that knowledge, they act ignorantly. Or, as one translation of the text in Isaiah puts it, "my people don't behave intelligently."[35]

The Nativity narrative in Luke seizes on that symbol and reverses it. In Isaiah, a manger signifies ignorance. In Luke, a manger signifies knowledge of God's presence in the world.

---

34. On March 4, 1850, Sen. John C. Calhoun's speech for delivery in the Senate cited the separations in Methodist and Baptist churches over slavery as indications that secession is possible and necessary. Calhoun wrote the speech but was too ill to deliver it, so Sen. James Mason of Virginia read it for him (see "John C. Calhoun's Speech").

35. Isa 1:3 CEB.

Lest the reader miss it, Luke repeats it three times. Mary gives birth and places her son in a manger.[36] Shepherds hear an angelic message about the birth of a Savior and learn that the sign to validate that message will be the baby in the manger.[37] With this knowledge, the shepherds go to Bethlehem, where they see the child in the manger.[38]

The manger thus becomes a symbol that ignorance is reversed by the knowledge that God reveals. The people of God can learn the truth of God, for God is present in the world.

A Matter of Acting

The shepherds woke from sleep, knowing what was revealed. And, according to Luke's narrative, they acted. Having learned from sources that were both mysterious (hearing the angel) and mundane (seeing the manger), the shepherds went public with their knowledge. They acted. They spoke openly about the end of their ignorance. Everyone who heard them was amazed.[39]

In Luke's imaginative telling, the shepherds become the first to report to the world what they know. Though they are never named or numbered, they are identified by their place in the social and economic order of the day. These shepherds are the least and the lowest in the labor market, and they lack any of the status that might be recognized by the religiously or politically established authorities. They lived not in homes but in fields. Their only credentials were what they had heard and seen. Yet none of those limitations inhibited them in amazing the world.

They acted. They are the prototype for Christians who take what we learn and turn it into a public witness. As key figures in this biblical version of Christ's coming, they are vital in the story of revealing what happens when believers woke. The manger is not a sign of their social location, economic condition, intellectual deprivation, or spiritual devastation. It signifies what they know, and it lures them to act. It is evidence of transformational hope.

That is what happens when the church woke. Ordinary time is filled with extraordinary promise. Mundane matters communicate mysterious meaning. Knowledge replaces ignorance and action transforms indifference. That the church woke is publicly amazing.

36. Luke 2:7.
37. Luke 2:12.
38. Luke 2:16.
39. Luke 2:17–18.

CHAPTER TWO

Religion and Religious Freedom in America

A Complicated Story

There is a classic way to tell the story of religion in America. But it is almost certainly wrong. It has too many errors and omissions. Yet that has never stopped people from telling it.

Americans have heard since elementary school about the Pilgrims who arrived in 1620 at Plymouth Rock, seeking religious freedom. These determined Pilgrims sought control over their own rules for worship and conduct, according to an account by Governor William Bradford, who used biblical imagery that made it into a sacred story.[1] It is a tale Americans love to tell.

The Pilgrims' saga of survival, despite danger and great suffering, is quite compelling. Five of the 102 passengers who were aboard the *Mayflower* died at sea. Illness claimed half of the settlers in the first winter. Still, these immigrants endured.

Their piety and persistence blends in Americans' popular imagination with the religious and political views of another sect of English immigrants who first arrived a decade later and in the following decades in much larger numbers, also settling in Massachusetts. Like the Pilgrims, these Puritans were ecclesiastical separatists who sought freedom to worship.

---

1. *A Relation or Journal of the Beginning and Proceedings of the English Plantation Settled in New England* (London, 1622). Bradford continued to write a journal of the colony until 1651.

John Winthrop, who led the first shipload of Puritans, delivered a sermon to his group aboard the *Arbella* in 1630 in which he told them that their adventure was both a civic and a sacred journey. They were experiencing a new Exodus, he said. They were bound in a covenant with one another and with God, like the one that the people received from the Lord in Scripture. They were going to build their spiritual and secular version of the "city upon a hill" that Jesus envisioned in his Sermon on the Mount.[2] But, unlike the Pilgrims, Puritans sought to impose their will on all, not just on themselves.

The Puritans' journey, as Winthrop told his shipboard congregation, involved "seeking great things for ourselves and our posterity." If they failed to fulfill their duties in this covenant, "the Lord will surely break out in wrath against us." In that spirit, the Puritans sought to settle their communities and to subdue their adversaries. Winthrop explained it this way:

> When God gives a special commission he looks to have it strictly observed in every article.... Thus stands the cause between God and us. We are entered into Covenant with Him for this work. We have taken out a commission. The Lord hath given us leave to draw our own articles.
>
> The Lord will be our God, and delight to dwell among us, as his own people, and will command a blessing upon us in all our ways. So that we shall see much more of his wisdom, power, goodness and truth, than formerly we have been acquainted with. We shall find that the God of Israel is among us, when ten of us shall be able to resist a thousand of our enemies; when he shall make us a praise and glory that men shall say of succeeding plantations, "the Lord make it likely that of *New England*." For we must consider that we shall be as a city upon a hill. The eyes of all people are upon us.[3]

Americans blend the Pilgrims, whose *Mayflower* landed in 1620, and the Puritans, whose first wave came on the *Arbella* in 1630, into one story that lets religiously and ethnically similar immigrants in the seventeenth century be the font from which religion in America flows. Thus, on Thanksgiving, Americans can recall their legacy of liberty as if it were a single saga of piety and politics, with gratitude for those who founded Americans' faith and freedom, granting it to the nascent nation. But the simplicity of this tale is part of its inaccuracy. It omits far too much.

---

2. Matt 5:14.

3. Winthrop, "Modell of Christian Charity," 46–47. The words quoted have been modified only to offer a modernized spelling of the original text. See also Hall, *Puritans in the New World*, 169.

First, there was plenty of religion in America before any immigrants landed. The First Peoples and the Native Nations, who lived in North America and were present when Europeans came, had many spiritually alert tribes, who respected the sky, the land, the water, and all the creatures that soared, ran, or swam in them. These people honored the creator and the creation through a variety of differing ceremonies and rituals.

Evidence of those religious practices as early as 1500 BCE has been found within burial mounds in the vicinity of the Great Lakes and in the lower Mississippi River valley. Agricultural, social, and religious activities—stretching from what is now Ohio to what is now Florida—can be traced to 500 BCE in the communities of the Adena and Hopewell peoples. The Mississippian tribes, including the Natchez people, who met Spanish and French immigrants and invaders, built temples and had cohorts of priests who led their religious rites.[4] Therefore, any recounting of America's religious history should include at least three thousand years of spiritual practices that occurred before the first Europeans came. And discussion of those centuries should acknowledge that much of the physical evidence of religion among hundreds of tribes of native peoples was either demolished or destroyed during displacements of the tribes after the Europeans arrived.

Second, adherents of other religious traditions came to the continent long before Pilgrims and Puritans brought their versions of Protestant Christianity. Roman Catholics landed in Florida more than a hundred years before the *Mayflower* reached Massachusetts. Roman Catholic Mass was celebrated in California in 1526, about a century before the Pilgrims came. Ten years before the Pilgrims settled in the northeast, Catholics built a church in Santa Fe in the southwest.

Also, not all who arrived in America from elsewhere were Christians. In 1528, almost a century before the *Mayflower* landed, a Moroccan Muslim reached the Texas coast—albeit not voluntarily, since he was a slave who had gone overboard and drifted ashore after surviving a shipwreck. In 1584, generations before the Pilgrims came, the first Jew settled on American soil.

If a story were to be told accurately about religious immigrants in American history, it would have to be an extremely long multi-faith saga.

Third, more than a year before the *Mayflower* arrived in Massachusetts, a ship called the *White Lion* arrived in Virginia. Aboard were more than twenty Africans, who had probably come from Ndongo (now called Angola). Their journey was far more harrowing than the troubles the Pilgrims faced. They were captives, who had been forced to march hundreds of miles to the port city of Luanda, where they were sold as slaves and shackled

---

4. See Edwards, "Mound Builders." See also Colavito, *Mound Builder Myth*, iii.

on the *San Juan Bautista*, a ship that Spain purchased from Japan a few years earlier. Whether they adhered to indigenous religions, to Catholic traditions that Portuguese missions brought to Central Africa, to Islam, or to apostolic Christian traditions that developed in Africa after the apostle Philip baptized an Ethiopian,[5] is unclear. In any case, they sailed to America on John the Baptist's namesake slave ship.

When the ship left Africa, it was carrying about 350 enslaved Africans and was headed to a market in Mexico. During the voyage, disease or deprivation claimed almost half of that human cargo. Then, as the *San Juan Bautista* approached Mexico, two English ships seized dozens of the Africans and turned north to Virginia. One of the attackers, the *White Lion*, carried the slaves to a port now called Hampton. Virginia's colonial governor and a merchant bought the captives and took their newly acquired property to Jamestown for resale at the slave market in 1619.

Pilgrims by Force Not Freedom

So, a year before the celebrated Pilgrims came to North America by choice in their search for religious freedom, Africans arrived in chains. They were sold as pieces of property, deprived of any political liberty, and denied any opportunity to exercise religious freedom. Whatever sort of spiritual identity or personal dignity they may have had in Ndongo had been stolen from them. They were marketed and managed like livestock.

But the arrival of the *White Lion* and the enslaved people aboard it in 1619 did not start the slave trading across the Atlantic to the Americas. A century earlier, King Charles I of Spain had authorized it in 1518, using power granted to his father in 1493 by Pope Alexander VI in decrees that divided the world between Spain and Portugal.[6]

King Charles I had inherited the Spanish monarchy at age sixteen, when his father died. Thereafter, as a political compromise between the

---

5. Acts 8:26–38. See McCaulley, *Reading while Black*, 98.

6. A member of the Borgia family, Pope Alexander VI had been elected to the papacy just a few months before Christopher Columbus reached North America for the first time in 1492. The political circumstance that surrounded his election included an eagerness on the part of the King of Spain to have good relations with the papacy. That led to a series of decisions, among which were a sequence of papal decrees (or bulls) on May 3 and 4, 1493, and a Treaty of Tordesillas, which Spain and Portugal ratified in 1494 and which divided the "new" world between them. The agreement lasted until other complicating factors, namely the rise of the Protestant Reformation on the continent of Europe and the emergence of England as a significant political and naval power, altered international perspectives about allowing a religious leader to divide the world between two countries.

French and Germans, the very young king of Spain acquired another title as Emperor Charles V of the Holy Roman Empire. So, the European slave trade began in 1518, under a license granted by a teenage monarch, based upon a religious edict to which he was heir. It was not his last entanglement with religion. Three years later, he presided over the proceedings against a Protestant preacher, Martin Luther, at the Imperial Diet.

Political and religious entanglements in continental Europe thus had direct and indirect connections to enslaving wars in Africa, commercial slave trading in the Americas, and early religious developments in North America. A century before any Protestant Pilgrims or Puritans reached the coast of Massachusetts, a Muslim who was enslaved by the Spanish explorer Cabeza da Vaca reached the coast of Texas. And a year before the *Mayflower* touched Plymouth Rock, the *White Lion* unloaded in Virginia its cargo of people whose religion is a cloudy mystery. The enslaved Africans on the *White Lion* possibly knew none of the European religious history that had abetted their enslavement. Nevertheless, their arrival in America meant they were losing their personal dignity, their political liberty, and their religious identity.

Religion in the American Colonial Context

So, the story of religion in America is an exceedingly complex one to tell. And it cannot be told apart from a variety of forces and factors that were shaping life in North America, locally and abroad, during the sixteenth century and thereafter.

The United States of America did not begin with one single event. The colonies declared independence from England in 1776. The country was first recognized by another head of state as an independent nation in 1777.[7] It did not seal its national status with a military victory until 1783. It solidified its governance with a Constitution in 1787. It inaugurated a president in 1789.

But its religious, economic, and social patterns had formed long before. They included buying and selling enslaved Africans, displacing (as well as occasionally enslaving) native tribes, seizing property without regard to the first peoples' prerogatives, and regulating religion in ways that ignored the spiritual heritage of the enslaved or the indigenous, who were deemed unworthy to be recognized for any religious purpose. Some religions were treated with indifference, others with ignorance, and still others with

---

7. The Muslim Sultan of Morocco was the first international head of state to recognize the independent status of the new nation called the United States of America.

intolerance. White immigrants assumed supremacy over the definitions of "faith" and "freedom" in America.

That made the story of religion in America a chronicle of domination. But within it were elements of diversity. From the colonizing period in the early 1500s to forming a new nation in the late 1700s, multiple types of religious life expressed themselves in America. The differences were manifest in styles of worship or liturgies, patterns of institutional order, languages used in rituals, systems of governance for operations, titles and selection methods for spiritual leaders, architectural features of gathering places, and points of view on how religious communities and institutions interacted with the larger society.

There was diversity among Christians. And there was multi-faith diversity, as well.

The Church of England was the religious preference of the English colonists who began Jamestown in 1607, leading the Virginians to adopt the Anglican Church with its parish system as the established religious pattern for colonial Virginia thereafter. Dutch Reformed Protestants, who made "New Amsterdam" (later "New York") their home in 1614, established their "classis" system of church polity and government. Another contingent of "reformed" Protestants arrived and established their first "presbytery" in Philadelphia in 1706. Sephardic Jews arrived in 1654, and the first synagogue was eventually built in New York in 1730. Pennsylvania was chartered as a colony in 1681 by William Penn, a Quaker who insisted on tolerance for all religions. The Maryland colony was chartered to a Roman Catholic named Calvert, who sought to provide a haven for Catholics. Heirs of the radical reformation brought other versions of community and separatism to America. The Amish, for example, reached Pennsylvania in 1760. They preferred disengagement from the broader social and political systems. But they were the exception.

Where the boundaries of religious and political establishments coincided, the powerful could impose their will. There were some dramatically disturbing persecutions, prosecutions, and executions of persons—most of them women—who were charged with engaging in witchcraft, sorcery, and uncouth occult behaviors in the 1680s and 1690s. The sacred and secular systems collaborated in Massachusetts, indicting people for spiritual offenses, trying them in civil courts, and inflicting judicial punishments on the convicted offenders.

Some spiritual developments crossed colonies' political boundaries and their religious establishments. One was the "Great Awakening" in the 1730s, a religious revival that involved profoundly emotional outbursts of weeping, shouting, falling, and other physical behaviors. That they were tolerated rather than outlawed may have been because they were led mainly by men.

The Entanglements of Religious Freedom in America

Although some colonial protections for religious liberty existed, not all religions were protected. In reality, not all religions were recognized. The institution of slavery suppressed any religion the Africans brought aboard the slave ships. Although the United States Constitution did show respect for religious rights of people, the enslaved were deemed not to be people. Further, the freedom of religion only applied to those covered by the Constitution, which Native peoples were not. They were deemed to be adversaries of those who wrote and ratified the Constitution. In fact, it was not until 1978 that the Congress passed, and President Jimmy Carter signed, the "American Indian Religious Freedom Act," which declares that it is

> the policy of the United States to protect and preserve for American Indians their inherent right of freedom to believe, express, and exercise the traditional religions of the American Indian, Eskimo, Aleut, and Native Hawaiians, including but not limited to access to sites, use and possession of sacred objects, and the freedom to worship through ceremonials and traditional rites.[8]

Religion has been a complicated aspect of the American story for a very long time. Even when religious liberty was constitutionally guaranteed, it did not assure spiritual liberty for all. And before religious rights were ever written into the Constitution, they had been compromised.

It was very difficult to disentangle religion from commercial and political forces, some of which were internal matters in English business, law, and politics. The Puritan venture in New England, which was officially known as the Massachusetts Bay Colony, was the initiative of the Massachusetts Bay Company, whose investors hoped to profit from their project. The religious vision to create the theocracy that John Winthrop defined and proclaimed was inseparable from the commercial venture that funded it. Whatever its pious principles may have been, profits and political priorities pervaded it.

Additional complications in the story of religion in America occurred as more and more colonizers arrived on North American shores. With the first year after the *Arbella* landed, many additional vessels had brought about a thousand more Puritans to Massachusetts. Among them

---

8. See 42 U.S.C. §1996. The law was amended in 1994 and 1996 further to protect religious ceremonies.

was a twenty-eight-year-old clergyman named Roger Williams, who had achieved recognition in England as a scholar and preacher. Indeed, John Winthrop considered him "a godly minister."[9] Williams, in fact, was such a thoroughgoing Puritan that his credentials could have compelled the Church of England to imprison him, if he had not found a home in New England.

And yet, within five years of his arrival, Williams acquired another reputation—not as a stalwart who supported the Puritan program but as an adversary who endangered it. He initially was offered a position at the Boston church. But he declined the post and went instead to be the preacher at the church in Salem. There, he began to proclaim his differences with the colonial authorities to such an extent that the leaders in charge of the Massachusetts Bay Colony found him much too troublesome. On October 6, 1635, the civil court in Massachusetts banished him from the colony and gave him six weeks to leave.

> Williams challenged both the government and the clergy . . .
> Nearly all other clergy in Massachusetts and most lay leaders believed he threatened the very vision that Winthrop had described. He threatened, they believed, the success of that city upon a hill. He threatened, they believed, God's vision.[10]

Williams had nowhere to go. Returning to England, which was the plan that the colonial authorities had in mind, was not an option. That would have separated him from his wife and children, who were not included in the order that banished him. Anyway, in England, he would be imprisoned. Quite possibly, he would be executed.

But he was an astute young man. He had made it his business to learn some of the native languages and to be familiar with Indian trails through the forests. Before colonial leaders could force him aboard a ship, he fled on foot and found refuge with a local tribe.[11]

After spending the winter in the company of native peoples who offered him sanctuary, Williams made his way southwest. During the summer of 1636, he settled in the area known as Providence, where he founded a colony called Rhode Island. He wrote a compact for the new colony that separated the beliefs and practices of religion from the authority of the state.

Others came to settle in his new colony, including some like him who fled the colony in Massachusetts Bay and also accepted the principle that

---

9. Barry, *Roger Williams*, 2.
10. Barry, *Roger Williams*, 3.
11. Barry, *Roger Williams*, 4–5.

civil courts could not decide doctrine. Williams believed that it was "monstrous" to compel a person to submit to the religious faith of another, or to compel anyone to conform to somebody else's beliefs.[12] And he sought a colony based on that principle. His religious struggles in Massachusetts resulted in Rhode Island.

Religious diversities developed in different directions elsewhere. There was no single expression of religion in America.

In 1632, a Catholic named Cecil Calvert gained a charter for a "Maryland Colony" along the mid-Atlantic coast. It was envisioned as a safe space for Roman Catholics to reside and to exercise their faith. Indeed, the first religious service in Maryland was a Catholic Mass in 1634. Still, these religious developments in the colonies could not be separated from English politics at the time. The Catholic sentiments of King Charles I of England put him in conflict with English Puritans, and some of those conflicts impacted the Maryland Colony. The person with the charter for Maryland was Catholic. But the leaders in its colonial assembly were Protestants.

In 1649, the same year that King Charles I was beheaded by the Cromwell government in England, the Maryland legislature passed "An Act Concerning Religion." It imposed a limited form of religious toleration for all groups that affirmed Trinitarian Christianity and declared any attempt to "blaspheme God, the Holy Trinity" a crime punishable by death. It also set fines for Maryland colonists who spoke in pejorative ways about any religious denomination.[13]

The situation in Maryland was further impacted by religious challenges that had arisen in neighboring colonies. In Virginia, the Church of England prevailed in religion.[14] It was encoded in colonial law and supported by public revenues. But, as in England, Virginia had Dissenting sects of Puritans. Some of them fled to Maryland to escape the Anglicans' control of the colonial assembly. To the north of Maryland, though Pennsylvania did not become a chartered colony (or a religious refuge) until 1681 when King Charles II authorized William Penn to establish it, the colonists in Maryland saw their northern neighbor as a possible threat.

It is tempting to view Pennsylvania and Rhode Island as prototypes of American religious freedom. William Penn and Roger Williams were both

---

12. Barry, *Roger Williams*, 252, 394.

13. "Maryland Toleration Act of 1649," para. 2. This act was enacted September 21, 1649.

14. The Church of England was the established religion of the Virginia colony from its founding until 1786, three years after the end of the Revolutionary War, and just a year before the Constitution was completed with its First Amendment prohibiting the establishment of religion.

seventeenth-century figures, though they came from different generations. The two of them illustrate some of the complexities of religion in America. Both affirmed religious liberty. Both believed that civil authority should not impose religious doctrines or sectarian perspectives on society. Both suffered for their beliefs. Williams had been banished from Massachusetts and was in jeopardy if he returned to England. Penn had endured several confinements in the Tower of London for his Quaker beliefs and sought to create a colony where no person could be treated that way.

Yet it is too simplistic to put Williams and Penn together as the architects of America's religious freedom. For one thing, Williams hated Quakerism. He considered Penn's Quakers to be a sect of "pernicious opinions" and heresies. He hoped any Quakers in Rhode Island would be removed.[15] And neither Penn nor Williams considered religious liberty to be the right of slaves.

Pennsylvania and Rhode Island were deeply embedded in the colonies' cultural and legal ethos, which limited religious freedom for enslaved people. Slavery was legal in Pennsylvania until 1780 and in Rhode Island until 1843, which was well after Massachusetts (1783) and New York (1827) had ended enslavement.

Enslaved Property and Racial Identity

America's complicated religious life occurred in the context of colonies' commercial, social, and political systems. Particularly pernicious among those systems was slavery. It fostered the transoceanic commerce that created and supplied markets with enslaved human property for sale. It operated under legal protections in most colonial regions, in the north and in the south. It had commodified enslaved people and their progeny as chattel to be managed in perpetuity. And it added an instrument for justifying restrictions on personal life and religious liberty.

The instrument was race. Chattel slavery had become deeply rooted in political, social, and religious systems of the colonies. Then laws that applied to it were written in racial terms. Legalized enslavement was linked with racialized identity.

Maryland received its charter in 1632. In 1638, its governing colonial council issued an edict, which became known as the "Maryland Doctrine of Exclusion." It provided that "Neither the existing black population, their descendents [sic], nor any other blacks shall be permitted to enjoy the fruits

---

15. Barry, *Roger Williams*, 374.

of White society."[16] This was four years before the first slaves were brought to Maryland. Race as a category was linked to slavery, but it also existed separately. And in Maryland, where religion mattered, race mattered. Race and enslavement had commercial value. Tobacco, the main product of the Maryland colony, required a lot of labor. Slavery offered a solution to that problem. Within eight years after the colony was created, Maryland imported its first slaves. All were Africans. During the ensuing years, the numbers of the enslaved in Maryland grew. To protect the property rights of those who enslaved them and to prevent the enslaved from fleeing to a colony where laws for their emancipation were more liberal, Maryland in 1664 enacted a law "making blacks and their children slaves for life."[17]

Further south, in 1669, another colony followed a similar pattern. A document called the "Fundamental Constitutions of Carolina" provided that "every freeman of Carolina shall have absolute power and authority over his negro slaves, of what opinion or religion soever."[18] Slavery in the colonies was a device for transforming people into property. Racial laws offered a means to codify the category of "negro" as a basis for denying personal identity and religious liberty. The church and civil authorities often collaborated in these racializing actions.

Some civil jurisdictions allowed enslaved persons to gain freedom by becoming "Christians" by a White definition, but enslaved persons could not be free by relying on a religion from Africa. In colonies such as the Carolinas, where religious and civil authorities were indistinguishable, "religious liberty" was a phrase with no value for those who were enslaved and Black.

---

16. Grear, "Why Vote?," para. 1. See also Alpert, "Origin of Slavery." The phrase "Slaves excepted" appears in 1638 legislative actions of the colony, which are available in Archives of Maryland at "Proceedings and Acts of the General Assembly of Maryland January 1637/8-September 1664," 1:41, 67, 69 (see https://msa.maryland.gov/megafile/msa/speccol/sc2900/sc2908/000001/000001/html/index.html).

17. "An Act Concerning Negroes & Other Slaves," in Archives of Maryland, edited by William Hand Brown, 1:533–34 (see https://babel.hathitrust.org/cgi/pt?id=mdp.35112103841641&view=1up&seq=596&q1=durante%20vita). Some colonies allowed slaves to be set free if they became Christians. Still others had differing policies regarding intermarriage between Blacks and Whites, including the issue of whether a Black slave who married a White person could thereby become free. This 1664 provision of law in Maryland made race an absolute and permanent identifying marker for enslavement.

18. As a document, the "Fundamental Constitutions of Carolina" was controversial, not because of the way it defined the "absolute" power of a slave owner but because it granted special governing privileges to a small group of English nobles who controlled most of the land between Virginia and Florida. It went into effect on March 1, 1669.

In the Carolinas, slavery had become common from the start of the Europeans' arrival. Charleston was settled in 1670 and quickly became central to the slave trade. As many as half of all the enslaved arrivals in America came through the port of Charleston. The city was governed by an appointee who was assigned by the king in London, and its system of local government came through parishes of the Church of England. Civic districts conformed to parish boundaries. Governing rested with churchwardens and parish vestries. Hence, overseeing the slave trade and organizing local efforts to recapture the runaway slaves became church business.

Slavery was practiced in Massachusetts before the Puritans arrived on the *Arbella* and officially was authorized under Massachusetts law in 1641. A slave market in Boston supplied the colonies in Connecticut, Rhode Island, and Virginia. Slavery was also one of the devices for dealing with native peoples who were viewed as adversaries. They could be captured, enslaved, and sometimes even traded for Africans, who arrived after they survived the Atlantic crossing.

Slavery was practiced in Manhattan as early as 1626, when the Dutch held the charter for "New Netherland." It continued when the English changed both the name of the colony and the type or nature of the enslavement. To the Dutch, slaves were servants in bondage to their owners. To the English, they were marketable commodities. Under the colonial regime in "New York," the slave trade expanded.[19]

Pennsylvania had toleration for religion. But it also tolerated enslavement. William Penn owned slaves when he received the charter for his colony in 1681.

Religious people and institutions not only shared these racist values but contributed to them. Colonists who came to North America in search of religious freedom conspired with the economic interests that enslaved people and that defined them racially.

So, some who came to America chose to get on ships and sail to unknown places, seeking liberty. Some chose to enslave other human beings, put them on ships, and sail them to unknown places, seizing their liberty. The enslaved, identifiable by their Blackness, were treated as if they were property to be bought, used, and sold. Being Black could be sufficient cause to be deprived permanently of liberty. And the church was a collaborator in this entire enterprise.

The problem was that the colonizers at the time did not see it as a problem. They did not recognize that the crisis was in fact a crisis. Churches

19. Harper, "Slavery in New York."

accepted it, abetted it, helped to impose it, and, when they considered it necessary, found theological reasons to justify it.

But even in the colonial era there were people of faith who took action to end it. Some individuals saw evil in slavery and chose to emancipate their slaves. Some saw a way to liberate individual slaves by recruiting them to become Christians and then citing their faith as a way to open a door to freedom. Some raised money to purchase enslaved persons in order to free them.

Yet structures of racialization, enslavement, and segregation were deeply entrenched. It was not enough that individuals acted within existing laws to liberate slaves. It would not be enough until the church woke and acted against a system of enslavement by breaking down the laws and the social patterns that were codified in those laws.

The Arrival of Methodism

Among the religious groups that established a presence in colonial America, Methodists were late arrivals. John and Charles Wesley, the founders of Methodism, had been in the Georgia colony in the 1730s. Charles was there for several months, primarily as a secretary working for James Oglethorpe. John, for nearly two years, was a chaplain. After they returned to England, neither was in North America again. But Georgia had a formative influence on them, especially on John and on the rise of Methodism.

Georgia was an unusual colony in a number of respects. It was founded in 1732, initially to fulfill what Oglethorpe envisioned as a place where persons who were poor or saddled with debt could build new lives in a setting designed to minimize the extremes of wealth and poverty.

Established under a charitable trust, rather than by a corporation like the Massachusetts Bay Company that hoped to earn profits for investors, Georgia was governed by a board of Trustees whose members were to receive no salary from it, own no properties in it, and acquire no benefits from it. The charitable trust supplied colonists with the clothing, transportation, and tools needed to turn the colonized property into productive land with livable housing. Oglethorpe envisioned that Georgia would produce "Silk, Wine, Oil, Dyes, Drugs, and many other materials" that could be marketed to make the colony financially viable.[20]

Others, including the King of England and members of the board of Trustees, also hoped that Georgia would achieve additional goals. It could be a buffer against the Spanish in Florida, the French in Louisiana, and

20. *Brief Account of the Establishment of the Colony*, 3–15, esp. 6.

unfriendly native tribes who might threaten the Carolinas and other English colonies.

One provision of the original charter for Georgia was that "Negro slavery" would not be permitted. The explicit reason was that absence of enslavement would encourage "English and Christian" people to settle there. Various "Christian" groups did settle in Georgia—Puritans, Anglicans, Lutherans, and Quakers, for example. However, Catholics were not permitted.

John Wesley served in the colony from March 1736 to December 1737. He conducted worship and led prayers for parishioners in Savannah and in a new settlement called Frederica. He also made contact with tribes of native peoples in the area, attempting—with approval from their leaders—to teach them Christianity.

In doing so, he honored the plea of Tomochichi, the chief of the Creeks, that he teach the Christian message before baptizing any of the tribal members into the church.[21] Besides visiting indigenous peoples, Wesley traveled beyond Georgia to South Carolina,[22] where he met enslaved persons. He drafted plans for visiting more slaves by traveling from one plantation to another.[23]

By the time Wesley left near the end of 1737, pressure was building in Georgia to change portions of the charter. Specifically, the colonists wanted to end the restrictions on the amount of land any individual could own and end the prohibition against "Negro slavery." They argued that Georgia could not successfully compete with South Carolina, where unpaid slave labor worked larger and more efficient plantations. And they added that defending against military incursions would require laborers working the land while colonial militia prepared to defend it. In 1750, the Trustees agreed to allow slavery. By then, both Oglethorpe and the young Methodists were gone.

Another tradition with Methodist ties arrived. Philip William Otterbein, a minister of the German Reformed Church, came to America in 1752 to serve German-speaking congregations in Pennsylvania. He shared some Pietist views that John Wesley experienced in Georgia, on his trip back to England, and in encounters with Moravians in London. Otterbein was familiar with the small-group practices in Wesley's class meetings, and he used them in his ministry. Otterbein moved to Baltimore in 1774. There, he

21. Heitzenrater, *Wesley and the People*, 62. Chief Tomochichi had told Wesley that this was superior to the techniques of the Spanish, who baptized first and then tried to teach. (Charles Wesley also worked in the Georgia colony as a secretary to Oglethorpe.)

22. In 1729, the colony of Carolina had been separated into North Carolina and South Carolina.

23. Heitzenrater, *Wesley and the People*, 67.

became the pastor of an Evangelical Reformed Church, which he led until he died in 1813. Soon after arriving in Baltimore, he had conferences with other preachers and coordinated plans for class meetings. One with whom he conferred was a young Methodist lay preacher who had arrived as an emissary sent by John Wesley.

Methodism was absent from the colonies after the Wesley brothers left Georgia in 1736 and 1737.[24] In 1763, Methodism arrived again in a new form. Its second coming was not through a chaplaincy or some other ordained ministry, but by the arrival of some Methodist laity. Robert Strawbridge, a Maryland farmer of Irish descent, became a Methodist before emigrating to America. He and his wife Elizabeth were likely the first to begin hosting meetings that could be called "Methodist" in America. Without any ecclesial permission or church authorization, they simply activated Methodism. Other lay Methodist immigrants followed a similar pattern when they settled along the east coast, particularly in New York and Baltimore, but elsewhere, too.

Then a twenty-one-year-old lay preacher named Francis Asbury arrived in 1771. Asbury came to North America in response to an appeal from John Wesley, who wanted to bring some order to American Methodists. Having a random assortment of laity define Methodism was too chaotic for Wesley's spirit and too dispersed for Methodism to be effective. Asbury was sent to bring some discipline to the movement. In that process, he met Otterbein in 1774 in Baltimore.

In that last quarter of the eighteenth century, these Methodists were a tiny, scattered few who started meeting amid the deeply rooted religious establishments in colonial America. They tended to live on the margins of commercial, cultural, religious, and political systems operating in the colonies while functioning within them. Those systems included slavery.

When Asbury reached North America, enslaved persons numbered in the hundreds of thousands in the colonies. Since the slave trade was a thriving business in those days, millions more were on the way.

---

24. In 1736, John and Charles Wesley served as Anglican chaplains in the Georgia colony, with Charles also assisting James Oglethorpe. Charles left in the fall of 1736, after working only about six months. John left in December 1737. See Kimbrough, *Charles Wesley in America*.

CHAPTER THREE

The Founding Generation

Methodism in the Context of Late Colonial America

Before Francis Asbury arrived in 1771, a slave trade had operated in North America for a hundred and fifty years. By then, English slave traders were more active in the Atlantic than the Spanish or Portuguese. Items produced in America, in significant part by enslaved labor, sailed aboard English ships to Europe. And shipments of slaves sailed west from Africa to America. So, Methodism emerged in a land that accommodated the enslavement of Africans and earned profits from their bondage.

Initially, Methodism's presence was led in the 1760s by individuals who were inspired under Wesley's influence in Europe before they came to America. Acting on their own initiative, with neither ordination nor authorization, they formed their versions of Methodism. Robert and Elizabeth Strawbridge came from Ireland, farmed land in Maryland, and held Methodist society meetings in their home. Thomas Webb retired from military service, settled in New York, and became a Methodist leader. Robert Williams (a Welsh Methodist) and John King (an English Methodist) traveled to America on their own. Barbara Heck, along with her husband Paul Heck and her brother Paul Ruckle, were Palatines from Germany who became Methodists in Ireland and reached New York, where her cousin Philip Embury (also an Irish Methodist) lived.

In 1769, Wesley sought to bring some order to the movement. He persuaded two of his lay preachers, Joseph Pilmore and Richard Boardman, to cross the Atlantic. Pilmore went to Philadelphia and Boardman to New York. But Wesley appointed them to "America." In 1771, he sent two more lay preachers—Richard Wright and Francis Asbury—to "America."[1] Wright and Asbury were in their twenties. Pilmore and Boardman were in their early thirties.

According to the official records in the *Minutes* of Wesley's conferences, these four lay preachers were the only persons appointed to Methodist work in the colonies at that time. Others, who had gone on their own, were not listed. But they could not be ignored.

Robert Strawbridge, for example, had been preaching and celebrating the sacraments for several years in Maryland on his own authority. In November 1769, Pilmore and Boardman had a hundred Methodists gather for a service in New York. But Webb was the preacher.[2]

Wesley's *Minutes* report that there were 316 Methodists in "America" in 1771 and 500 in 1772.[3] So Methodism—with four preachers and a few hundred members in four colonies—was a tiny fragment of the 2,500,000 people living in the thirteen colonies when Americans began to talk of revolution.[4] Of course, that total reported population did not include another estimated 500,000 enslaved Black people, perhaps 50,000 non-enslaved Black people, and countless native peoples within the thirteen colonies. Anyway, Methodism was a minimal percentage of the populace.[5]

In 1773, Methodists in America began to hold conferences, report on their work, keep their own *Minutes*, and list places where preachers were to be "stationed." They still considered themselves to be under the authority of Wesley and his conference, though, as their *Minutes* very clearly state.[6] Separate conferences in America and Britain kept their own lists of the preachers' appointments, beginning in 1773.

The names of those "stationed" differ. Wesley's list has eight preachers. The American list has ten, with Robert Strawbridge among them. The American list is by colony. Wesley's list says "America." Both sets of *Minutes* publish statistics on the number of members in societies until 1785,[7] when

---

1. Richey et al., *Methodist Experience in America: A History* (hereafter *MEAH*), 1–13. See also Heitzenrater, *Wesley and the People*, 244–46.

2. *MEAH*, 1:12.

3. Wesley, *Works of John Wesley*, 10:400, 410.

4. The largest colony by far was Virginia. With about 450,000 people, it was almost double the size of the next largest. Nearly half of the colonists lived in the four largest colonies: Virginia, Pennsylvania, Massachusetts, and Maryland. (See "Thirteen Colonies Population.")

5. See "Statistics on Slavery."

6. "Minutes of the Methodist Conferences . . . 1773 to 1784," in Richey et al., *Methodist Experience in America: A Sourcebook* (hereafter *MEAS*), 56–57.

7. Wesley, *Works of John Wesley*, 10:573–77.

Wesley's *Minutes* in England significantly changed their format. Until then, both sets of *Minutes* asked, "What numbers are there in the society?" Wesley's *Minutes* offered a number for "America," while the American *Minutes* gave data for each colony.

These signs indicate that the organizations were evolving as separate institutions before the end of the Revolutionary War. In 1784, with John Wesley's blessing, American Methodists declared themselves an independent "church." Until then, they were only a "society" of persons committed to a disciplined way of Christian life within Wesley's movement.

But even as a new American "church," Methodists were almost too few to be noticed in America—almost, but not quite. American Methodism had at least two distinguishing features. One was its structure. Another was its attitude to slavery.

Methodist Structure

Christians created various organizational forms as they developed their institutional and spiritual homes in America. Catholics planted missions and later sent bishops to settle a diocese. Anglicans defined the geographical boundaries of a parish, within which they conducted worship and other activities. Some Protestants—Lutherans, Baptists, and Presbyterians—organized their systems around congregations that called their own pastors. Methodists developed a different system. They met in small groups or classes for spiritual discipline, prayer, and study. They also had larger assemblies for worship, singing, and preaching.[8] Lay leadership was vital.

The whole operation, including property, was connected. The key to the Methodist connection was what Wesley called a "conference." It was a group of preachers, not a meeting of them but a membership body of them. They were present by invitation. They conferred with each other. They trained and examined prospective members. They were deployed, stationed, or sent to places of service. Their assignments were for short periods. They travelled circuits and moved from one circuit to another in a process called "itinerancy."[9] Hence, a preacher was not bound to being called by a congregation, or limited to the geographical space of a parish, or restricted by the oversight of a diocesan bishop. Each member itinerated, visited, ministered, and preached as opportunities presented themselves. It was an organized version of what John Wesley had done during his days as a colonial chaplain

---

8. Wesley avoided the word "church" for his movement, preferring "society" in "connexion" with him.

9. Heitzenrater, *Wesley and the People*, 102.

in Georgia, when he itinerated from one tribal community to another for his ministry among the native peoples, as he had planned also to do among slaves.

This itinerant system generated an image of Methodism's preachers as dedicated people on the move for the sake of the Christian faith. Often, they traveled in pairs, even sharing a horse that they took turns riding. Itinerants acquired a public image for their determination to travel in any circumstances. An adage for extremely bad weather emerged: "There's no one out today but crows and Methodist preachers."[10]

Itinerancy was the engine that made Methodism function. Asbury, for example, objected to any preachers who became accustomed to a settled life in ministry. In 1771, soon after his arrival, he criticized both Pilmore and Boardman for getting comfortable in their cities. He said, itinerancy created "a circulation of preachers, to avoid partiality and popularity."[11]

Complementing the conferences where preachers gathered annually were the "quarterly conferences" in the appointed circuits where the itinerating preachers were sent.[12] Blending basic business—like raising funds to pay the preacher—with spiritually elevating celebrations of the sacraments, the "quarterly conference" included lay members, preachers, and the presiding elder. They became an increasingly vital element for organizing Methodists in a coherent system.

The Methodist structure, with conferences and itinerating preachers, proved to be agile and very effective in the American context. Moving across the borders of colonies and religious establishments, Methodism was not constrained by congregational or parish boundaries and was not restricted to specialized facilities. Methodists could meet in homes, barns, or buildings they borrowed from families or other groups. They could meet in open-air settings, forest clearings, or public spaces, as Wesley discovered when he adopted the "vile" technique of field preaching.[13]

Additionally, the system of itinerating preachers created contacts with a wide variety of constituencies. The Methodists could, more readily than others, make connections with native peoples, with enslaved and free persons, with remotely rural households, and with residents of urban centers.

Yet, for all its distinctiveness and effectiveness, the Methodist system of conferences and itinerancy was expanding within the context of colonial America, whose socioeconomic order assumed legal enslavement.

---

10. Powell, "Methodist Circuit Riders in America," 34.
11. *MEAH*, 18.
12. *MEAH*, 20.
13. Heitzenrater, *Wesley and the People*, 99.

The Founding Generation

Methodism was not merely an evangelical enterprise that achieved institutional growth. Methodism was also a part of the American landscape, with enslaved and racially identified people who lived in racialized social patterns. Early Methodist meetings were ethnically diverse. But they were touched by the tensions of race and slavery.

In a November 1769 letter from New York, Richard Boardman wrote to John Wesley about "the number of Blacks that attend the preaching" in Methodist meetings, noting that their presence "affects me much."[14] In a November 1771 letter from New York, Joseph Pilmore wrote to John Wesley that "even the poor Negroes are turning to God, & seeking to wash their robes and make them white in the Blood of the Lamb." He added that one of the classes in New York included "about twenty Black women" as well as "people of superior rank."[15] The implications that Black people are stereotypically "poor" and "Black women" are inferior is painfully clear.

Such letters reveal how the identifications by race and the brutalities of a culture of enslavement were the accustomed background for Methodist activities. Boardman's 1769 letter recounts his conversation with an enslaved woman who had heard him preach.

> One of them came to tell me she could neither eat nor sleep, because her Master would not suffer her to come to hear the word. She wept exceedingly, saying, "I told my Master I would do more work than ever I used to do, if he would but let me come; nay, that I would do every thing in my power to be a good servant."[16]

Pilmore's 1771 letter also reports on someone who attended a Methodist gathering.

> A few days ago the Lord was pleased to manifest his Love to a poor Black, her Mistress has persecuted her very much because she came to The Methodist Church, but she thought it was better to be "beaten for hearing the word of God here; than to burn in Hell to all eternity."

And Asbury wrote in his journal about the presence of Black slaves in an assembly,

> To see the poor Negroes so affected is pleasing; to see their sable countenances in our solemn assemblies, and to hear them sing

---

14. *MEAS*, 53.
15. *MEAS*, 54–55.
16. *MEAS*, 53.

with cheerful melody their dear Redeemer's praise, affected me much, and made me ready to say, "Of a truth I perceive God is no respecter of persons."[17]

Racism, Enslavement, and American Methodism

Signs of Black presence were common. Signs of White supremacy were also. The Black slaves who deeply warmed Asbury's heart in New York in 1771 were a subordinated, segregated segment of a mostly White assembly. He described the White attendees as a social mix of "well established" business figures, "simple people," and "important leaders."[18] The Blacks were just identified by color or were characterized as "poor." That pattern endured.

One of Asbury's companions in itinerancy was a Black lay preacher named Harry Hosier. The two of them met with Methodists and preached to groups in mixed-race gatherings. Yet an apparently desegregated approach to Methodist meetings was neither a commitment to racial equality nor a bold declaration that Methodists were going to end racist social divisions. Instead, it was evident that racial inclusion was actually a form of White supremacy, which was soon openly acknowledged as standard Methodist practice. Black persons were not allowed to meet by themselves in Methodist gatherings unless a White person had oversight.[19]

Although early American Methodists mirrored the prevailing public acceptance of racial separation and stratification, they were also advocates of anti-slavery perspectives. Methodists offered public opposition to the slave trade and condemned the existence of enslavement. John Wesley, the scholarly English cleric who founded Methodism, was well informed about the evil enslavement of Africans. He acted publicly to stop the marketing of enslaved persons. One of the last things he read was a slave memoir.[20] One of the last things he wrote was a plea for ending the slave trade and American enslavement, which he called "the vilest that ever saw the sun."[21]

In 1774, John Wesley published his "Thoughts upon Slavery." He insisted that the concept of enslaving other people was based on "false foundations." He described the horrific evils of the slave trade, beginning with the ways Europeans had motivated some Africans to make war on their

17. Asbury, *Journal of Rev. Francis Asbury*, 1:17.
18. Moss, "Methodism in Colonial America," 1:104.
19. *MEAH*, 39.
20. *Gustavus Vasa*, the biography of a former slave named Olaudah Equiano (Heitzenrater, *Wesley and the People*, 307).
21. Heitzenrater, *Wesley and the People*, 307.

neighbors, capture their foes, and sell the captives as slaves. Wesley wrote that "white men" did this. He addressed the abuse to which slaves were subject on board the ships, in markets, and at places where they were forced to work in bondage. He rejected the notion that one can be excused from judgment about collaborating with the evils of slavery on the grounds that one was not personally a slave-owner. Merely tolerating the existence of an enslaving system, Wesley said, was an accommodation with evil.[22]

As an evangelical Christian, he considered slavery incompatible with Christian teaching. In addition, the early leaders of Methodism in America found common cause with the antislavery movement and made it part of Christian discipline.

In 1780, Methodists in Virginia were discussing, debating, and disputing a variety of issues. They pondered certification for celebrating sacraments, their loyalty to John Wesley in England, and the authority of a regional body to ordain persons for ministry. They sought clarity about the status of "Asbury as Mr. Wesley's representative." They insisted that their preachers refrain from smoking, chewing, or snuffing tobacco. And they addressed enslavement.

On slavery, these Virginia Methodists spoke with clarity and precision. The "travelling preachers who hold slaves [were] to give promises, to set them free," they decided. In addition, their sermons should address the evils of slavery and instruct the people to set their slaves free.[23] And they required that these regulations be read every year.

Hence, all the preachers in Virginia would be reminded annually about their obligations. They were to emancipate their slaves, preach against slavery, and discipline their members by teaching them to free any slaves they owned. In 1780, amid the war for independence, they left no doubt about the spirituality of their actions or the seriousness of purposes.

> [Question.] Does this conference acknowledge that slave-keeping is contrary to the laws of God, man and nature, and hurtful to society; contrary to the dictates of conscience and pure religion, and doing that which we would not others should do to us and ours?—Do we pass our disapprobation on all our friends who keep slaves, and advise their freedom?
> Answ. Yes.[24]

---

22. Wesley, "Thoughts upon Slavery," Sections III.2 (65–66), III.5–11 (67–69), IV.3 (70–71), IV.6 (72–73).

23. *MEAH*, 38.

24. *MEAH*, 38–39.

Transition to Political and Ecclesial Liberty

With a treaty signed on September 3, 1783,[25] Americans gained the world's recognition of their political independence. With a letter sent on September 10, 1784, American Methodists gained John Wesley's acknowledgment of their ecclesiastical independence.

"English Government has no Authority over them either Civil or Ecclesiastical," John Wesley wrote to Thomas Coke and Francis Asbury. As for "our Brethren in North America," he added, "no one either exercises or claims any Ecclesiastical Authority at all." Further, because "thousands of the inhabitants of these States desire my advice," he advised these independent American Methodists to have Coke and Asbury as "joint *Superintendents*" and also to recognize Richard Whatcoat and Thomas Vasey as "*Elders*."

He did more than advise the Methodists in America about the offices and persons to lead them. He proposed liturgies for Sunday worship, daily prayers, and celebrations of "the Supper of the Lord on every Lord's Day."[26]

John Wesley may have imagined that an independent American Methodism would still continue to be his movement, supervised by Coke and Asbury, who would jointly select and deploy preachers using the authority of the ordained elders he named. But others envisioned an independent Methodist body that decided whom to ordain and assign. The latter vision prevailed.

Coke carried Wesley's letter of September 10, 1784, with him to America. He arrived on November 3 and made his way to Delaware. On November 14, 1784, Coke preached at Barratt's Chapel. Afterwards he met Asbury for the first time. In a discussion that followed dinner, hosted at the Barratt family home, Coke realized that Americans would chart the course of American Methodism. Asbury had arranged for the quarterly conference[27] at Barratt's Chapel to assemble at a meeting around the time of Christmas. Coke and Asbury directed a preacher named Freeborn Garrettson to have "messengers" summon all the preachers to gather for the Baltimore meeting.

After their conversations concluded, Coke noted in his journal that Asbury gave him a route along which he was to itinerate between their visit at Barratt's and Christmas, when they would assemble in Baltimore. It would cover "about eight hundred or a thousand miles." Further, Coke added, "He

---

25. This was the date when British and American representatives signed the Treaty of Paris.
26. *MEAS*, 72–73.
27. *MEAH*, 50.

has given me his black (Harry by name,) and borrowed an excellent horse for me."[28] Two weeks later, Coke put the following note in his journal.

> I have now had the pleasure of hearing *Harry* preach several times. I sometimes give notice immediately after preaching, that in a little time *Harry* will preach to the blacks; but the whites always stay to hear him. Sometimes I publish him to preach at candle-light, as the negroes can better attend at that time. I really believe that he is one of the best preachers in the world, there is such an amazing power [that] attends his preaching, though he cannot read; and he is one of the humblest creatures I ever saw.[29]

Christmas Presence in Baltimore

The Christmas Conference solidified the leadership of Coke and Asbury. They both were in their late thirties in 1784 but differed significantly. Coke was born in Wales, ordained by the Church of England, held a Doctor of Civil Law degree, had missionary interests in many parts of the world besides the newly independent United States, and spent only a limited amount of time in America. Asbury was born in England, but he had been in America since 1771 and remained during the Revolution.[30] He had a working-class background but no higher education. Asbury's resume included serving a privileged household and laboring in a blacksmith shop.

Coke had the letter from Wesley that he presented to Asbury. Asbury had the Methodists in America whom he presented to Coke.

The Baltimore meeting was an unusual quarterly conference. Methodists mark it as the moment when sixty preachers founded their church.[31] Two of them, Harry Hosier from North Carolina and Richard Allen from Philadelphia, were Black. The others were White. During the meeting, they took actions by which they claimed authority to become a Methodist church. They ordained Asbury to be deacon, elder, and superintendent on

---

28. *MEAS*, 79, in a quote from Coke's Journal entry on November 14, 1784; Coke, *Extracts of the Journals*, 16.

29. *MEAS*, 79, in a quote from Coke's Journal entry on November 29, 1784, Coke, *Extracts of the Journals*, 18.

30. *MEAH*, 29.

31. *The Book of Discipline of the United Methodist Church 2016* (11) begins a list of bishops with Coke and Asbury in 1784. The Christian Methodist Episcopal Church similarly cites 1784 as the year that the church began (thecmechurch.org). There is no exact list of those who attended the Christmas Conference.

successive days. They welcomed Otterbein to participate in the ordinations. They elected others to be ordained deacons and elders. They called themselves "an Episcopal Church" and established a plan of church government. They defined their mission, saying that God's will for them was "To reform the Continent, and to spread scriptural Holiness over these Lands." They set rules for welcoming members. They gave directions for administering Baptism and the Lord's Supper. And they made unmistakably clear that the Methodists opposed slavery.

All of these actions became publicly known when, after the session adjourned, they were published in 1785 as the conference *Minutes*, which thereafter became known as the first *Book of Discipline* produced by American Methodists. The records reveal the position of the new church on race and slavery. Three questions on the agenda demonstrate this.

> Q. 41. Are there any Directions to be given concerning the Negroes? . . .
>
> Q. 42. What Methods can we take to extirpate Slavery? . . .
>
> Q. 43. What shall be done with those who buy or sell Slaves, or give them away?

The answers show Methodists' views on slavery were blunt. A member who buys or sells slaves is "immediately to be expelled" from membership, "unless they buy them on purpose to free them."[32] This must happen because God's law compels Methodists to act against slavery.

> We view it as contrary to the Golden Law of God on which hang all Law and the Prophets, and the unalienable Rights of Mankind, as well as every Principle of the Revolution. . . . We therefore think it our most bounden Duty, to take immediately some effectual Method to extirpate this Abomination from among us.[33]

They defined five steps to be taken in an orderly process. First, "Every Member of our Society who has Slaves in his Possession" must emancipate those slaves in a specified period, and any child born into slavery was to be free "immediately on birth." Second, circuit-riders must write the names and ages of every enslaved person on the circuit along with the record that has been filed with civil court to certify the emancipation plan for the person. Third, a Methodist who refuses to comply with the process will leave

---

32. *UMAS*, Q. 43, 85.
33. *UMAS*, Q. 42, A. 1, 84.

the church voluntarily or will be excluded by the preacher. Two other steps involve ways to restore departed members or receive new ones.

> No Person so *voluntarily withdrawn*, or so *excluded*, shall ever partake of the Supper of the Lord with the Methodists, till he complies with the above-Requisitions. No Person holding Slaves shall, in future, be admitted into Society or to the Lord's Supper, till he previously complies with these Rules concerning Slavery.[34]

Yet, for all their clarity regarding slavery, the preachers in Baltimore in 1784 were also clear that they did not affirm racial equality. The "Directions" that they provided "concerning the Negroes" were to include them in class meetings but required them to have "a proper White Person as their Leader."[35] White supremacy coexisted with opposition to Black enslavement.

In 1800, the General Conference of all preachers issued a "Pastoral Letter on Slavery." Signed by the three bishops of the church (Coke, Asbury, and Whatcoat), the letter declared that enslavement of Black people was "the great national evil" of the nation. It said that "the whole spirit of the New Testament militates in the strongest manner against the practice of slavery." It directed annual conferences to appeal to their state legislatures for the emancipation of slaves in the state. And it called for "the universal extirpation of this crying sin."[36]

Not Yet Fully Awake

Thus, early Methodists opposed slavery and assumed White supremacy. By regulation and practice, they racially stratified the church. In 1785, a year after he attended the Baltimore conference, Richard Allen received a request from Francis Asbury to itinerate with him.

> He told me he wished me to travel with him. He told me that in the slave countries, Carolina and other places, I must not intermix with the slaves, and I would frequently have to sleep in his carriage, and he would allow me my victuals and clothes. I told him I would not travel with him on these conditions.[37]

---

34. *UMAS*, 85.
35. *UMAS*, Q. 41, 84.
36. *UMAS*, 134–36.
37. *MEAS*, 117.

Two years later, the chasm between Black and White Methodists widened. Richard Allen and other Black Methodists in Philadelphia formed the Free Africa Society[38] for ministry to thousands of free (i.e., not enslaved) Black people in the city. With this institution in 1787, they sought recognition for their initiative.

They also requested a place to worship under their own leaders.

> In November, 1787, the colored people belonging to the Methodist Society of Philadelphia convened together, in order to take into consideration the evils under which they labored. Arising from the unkind treatment of their white brethren, who considered them a nuisance in the house of worship, and even pulled them off their knees, while in the act of prayer, and ordered them to the back seats. For these, and various other acts of unchristian conduct, they considered it their duty to devise a plan in order to build a house of their own, to worship God under their own vine and fig tree. In this undertaking they met with great opposition from an elder of The Methodist Church . . . who threatened that if they did not give up the building, erase their names from the subscription paper, and make acknowledgements for having attempted such a thing, that in three months they would all be publicly expelled from the Methodist Society. Not considering themselves bound to obey this injunction, and being fully satisfied that they would be treated without mercy, they sent in their resignations.[39]

Those were days when Allen, his colleague Absalom Jones, and other Black Methodists were usually in their seats for Sunday worship at St. George's Church in Philadelphia. As their numbers grew, the White persons in charge of seating moved the Black worshipers from the pews and told them to stand around the wall. Then, on a Sunday in 1792, according to Allen,

> the sexton stood at the door and told us to go in the gallery. He told us to go, and we would see where to sit. We expected to

---

38. Dickerson, "Our History."

39. Flipper et al., "Historical Preface," 10. This preface is significant both as an official denominational account of the founding events and as a manner of expression of that history just one year after three other Methodist bodies (Methodist Protestant, Methodist Episcopal Church, and the Methodist Episcopal Church South) had merged in a "reunion" in 1939 to form the Methodist Church. The Black denominations in the larger story of American Methodism were not included in the 1939 "reunion." That was a consequence both of the White Methodists' reluctance to desegregate American Methodism and the Black Methodists' reluctance to surrender any liberties they might have in their own denominations to one whose "reunion" would be built on a basis of racial separation and White supremacy.

take the seats over the ones we formerly occupied below, not knowing any better. We took those seats. Meeting had begun, and they were nearly done singing, and just as we got to our seats, the elder said, "Let us pray." We had not been long upon our knees before I heard considerable scuffling and low talking. I raised my head up and saw one of the trustees . . . having hold of the Rev. Absalom Jones, pulling him up off of his knees, and saying, "You must get up—you must not kneel here." . . . Mr. Jones said, "Wait until prayer is over, and I will get up and trouble you no more." . . . By this time the prayer was over, and we all went out of the church in a body, and they were no more plagued with us in the church.[40]

The Founders and Religious Freedom

In the same year (1787) and in the same city (Philadelphia) that Richard Allen and other Black leaders sought religious freedom in Methodism, fifty-five White men were dealing with the issue of religious freedom as they drafted a constitution. Their thirteen states had different approaches to religion. Maryland was to be a home for Catholics, but not everyone in Maryland was Catholic. Virginia, where the Anglican parish was the norm, had Baptists, Deists, and others.

Thomas Jefferson had deep religious inclinations. As a student at William and Mary, he worshiped at the Bruton Parish church in Williamsburg. As a learned adult, he both interpreted Scripture and rewrote it.[41] In 1786, he drafted, and the Virginia General Assembly approved, a Statute for Religious Freedom, which includes these words:

> Be it enacted by the General Assembly, that no man shall be compelled to frequent or support any religious worship, place, or ministry whatsoever, nor shall be enforced, restrained, molested, or burthened in his body or goods, nor shall otherwise suffer on account of his religious opinions or belief; but that all men shall be free to profess, and by argument to maintain, their opinion in matters of religion, and that the same shall in no wise diminish, enlarge, or affect their civil capacities.[42]

---

40. *MEAS*, 118.
41. Edwards, "How Thomas Jefferson Created His Own Bible."
42. "Thomas Jefferson and the Virginia Statute," para. 7.

Jefferson was not a delegate to the Constitutional Convention in Philadelphia in 1787.[43] But his fellow Virginian James Madison was. And lobbyists sought Madison's help in ensuring that the new Constitution would protect the freedom of religion from any governmental control. One lobbyist, Baptist preacher John Leland, wrote to Madison,

> If a Majority of Congress with the President favour one System more than another, they may oblige all others to pay to the support of their System as much as they please.[44]

Yet others wanted close ties between church and state in the new Constitution. George Washington, a member of the Virginia delegation and a member of the vestry in his Anglican parish, favored it. Alexander Hamilton, a New York delegate, considered religion to be a vital component of government by the people, and he sought a constitution with an "authoritative" word on it. John Adams, though he was not a Massachusetts delegate, wanted the government to levy religious taxes on everyone, with the revenue transferred to the church of each citizen's choice.

In the end, the drafters of the Constitution chose to include barely a dozen words about religion in the document that thirty-nine of the fifty-five delegates signed. The only reference was in Article VI, which said (and still says) that "no religious Test shall ever be required as a Qualification" for holding public office.[45] A delegate from South Carolina, Charles Pinckney, had proposed that language on August 20, 1787, and the delegates approved his text ten days later.

That brief statement upset people on all sides. Those who wanted religion to be affirmed by the Constitution, perhaps as a basis for public morality, said that the draft document insulted or ignored God. Those who wanted a strong statement separating religion from the government found the draft document lacking in clarity and vigor on this point. The absence of a sufficiently clear position on religion was one issue among others that some believed could threaten chances of ratification by the minimum three-fourths of the thirteen states. Such issues, for instance, may have led four of the seven Virginia delegates not to sign the draft Constitution. One was George Mason. He had written a Virginia Declaration of Human Rights in 1776.

The constitutional convention ended on September 17, 1787, and the draft Constitution went to the states. The ratification convention in Virginia

---

43. See "America's Founding Documents," https://www.archives.gov/founding-docs.
44. "Religion and the Federal Government, Part 1," para. 10.
45. "Religion and the Federal Government, Part 1," para. 1.

proposed a number of amendments to the document. Among them was a phrase adapted from Mason's Declaration of Human Rights, stating "that no particular religious sect or society ought to be favored or established by Law in preference to others."[46]

In an effort to secure support from the states, a plan emerged to add amendments to the draft Constitution, using the Congressional legislative process. The plan included a promise to name specific rights. The proposal succeeded, and every state but Rhode Island ratified it.[47]

When Congress met for the first time in the spring of 1789 under the new Constitution, Madison submitted legislation with a set of amendments to fulfill the promise that paved the way for ratification. The amendments covered individual and communal liberties, including religion. Congress adopted twelve, which went to the states for ratification. The third of the amendments addressed religious liberty. It drew upon a motion that Madison had proposed on religion.

> The civil rights of none shall be abridged on account of religious belief or worship, nor shall any national religion be established, nor shall the full and equal rights of conscience be in any manner, or on any pretext infringed.[48]

Of the twelve amendments that the Congress adopted as a Bill of Rights, the first two were not ratified by three-fourths of the states. The other ten, including the approved text of one that addressed religion, were ratified. The order in which they survived the ratification process remained in place. So, the third one became the First Amendment to the Constitution, which begins with a clear constitutional principle on separation of church and state: "Congress shall make no law respecting an establishment of religion, or prohibiting the free exercise thereof."[49]

Out of One Era and into Another

In effect, the founding era had ended, and the functioning era had begun. From 1783 to 1792, remarkable political and ecclesial transformations occurred. The United States of America won its independence in war but found that an attempt to govern itself freely through Articles of Confederation was

---

46. "Religion and the Federal Government, Part 1," para. 9.
47. Rhode Island finally voted in favor of ratification in 1790.
48. "Religion and the Federal Government, Part 1," para. 11.
49. The Constitution of the United States, Amendment 1 (see "Religion and the Federal Government, Part 1," para. 8).

not going to prevail in peace. A new Constitution guaranteed that the nation would have neither an established religion nor a capacity to prohibit the free exercise of religion. American Methodists adapted Wesley's permission for their "full liberty" and became a new church with an emerging new vision by the time he died in 1791.

By 1790, the Methodist Episcopal Church had 57,858 members and claimed 1.5 percent of Americans.[50] It was not the official religion of any one state, but its conferences connected an itinerant ministry overseen by two bishops in all states and territories.[51] It defined itself as a religion opposed to slavery and had a polity designed to impose antislavery disciplines.

American Methodism had established a new church. And the American people had a new Constitution. Even Rhode Island, which had not bothered to send delegates to the convention that wrote the Constitution, ratified it, and thus became the last of the thirteen original states to do so.

Besides the Sixth Article in the Constitution, which established that religion was never to be used as a factor for determining fitness to serve in public office, the First Amendment established that no religion was ever to become an official one and that no religion would ever be prohibited by law from being exercised in the United States.

Both the new nation and the new denomination also decided about race. Racial separation and White supremacy would govern America's cultural preferences and constitutional principles. The same would be true of Methodism's ecclesial polity.

The history of religion in America is as complex as the history of America. One of the complicating factors is basic terminology. Neither America nor American Methodism had been "discovered." Nobody had "found" the United States of America or the Methodist Episcopal Church. People "founded" them. Flawed human beings established the political and religious bases of the nation. Then they used their political and religious processes to form institutions on those foundations. Among the flaws were the fault lines drawn by the boundaries of race.

So, the Methodists' church formed under the American constitutional system, which set it free from restraints, constraints, or obligations enacted by the Congress of the United States. The government of the nation could not establish any religion, prohibit the practice of any religion, or set religious requirements for public service to the nation. Religious communities and institutions would determine their own policies, practices, and

---

50. *MEAS*, 22.

51. In 1786, Coke and Asbury began using the title "Bishop" rather than "Superintendent."

procedures for choosing whom to receive as members, whom to choose as leaders, and whom to consider equal partners in experiencing the benefits of their beliefs.

When the church woke to this new reality, the Methodist Episcopal Church in America had to choose how it would deal with matters of slavery and race. The church was founded on anti-slavery commitments with a discipline that would enforce an end to enslavement of other persons by Methodists. But it had also been founded on the social, cultural, and racial practices in America that valued White superiority and assumed Black inferiority.

The church would have to decide how to act on these matters. These early Methodists concluded that theirs was not a time filled with enough promise or possibilities to wake from sleep and take actions against an evil system they had previously deplored. Though the church had been stirred by an awareness of the evils of enslavement, it never woke to the task of dismantling White supremacy.

CHAPTER FOUR

From Founding a Church to Forming Separated Methodism

An Independent Church in an Independent Nation

In 1790, Black Methodists in Philadelphia were seeking the dignity and the respect that the systems of their church failed to offer. A key element in receiving such recognition was to have a house of worship that they controlled. They received financial support for a building on some land that Richard Allen owned in the city. But White preachers resisted the plan.

> As soon as the preachers of The Methodist Church in Philadelphia came to the knowledge of this, they opposed it with all their might, insisting that the house should be made over to the Conference. . . . However, the building went on, and, when [they] finished, they invited Francis Asbury, then Bishop of the Methodist Episcopal Church, to open the house for divine service, which invitation he accepted, and the house was named Bethel. (See Gen. xxviii. 19.)[1]

Asbury's willingness to participate in consecrating the building did not mean that the opposition had disappeared, however. The same White elder who had threatened Black members with expulsion if they pursued their building project recommended that the new Bethel African Methodist Church become incorporated. In that way, he argued, the congregation

---

1. Flipper et al., "Historical Preface," 11.

could receive donations and bequests. The Black members were agreeable, and he generously offered to have the incorporation papers prepared.

> But they soon found that he had done it in such a manner as entirely deprived them of the liberty they expected to enjoy; so that, by this stratagem, they were again brought into bondage by the Methodist preachers.[2]

Attempts to negotiate a resolution included proposals for Bethel to pay an annual sum to the Conference. But they were complicated by additional demands from the presiding elder that he be given the keys to the building, the control of all books and papers within it, and the power to determine when or whether meetings could be held in the structure. These conditions were yet another sign that White Methodists assumed a supremacy to control Black Methodists.

Eventually, after years of litigation, the Supreme Court of Pennsylvania decided this was a dispute about property, not about piety, and ruled in favor of Bethel. The Black Methodists had secured legal control of the property. Allen was their pastor. But race-based problems remained.

A similar situation in Baltimore led Black Methodists to meet in a "general convention" where they formed the African Methodist Episcopal Church as a denomination in the Wesleyan tradition in 1816. But gaining their identity required securing their liberty from Methodists who refused to acknowledge their equality. What began with Richard Allen's rejection of Asbury's invitation to itinerate in a segregated system evolved thirty years later into the creation of a new denomination—not because the church woke to know the evils of a religion based on a principle of racial superiority, but because a civil court treated problems of piety in terms of property.

Separations and Schisms

The Methodist Episcopal Church in the United States functioned in its earliest years in a system of racial separation based on a principle of White supremacy. It transformed antislavery appeals of John Wesley and the abolitionist views of American Methodists into toleration for the enslavement of Black people. It supported separation—in the American church as well as in the American society—of European immigrants and their descendants from the Africans and their descendants. It assumed that Black Methodists would function as inferiors under the superior authority of White Methodists.

---

2. Flipper et al., "Historical Preface," 12.

Asbury, in the earliest version of his journal, had published antislavery sentiments. But in later editions, he revised and suppressed those sentiments.[3] In the complex religious history of America, Methodists chose to create their own complications for the sake of racial segregation and White supremacy. At times, they preferred separation to finding a solution for their racism.

Before the denomination reached its fortieth birthday in 1824, it had endured at least five schisms. Three of those five splits involved race.[4]

The first, led by Richard Allen, began shortly after the denomination was established in 1784. He declined the overture from Asbury and formed the Free Africa Society soon after he attended the Christmas Conference. His initiative became a new denomination in 1816, with the creation of the African Methodist Episcopal Church.[5]

The second, led by Peter Spencer, occurred in Delaware and formed the "African Union Church" in 1813. It involved some complaints by White Methodists that Black Methodists were boisterous, noisy, and dirty. It also involved some complaints by Black Methodists that the only preachers appointed to lead them were White Methodist ministers. There were demands from White worshipers that Black worshipers be banished to the balcony. There were demands from Black members to have their own building. Eventually, Black Methodists did acquire a facility in Wilmington, Delaware. Asbury preached there in 1810, referring to it as "the African Chapel in Wilmington."[6] But it remained under the authority of the White Methodists. The dispute in Wilmington, like the one in Philadelphia, landed in the civil courts. But the Delaware court ruled in favor of control by White Methodists. Spencer and his group then formed the African Union Church as a separate denomination.

---

3. *MEAH*, 31.

4. The other two were primarily the consequences of internal polity disputes. First, James O'Kelly of North Carolina left in 1792 to form the Republican Methodist Church. He had tried and failed to persuade the denomination that a preacher who objected to his (only men were appointed as preachers in those days) appointment to a circuit could appeal to the conference. Second, some New England Methodists in 1814 created the Reformed Methodist Church. They objected to an organizational system that included bishops and that diminished congregational authority. They also objected to some of the denomination's doctrinal and structural patterns, both of which related at least indirectly to race. The Reformed Methodists sought more emphasis on moving through entire sanctification toward Christian perfection. They also wanted the church to adopt positions that had anti-war and anti-slavery emphases.

5. In addition to the discussion above, see *MEAS*, 197–98.

6. Maser and Singleton, "Union American Methodist Episcopal Church," 1:615.

From Founding a Church to Forming Separated Methodism

The third centered around Peter and Mollie Williams of New York, where Methodism in America had planted some of its earliest roots. The Methodists, who met in Wesley Chapel,[7] were a diverse group, both socioeconomically and racially. Francis Asbury preached there in 1771 to an assembly of prosperous business leaders, skilled laborers who worked at a tannery, and slaves. Among the "poor Negroes" whom Asbury saw in worship were the Williamses.[8] An enslaved couple, they were the property of a local tobacconist, to whom Peter Williams was an apprentice and from whom he learned the business of rolling and selling cigars. He encouraged them to attend Wesley Chapel, where Peter Williams became the church sexton.

When their owner decided to return to England rather than await the outcome of the revolutionary war, he sold Peter and Mollie Williams to the church with the understanding that they could work to acquire their freedom. By 1778, Peter Williams began getting compensation for his services as sexton. That, plus his income from selling tobacco products, enabled him to buy his freedom from the church in 1785. Later, his success in the tobacco business enabled the couple to purchase a home in New York.

Peter Williams became a leader at Wesley Chapel. In 1796, twenty-five years after he had first heard Asbury preach, he was part of a delegation that asked Bishop Asbury's permission for Black Methodists to meet and worship separately from the Whites. They based their petition on grievances similar to those that had been voiced by Black Methodists elsewhere: Blacks were rarely allowed to preach to Whites; and Black preachers were prohibited from the itinerancy.[9] A later account described the grievances more specifically.

> When the Methodist Society in the United States was small, the Africans enjoyed comfortable privileges among their white brethren in the *same meeting-house*, but as the whites increased very fast, the Africans were pressed back; therefore, it was thought essentially necessary for them to have meeting houses of their own, in those places where they could obtain them, in order to have more room to invite their coloured brethren yet out of the Ark of safety to come in;—and it is well known that

---

7. The Methodist community that began as Wesley Chapel is now John Street United Methodist Church.

8. Technically, Mollie (née Mary Durham) Williams was an indentured servant, not a slave, so she could achieve liberty through repayment of her debt by a specified period of work. Peter Williams was a slave, and his only path to freedom was a grant of emancipation or the purchase of his identity at the market price from whoever owned him.

9. Maser and Singleton, "Union American Methodist Episcopal Church," 1:607–8.

the Lord has greatly enlarged their number since that memorable time, by owning their endeavors in the conversion of many hundreds. Many preachers have been raised up among them, who have been very useful in a located state; but they have been hitherto confined; they have had no opportunity to travel . . . and their coloured brethren have been thereby deprived of those blessings Almighty God might have designed to grant to their instrumentality.[10]

Asbury approved their request for a separate worship site in New York. They began using a structure that previously served as a stable and a carpentry shop. Within three years, the group of Black worshipers outgrew that space, and they hoped to find a property for a new building. In 1801, they incorporated the "African Methodist Episcopal Church (Called Zion Church) of the City of New York" and named a Board of Trustees, one of whom was Peter Williams. By written agreement, the Methodist Episcopal Church would appoint the preachers, and the Trustees—all Africans or of African descent—would control the property.

The path forward was hardly a smooth one. Internal dissents and disputes in Zion Church led to a loss of members. Talks about a possible union with Richard Allen's group occurred but did not bear fruit. Other Black congregations in Connecticut as well as in New York approached Zion Church about connecting with them, but without achieving unity. Meanwhile, difficulties with White leaders of the Methodist Episcopal Church persisted.

When the delegation received Asbury's support in 1796 for a separate Black worship site, James Varick—a Black class leader at John Street Church—received approval to preach and lead prayers for the Black congregation. But he could only do so under White supervision.

In the following years, Varick continued to preach at Zion Church, which became known as "Mother Zion." He built connections with Black Methodists elsewhere and with Black groups that were not Methodist. In public, they held antislavery rallies. In church, they sought to be free of White control. After Asbury died in 1816, the search for freedom became more complicated. The next generation of White church leaders delayed or deferred decisions on embracing Black preachers among the itinerant ministers. Whites insisted that the church laws would have to be changed to allow this, thereby postponing any decision to the 1824 General Conference.

Varick, who had been ordained as a deacon in 1806, might have been ordained elder in 1821 at a Black conference with White elders as

---

10. See Christopher Rush, "A Short Account of the Rise and Progress of the African M.E. Church in America," in *MEAS*, 199–200.

the presiding officers. But no bishop attended, so no ordination occurred. Varick was ordained elder in 1822, but it was at an irregular service led by "renegade Methodist elders," some said.[11] When the General Conference met in 1824, the delegates decided that the Black Methodist conference lacked authority to elect preachers to the itinerancy or to ordination. Instead of acting to affirm Varick's ordination, they annulled it.

That decision sealed the situation. Schism followed. The Methodist Episcopal Church, in its 1824 General Conference, made clear that racial inclusion and racial separation both meant racial subordination. Black Methodists could only have whatever authority White Methodists granted. In 1826, the African Methodist Episcopal Zion Church conducted its own General Conference for the first time. Varick was elected bishop at the meeting. He died the next year.

The formation of these denominations—African Methodist Episcopal, African Union, and African Methodist Episcopal Zion—did not mean that all Black Methodists fled to Black churches. But it did mean that American Methodism would be a racially divided movement afflicted by White supremacist views in a segregated nation.

This became the pattern in Methodism's American expansion. On February 24, 1824, after learning about Richard Allen and the African Methodist Episcopal Church, two Black preachers in Cincinnati—an enslaved man named James King and another man named Phillip Brodie—offered an option to the Black worshipers in Methodist Episcopal churches in the city. They "decided they would no longer tolerate the prejudicial treatment they had received during their worship experiences," and they formed Allen Temple African Methodist Episcopal Church,

> the first organized Black congregation west of the Allegheny Mountains out of a need to provide more freedom and autonomy for worship, while influencing positive change toward racial equality and community empowerment.[12]

In 1836, the General Conference of the African Methodist Episcopal Church met in Pittsburgh and decided to launch a westward mission. The Rev. William Paul Quinn, one of the founders of the AME in 1816, traveled to the middle of the continent. He moved through Illinois. But he was prohibited from entering Missouri because, by the terms of the Missouri Compromise in 1820, Missouri was admitted to the Union as a slave state.

---

11. *MEAH*, 113.
12. "Allen Temple History."

The presence of any non-enslaved Black preacher in Missouri would have provoked problems.

In 1840, Quinn devised a plan. He stood on the Illinois side of the Mississippi River and preached to people—including slaves—who gathered on the Missouri side. By some accounts, he adopted a tactic of preaching from a boat in the middle of the river to those who gathered on the Missouri side. In 1841, a group in St. Louis organized St. Paul African Methodist Episcopal Church, which still identifies itself as "the oldest African Methodist Episcopal Church west of the Mississippi River."[13]

Within forty years after the founding of the Methodist Episcopal Church in the United States in 1784, new Methodist denominations and churches formed because of persistent racism and prevailing practices of White superiority. By separating from the existing denomination and by forming new institutions in the first half of the nineteenth century, Black people were calling attention to the "legalized" brutality of enslavement and to "civilized" systems of segregation and subordination that were the realities of life in Methodism across the United States. In these decades, White Methodists did not want an American Methodism that woke to the truth about race. So, the church never quite woke, and the church never reacted to alarms about it.

Suppressing Antislavery in Methodism

These Black denominations in Methodism formed because of racist behaviors and White supremacist beliefs—not just about enslavement. But, by the time American Methodism should have been marking the sixtieth birthday of the Methodist Episcopal Church in 1844, it divided into two big pieces over slavery.

A church that had been "constitutionally, legislatively, and programmatically committed to antislavery"[14] shifted from its foundations. The Pastoral Letter approved by the 1800 General Conference and signed by the bishops had provoked complaints in slave holding states. After the 1804 General Conference, a separate edition of the *Discipline* was published for South Carolina, without regulations regarding slavery. The 1808 General

---

13. The church has connections to a number of significant developments in the community and the country. It was the birthplace of the St. Louis Chapter of the NAACP in 1913. It was also the home church of Ethel Hedgeman Lyle, one of the founders of Alpha Kappa Alpha Sorority (see https://stpaulamestl.net/). Quinn's influence and impact were widespread. An academic institution of the African Methodist Episcopal Church, Paul Quinn College in Dallas, was established in 1872 in his name.

14. *MEAH*, 86.

Conference decided that each annual conference would set its own policies regarding the slave trade and the practice of enslavement. In 1816, the General Conference received a report that said, "little can be done" to end slavery and "the evil appears to be past remedy."[15] The church surrendered to slavery.

The church also supported enslavement. In 1827, the Mississippi Conference addressed a pastoral letter to its members that emphasized an "overlooked or neglected" ministry, namely "the religious cultivation of your slaves." The letter demonstrates that Mississippi Methodism accepted—and, with passages of Holy Scripture, substantiated—that slavery was biblically legitimate. It simply added that slave owners had an obligation to teach their slaves to read so they could "read God's holy word." The letter said that the biblical perspective, "requiring the submission of the slave," also encourages "religious instruction" of slaves.[16]

Thus, the church surrendered its antislavery mission. It yielded to the social, cultural, and economic practices of maintaining enslaved people as if they were property. The denomination that had labeled slavery a "crying sin" in 1800 now called slavery biblically legitimate in "our Lord's plantation," in the words of the Mississippi Methodists. The church even produced slave catechisms for Methodists in South Carolina to guide the religious instruction of the enslaved. Methodists decided that slaves, with no hope of liberty on earth, could spiritually "escape from their earthly woes" and find hope in heaven.[17]

Some Methodists opposed this shift. They advocated the abolition of slavery, in words and in actions. La Roy Sunderland, who became the editor of *Zion's Herald* in 1836 at the age of thirty-four, made it a voice of Methodist abolitionism.[18] Orange Scott, who was a presiding elder in New England, defended the right of abolitionist Methodists to serve as delegates to the General Conference. Denmark Vesey, an enslaved South Carolina Methodist who had bought his freedom in 1820, was arrested, convicted in a secret trial, and executed in 1822 allegedly for organizing a slave rebellion.

Vesey, who helped found an African Methodist Episcopal Church in Charleston in 1818 that later was called "Mother Emmanuel,"[19] became a

15. *MEAH*, 88.

16. See "Address of the Mississippi Annual Conference" (February 22, 1828) in *MEAS*, 209.

17. Leonard, *Sense of the Heart*, 194.

18. *MEAH*, 178–79. See also Leonard, *Sense of the Heart*, 145.

19. On June 17, 2015, Dylann Roof killed nine people inside the church: Clementa Pinckney, Cynthia Hurd, Depayne Middleton Doctor, Sharonda Coleman-Singleton, Susie Jackson, Ethel Lance, Tywanza Sanders, Daniel Simmons, and Myra Thompson. See Costa et al., "Church Shooting."

martyr to remember. Frederick Douglass called for Black people to honor pioneers like Vesey who had fought for freedom instead of just waiting for freedom to be given. He lauded their awakening to truth and taking action. Douglass often exhorted crowds with the words, "Remember Denmark Vesey of Charleston!"[20]

Dividing Instead of Awakening

Many members of the African Methodist Episcopal Church, the African Union Church, and the African Methodist Episcopal Zion Church had endured the cruelties of enslavement. Many, including Frederick Douglass, encountered Methodism when they were still enslaved.

In 1833, Douglass received permission from his master, Thomas Auld, to attend a Methodist camp meeting with him. To be clear, in the culture of enslavement, a slave did not participate "with" the master in the meeting. However, the slaves could observe the spectacle of the camp meeting, see the tent city that had been constructed, smell the meat cooking over the campfires, and hear sounds from the space where the White "mourners" were being moved by the preachers to utter their groans and shouts of spiritual ecstasy as their faith was revived.[21]

To Douglass, the camp meeting was proof that Methodists were like most Christians. They were hypocrites. They could praise the Lord one day and then pummel their slaves the next without sensing that there was any irony in the situation or any reason to ponder the question of divine justice on earth.

By 1836, abolition of slavery was no longer on the agenda of the Methodist Episcopal Church. Resolutions in the Georgia and South Carolina annual conferences declared that slavery was "not a moral evil." Bishops had become convinced that the real issue troubling the church was not enslavement but abolitionism. In a plea to the 1836 General Conference, the bishops implored Methodists to cease any affiliation with abolitionists. Four years later, in their 1840 message, they lamented that many Methodists did not follow their 1836 instructions to cease abolitionist activities. That may have been persuasive. The 1840 General Conference elected opponents of abolitionism to key positions like editor of *Zion's Herald*.[22]

---

20. Blight, *Frederick Douglass*, 287, 395. Metropolitan AME in Washington became Douglass's home church. See Blight, *Frederick Douglass*, 679.

21. Blight, *Frederick Douglass*, 58, 161, 198.

22. *MEAH*, 180–81.

From Founding a Church to Forming Separated Methodism

For many Methodists, both Black and White, the shift away from opposition to slavery was intolerable. In 1842, Orange Scott and La Roy Sunderland announced that they decided to depart from the Methodist Episcopal Church, characterizing it as "not only a slaveholding but a *slavery defending church*."[23] The following year, 1843, they convened a meeting and formed the "Wesleyan Methodist Connection" as a new antislavery denomination.

At the next General Conference of the Methodist Episcopal Church in 1844, all of the tensions surrounding slavery coalesced in a single matter. It involved Bishop James O. Andrew. After his election to the episcopacy in 1832, he had been widowed. He then married a widow, whose late husband had owned slaves. By marrying her, Bishop Andrew became the owner of her property. Thus, Methodist Bishop James O. Andrew became a slaveowner.

The church had to face the issue of whether a bishop could own slaves. That church also had to face a dilemma in its polity. A decision had to be made whether it was the responsibility of the General Conference or the responsibility of the bishops in the Episcopacy to discipline a bishop for some questionable behavior, regarding slavery or anything else.

The 1844 General Conference lasted more than a month. Instead of resolving the issues, its eventual outcome divided the denomination into northern and southern churches. Some tried to say this was neither a "schism" nor "secession."[24] But it clearly split the denomination based on state laws and practices involving slavery. The next year, a convention of southern delegates in Louisville met and planned a General Conference of a "Methodist Episcopal Church, South," in 1846. Methodists in the north, meanwhile, kept the name Methodist Episcopal Church, but they muted any remaining abolitionist voices at their 1848 General Conference.

So, the southern Methodists became a denomination that accepted, affirmed, and justified slavery. In the same era, northern Methodists—in an effort to retain all of their churches, circuits, and conferences within their state borders—abandoned any antislavery missions they previously supported in their resolutions or regulations, lest they antagonize some constituents.[25]

People in the nation's capital got the message. South Carolina Senator John C. Calhoun drafted a speech for delivery on the floor of the Senate in which he cited the separation of the Methodists over slavery as a sign that the nation was likely to split on the same issue.

---

23. See Orange Scott, "The Grounds of Secession from the M.E. Church," in *MEAS*, 257.

24. *MEAH*, 187.

25. *MEAH*, 193.

Forming a Racially Divided Church in a Racially Divided Nation

The Methodists never quite woke or acted to fulfill their mission that had once included opposition to slavery. The outcome of the Civil War, the Emancipation Proclamation, and the ratification of constitutional amendments ended slavery. But the War Between the States did not solve things, nor did it end the problems and practices of White supremacy. Frederick Douglass believed another fight would have to be won. He said America would soon have to contend with "the fight over the memory of the war."[26] Douglass was correct.

In 1866, the editor of the *Richmond Examiner*, Edward Alfred Pollard, used the phrase "the lost cause" in writing about the southern way of life and the "many noble and generous virtues" that southern culture generated.[27] The memory of the war in the north may have been that the Union had prevailed. But the memory of the war in the South became a mythic ideology about a great cause that was temporarily lost but would be revived.

Pollard referred to slavery as "the peculiar institution of labor in the South" that English interests imposed but southerners improved by the "legislative checks and Christian sentiments which were the constant employment of the South."[28] He said the "ethics of negro servitude in the South" could be summarized in two principles:

1. The white being the superior race, and the black the inferior, subordination, with or without law, must be the status of the African in the mixed society of whites and blacks.

2. It thus becomes the interest of both races, especially of the inferior race, that this status should be fixed and protected by law; and it was simply the declaration and definition of this principle that went by the name of negro slavery in the South.[29]

Pollard said the ethic of racial inferiority was constitutional, because the Constitution of the United States counts the "negro population, five of which in the basis of representation were made equal to three white men."[30]

---

26. Blight, *Frederick Douglass*, 530.

27. Pollard, *Southern History of the War*, 2:568. The phrase "lost cause" was more than a caricature offered by Pollard. It became an origin story of southern culture. Confederate General Jubal Early in 1872 and Confederate President Jefferson Davis in 1881 spoke and wrote about "the lost cause." General Early claimed that the idea of the "lost cause" originated with Robert E. Lee.

28. Pollard, *Southern History of the War*, 2:562.

29. Pollard, *Southern History of the War*, 2:563.

30. Pollard, *Southern History of the War*, 2:568.

The war was an effort by the north to crush the southern way of life, he said, to undo a natural order of creation that provided inferior beings for "the demands of physical and manual labor" so that "the better classes in the South" were set free to create an "extraordinary intellectual culture" and produce great "statesmanship."[31]

The myth of the "lost cause" also included a promise.

> When Jefferson Davis, the President of the Confederate States, was seeking safety in flight, a fellow traveler remarked to him that the cause of the Confederates was lost. He replied: "It appears so. But the principle for which we contended is bound to reassert itself, though it may be at another time and in another form."[32]

Frederick Douglass was correct to fret over the way the people would remember the war. He had experienced almost everything, ranging from the horrors and hostilities of enslavement to the hypocritical holiness of American Methodism. He knew that treasures like faith and freedom could be twisted by some persons and systems to excuse the indignities they imposed on others.

The myth of the "lost cause" proved to be pervasive and durable. It rewrote the history of enslavement, the acts of war, the conditions of peace, the terms of justice, and the memories of a social order. It became an archetype of cultural identity for many White southerners.

In June 1891, a St. Louis newspaper reported that 25,000 people had gathered in Jackson, Mississippi, with speeches, prayers, and poems to unveil a monument honoring Jefferson Davis. The event was "all that the most ardent lovers of the lost cause hoped it would be."[33]

In June 1892, a Black man named Homer A. Plessy was jailed in Louisiana for boarding a rail car designated for White passengers. Four years later, in *Plessy v. Ferguson*, the Supreme Court ruled that "separate but equal" accommodations were permissible under the Constitution.

In March 1898, the chair of the North Carolina state Democratic Party met with the editor and publisher of the state's most influential newspaper to discuss "the Negro problem" in the state's largest city, Wilmington. The party chair publicly insisted, "The Negro shall know his place."[34]

On November 10, 1898, an organized and well-armed force of about 2,000 White people launched an assault against Black people and their

---

31. Pollard, *Southern History of the War*, 2:568.
32. Pollard, *Southern History of the War*, 2:582.
33. See "Great Day for the South."
34. Zucchino, *Wilmington's Lie*, 65.

property in Wilmington. Estimates are that as many as three hundred Black persons were killed in the action, which some called a "race riot" but others more accurately identified as a "massacre." Besides those who were killed, thousands of Black people either fled or were formally banished from the city, some in forced marches. The event also was a *coup d'état* that removed elected leaders from the city government and installed instigators of the massacre as new city officials.

Among the White participants in the action were White ministers, who took their rifles to the streets and became part of the violent mob. Then on Sunday, November 13, they stepped into their pulpits to speak about the events that occurred three days earlier. The preachers made clear that White supremacy was the message of the gospel.

A Baptist preacher, who had taken his firearm on Thursday and joined the mob, said on Sunday, "God from the beginning of time intended that intelligent white men should lead the people and rule the country." Similarly, a Presbyterian preacher, who also carried his rifle in the streets on Thursday, said on Sunday, "The city . . . has been redeemed for civilization, redeemed for law and order, redeemed for decency and respectability. . . . For these things, let us give God glory." He followed those words with a pious appeal for his White congregation to "pity" the Black people in Wilmington, to "sympathize" with them, and to offer "a helping hand."[35]

Some church leaders, like John C. Dancy, expressed hope that the Black people of Wilmington might be more willing to accommodate themselves to the interests of the Whites. Others simply remained silent about the events in the city.[36] It was a story too painful to tell.

The violence in North Carolina's largest city dramatically escalated. Officially sanctioned and publicly supported attacks on Black people by White groups occurred on multiple occasions. From September 22–24, 1906, a race riot in Atlanta claimed upwards of a hundred lives. From May 31 to June 1, 1921, in Tulsa, Oklahoma, a White mob—with encouragement from local officials—destroyed the Black business center of the city and caused the deaths of an estimated three hundred Black people. Thousands of others were injured and required medical treatment.

These events showed that White supremacy, motivated by the mythology of a lost cause, could justify violent suppression of Black people. Monuments of stone and metal, ostensibly to celebrate participants in the war for the lost cause, echoed it. State legislatures enacted Jim Crow laws to codify

---

35. Zucchino, *Wilmington's Lie*, 262–63.

36. John C. Dancy attended an African Methodist Episcopal Church in Wilmington and edited two of the official publications for the African Methodist Episcopal Zion Church (Zucchino, *Wilmington's Lie*, 57–58).

it. Politicians found they could gain votes by supporting it. Churches—including Methodists—endorsed it or tolerated it but never quite woke to the wickedness of it.

That was the case even when the events were episodes of lynching. According to the Equal Justice Initiative, more than 4,000 African Americans were victims of lynching between 1877 and 1950.[37] The Tuskegee Institute estimates that 72.7 percent of the victims of lynching were Black.[38] In places across the nation, these murders of Black people involved lawless actions, approved or unopposed by lawful authorities, that served as public entertainments.

When the church woke to the hideous injustice of lynching, taking action proved to be difficult. Jessie Daniel Ames was a Texas Methodist who, early in the twentieth century, became a suffragist. She was a leader in forming the Association of Southern Women for the Prevention of Lynching. She had contacts with other women's organizations, including the Commission on Interracial Cooperation, that made her attentive to the evils of lynching and the horrendous forms of violence directed at Black people.

Ames's 1934 essay, "The Shame of a Christian People," offered two points of emphasis. First, she addressed the savagery of lynching and the wickedness of the public officials who are its enablers. Second, she demonstrated that, in a nation that established constitutional liberty for religion, it is the responsibility of the religious community to act rather than to wait for some other authority to do so.[39] This second point was a critical, prophetic witness directed against the church people who remained "silent and cowardly." As Ames suggested, when the church woke, the church must act.

But complications arose for Ames. A women's organization created by the NAACP and known as the "Anti-Lynching Crusaders" began eight years before Ames formed the Association of Southern Women for the Prevention of Lynching. Ironically, it put Ames and the NAACP at odds. Though the data demonstrate that, by far, most lynching victims are Black, Ames declined to have her White organization collaborate with the NAACP "Crusaders." Moreover, her group opposed the political strategy that the "Anti-Lynching Crusaders" adopted. In brief, the Black women wanted a national law against lynching, while Ames wanted the states to deal with it.

That difference in strategy then became entangled in the power politics of the Congress. The Black women associated with the NAACP had

---

37. See https://lynchinginamerica.eji.org/.

38. See https://law.umkc.edu/ (see also "History of Lynching in America").

39. See Jessie Daniel Ames, "The Shame of a Christian People," in *MEAS*, 540–41. On the first point, she condemned Governor James Rolph of California, who congratulated members of the mob that lynched an alleged offender.

organized their efforts in support of a bill that would have made lynching a federal crime. It passed the House of Representatives in 1940, but it faced a filibuster in the Senate. Ames favored the substance of the House bill but opposed the effort to create a federal law. She wrote to one of the Senators from Texas, who then used her letter to announce that the leader of the Association of Southern Women for the Prevention of Lynching opposed the legislation. In the end, the Congress enacted no anti-lynching law.

As a result, whatever had stirred the church to acknowledge the evils of lynching did not mean that the church woke to act in a nationally strategic way that forced an end to the lynching of Black people in America. The church never quite woke, and it never acted nationally against such wickedness.

When the church fails to act, it rejects the sacred promises that apply to the circumstances of the moment. When the church woke but then failed to address something as patently wicked as lynching, the church was, in the words of Jessie Daniel Ames, "silent and cowardly."

In its founding era, American Methodism had adopted an antislavery discipline. But as decades unfolded, the church abandoned that mission. What's more, the church tolerated and enabled the sinister sin of White supremacy. Instead of acting upon what it knew about the spiritual power of the gospel, the church became silent and cowardly about the gospel. That meant the gospel was ashamed of the church.

Meanwhile, in the decade when Tulsa was torched and when the church failed to be a force against lynching, Methodists in America put forward a plan to create a reunited Methodist denomination. The reunion was envisioned as a way to overcome the schisms of the nineteenth century, including the one that split the church over slavery. However, the emerging plan for a Methodist reunion not only failed to address the internal problems of White supremacy and the public problems of social injustice, but it also codified a constitutional structure for the reunited church in which race was the major factor in its organization.

A Segregated Reunion

In the late 1930s, amid a growing European war and an enduring Depression, American Methodists were drafting plans to reunite a denomination that had broken apart in the previous century. The Civil War that restored the Union of the United States had not reunited the church.

But leaders of the Methodist Episcopal Church, South, and the Methodist Episcopal Church had been talking for decades about bringing together the pieces that had separated over slavery in 1844. Each denomination had created a global missionary enterprise in the time they were apart. Each had established institutions of higher education and theological education. Each had organized social service initiatives including hospitals, homes for orphaned children, and other ministries. And each had priorities for the ways a reunited church would be structured. The southern church had created a Judicial Council as a constitutional body to review actions taken by the General Conference and wanted it to be part of denominational government, for example. And Methodist Protestants, who were in the discussions, seemed ready to accept bishops again.

The defining factor, however, was race. When the reunion officially occurred in 1939, it united three overwhelmingly White Methodist denominations: the Methodist Protestant Church; the Methodist Episcopal Church, South; and the Methodist Episcopal Church. Black Methodist denominations that had formed early in the nineteenth century (the African Methodist Episcopal Church, the African Methodist Episcopal Zion Church, and the African Union Church) were not included in the reunion. Nor was the Colored Methodist Episcopal Church, which had been split from southern Methodism in 1870. The Methodist Church, as the new denomination was called, had a global presence with a constitution to establish governing authority for a new international profile. But the constitutional system was driven by the American Methodists' decision to base this reunited denomination on racially binary practices and White supremacy principles.

The Constitution for the Methodist Church contained an entirely new structural unit of government called "jurisdictional conferences" that only existed in the United States. There were six of them. Five were defined by American geographical regions: Northeast, Southeast, North Central, South Central, and Western. The sixth was defined by race.

Designated as the "Central Jurisdiction," it geographically overlapped the other five. It could have been called the Black Jurisdiction. It ensured that Black preachers in the Methodist Church were clergy members of Black annual conferences, consisting of Black Methodist local churches. By assigning responsibility for electing bishops to the six individual jurisdictions, the Constitution of the Methodist Church effectively gerrymandered a guarantee that the White clergy and congregations would only be overseen by White bishops. In the Central Jurisdiction, Black Methodists would be elected to the office of bishop, but they would oversee only Black preachers and appoint them to Black local churches. At the General Conference, Black annual conferences would have delegates, but they would be substantially outnumbered by delegates from the White annual conferences in their regional jurisdictions.

What happened in 1939 is often called a "reunion" of the northern and southern churches. That term, however, gives a patina of reconciliation to cover what was formally and functionally a deeply racial estrangement. It was not the only racially motivated division of Methodism.

Most Black clergy, conferences, and congregations that had been part of the Methodist Episcopal Church South after 1844 were excised from the denomination after the Civil War to become the Colored Methodist Episcopal Church in 1870. So, the "reunion" of the northern and southern Methodists was actually the creation of a new denomination that embodied principles and premises of White superiority and Black segregation.

Additionally, it occurred at a time when the "local church" was becoming the *de facto* center of American Methodism. Since most local churches had long been racially or ethnically homogeneous, the new denomination formed by a twentieth-century "reunion" in 1939 was in fact both culturally and constitutionally segregated by color into Black and White.

CHAPTER FIVE

Divided in Church and Society

The Complex Communities of Methodism

Methodism in the twenty-first century is a global phenomenon with many church groups and eighty million members in 138 countries.[1] The Methodist institutions that arose from American roots in the colonial era are part of the story. They developed institutions for ministry that benefit society, in addition to tens of thousands of local churches and multiple denominations. And these Methodist denominations that emerged in America are not just in America. Each denomination has an international presence. Their roots grew many branches across the world.

The African Methodist Episcopal Church has about three million members, with some in sub-Saharan Africa and in the Caribbean. The African Methodist Episcopal Zion Church (about 1.4 million members) and the Christian Methodist Episcopal Church (about 1.2 million) have constituents in the Caribbean and in multiple African nations. The United Methodist Church has nearly half of its members outside the United States—in Africa and Asia, as well as in parts of Eastern, Western, and Central Europe. What formed in North America has many global forms.

This Methodist presence can be confusing. In southern California, one can belong to a "Korean Methodist Church" and be affiliated with a body based in Seoul. Or one can belong to a "Korean United Methodist Church" and be part of the California Pacific Annual Conference of the United Methodist Church overseen by a bishop in Los Angeles. Such situations also

---

1. See "Statistical Information."

exist in other states of the nation and in other annual conferences within American Methodism.

And similar confusion also is possible elsewhere. In Nigeria, the most populous country in Africa,[2] one can be a Methodist in the "Methodist Church Nigeria," which has seventy-four diocesan bishops. Or one can belong to "The United Methodist Church," which in Nigeria has four annual conferences and one bishop.

Each Methodist body that formed in the United States has its own ecclesiastical history. The African Methodist Episcopal Church celebrated two hundred years as an independent church in 2016. The African Methodist Episcopal Church Zion celebrated two hundred years in 2021. The Christian Methodist Episcopal Church marked its one hundred fiftieth anniversary in 2020, though the coronavirus crisis caused a delay in the festivities for celebrating the occasion. With more than a million members and ministries in Haiti, Jamaica, and fourteen African nations in addition to the United States, the Christian Methodist Episcopal Church has plenty to celebrate. But the unique situation that brought the church to life in 1870 involves both pride and pain.

Racism as an Irresistible Force in Forming the Church

Black Methodists in Philadelphia, New York, and elsewhere had created their own new denominations to escape the disrespect, neglect, and abuse they endured from White Methodists. They cherished worshiping without White oversight, acquiring property without White control, and affirming preachers without the impositions of White limitations on the itinerancy of Black clergy. As independent African Methodist churches, they pursued the Christian mission, while emphasizing their Wesleyan heritage.

But the Christian Methodist Episcopal Church is unique. By Juneteenth,[3] two months after the Civil War ended, word of Emancipation had spread. Six months later, enough states had ratified the Thirteenth Amendment to the Constitution to end slavery in the nation. An estimated 100,000 formerly enslaved Black members of the Methodist Episcopal Church, South, acquired their political emancipation and their

---

2. The estimated population of Nigeria in 2021 is 214 million, nearly twice that of Ethiopia, which is second.

3. On June 19, 1865, slaves in Texas finally heard about Emancipation. The date, known as Juneteenth, became a national holiday by the action of the United States Congress and the president's signature in June 2021.

constitutional freedom of religion. By the end of 1865, they were people, not property. And they were Methodists.

A question arose at the 1866 General Conference of the Methodist Episcopal Church, South: "What shall be done to promote the religious interests of our colored members?"[4] One proposal was to create a separate "jurisdiction" of Black annual conferences under the General Conference. Another option was uniting the Black members with one of the African Methodist churches. But the prevailing view among newly liberated former slaves, expressed by the voices and the pens of Black leaders, was clear.

> Isaac Lane of Tennessee, and later Founder of Lane College, said, "At once we made it known that we preferred a separate organization of our own . . . established after our own ideas and notions." Lucius Holsey of Georgia, and later Founder of Paine College, wrote, "After emancipation a movement was at once inaugurated to give the Negroes a separate and independent organization."[5]

In 1866, the Methodist Episcopal Church, South, decided to place their Black preachers and laity "into an entirely separate Church and thus enable them to become their own guides and governors."[6] On December 16, 1870, forty-one former slaves officially formed "The Colored Methodist Episcopal Church."[7] To be clear, not all of the Black Methodists in the South joined this new denomination. In 1873, when previously enslaved people founded St. Paul Methodist Church in Dallas, they were in connection with the Methodist Episcopal Church, South.

But the Christian Methodist Church, like all Black Methodist denominations that began in America, has its own story. They have an international mission and control their own policies, practices, and systems of order. They also offer enduring evidence of the racism that forced them to form separate Methodist churches. Subjugation, subordination, and segregation deprived them of religious liberty and their human dignity in a church that tolerated injustice within society.

It happened in all regions, not only in the South. Northern White Methodists segregated the church, too. In 1864, their General Conference

---

4. Lakey, "History of the CME Church," para. 2.

5. Lakey, "History of the CME Church," para. 3.

6. Isaac H. Anderson, "Report of the Committee on Church Organization," in *MEAS*, p. 368.

7. Lakey, "History of the CME Church," para. 1. The meeting that established the new church was in Jackson, Tennessee. In 1954, the denomination changed its name to "Christian Methodist Episcopal Church."

gave full clergy rights to Black preachers (i.e., the men) but also created Black-only annual conferences. Their newly affirmed Black preachers in full membership could itinerate, but only among Black constituencies.[8]

Several factors contributed to the segregation and racial subordination within American Methodism. One was Black Methodists' search for freedom from White authority over worship, property, and ministry. Another was White Methodists' political control over the doctrine and disciplines of the church. These patterns limited Black constituencies to choosing Black leaders and discussing Black concerns, while diluting Black Methodists' impact on any broader church matters. The church crafted a racialized identity. American Methodism was racially segregated. And American Methodists worshiped in racially separate, racially homogeneous congregations.

Another was that American Methodists lived in a context of racial division, animosity, and violence in the nation. White terrorists massacred Black people in various locations: Colfax, Louisiana, in 1873; Vicksburg, Mississippi, in 1874; Wilmington, North Carolina, in 1898; New Orleans in 1900; Charleston, South Carolina, in 1919; and Tulsa, Oklahoma, in 1921. Supremacy by Whites in America was the norm at local, state, and federal levels of government.

Woodrow Wilson had written that White people should persist in the determination "that the negro race shall never again rule over them" and also in their "united resistance to the domination [by] an ignorant race." When he was president, Wilson had his cabinet watch "The Birth of a Nation." When members of the National Association for the Advancement of Colored People (NAACP) visited him to insist on equal justice, he evicted them from the Oval Office.[9]

Putting a Segregated Church in Order

When northern and southern Methodist denominations reunited in 1939 after a century of separation, *The Book of Discipline* for the new church included a map[10] of the United States. It outlined geographical boundaries of five jurisdictions and had shading that defined a sixth one, the Central Jurisdiction, which overlapped the regional ones. Black conferences, congregations, and clergy were assigned to the Central Jurisdiction. The church was constitutionally segregated.

---

8. Thompson, "Invisible Made Visible," 6–7. See also *MEAH*, 259.
9. Woodard, "Woodrow Wilson," para. 10. See also Berg, *Wilson*, 347–50.
10. *Doctrines and Discipline of the Methodist Church 1939*, 448.

White members might never interact with Black bishops, pastors, or laity. And there were inequities. Any Black bishop of the Central Jurisdiction had the same expense allowance as any White bishop. But Black bishops had to cover two-thirds of the nation. Expense accounts were equal in dollars, but they were inequitable in distribution.

With its regional jurisdictions, the Methodist Church essentially preserved the territory of the Methodist Episcopal Church, South, in two jurisdictions—the Southeastern and the South Central—which basically adhered to the boundaries of the old Confederate States of America. It defined the Central Jurisdiction as a region consisting of "The Negro Annual Conferences, the Negro Mission Conferences and Missions in the United States of America."[11] The Methodist Church thus established an ecclesiastical system of racial segregation through its Constitution.

Besides segregating the Methodist Church constitutionally, the new denomination also practiced segregation congregationally. In Methodism, the word "church" had not been used as a term with a "local" meaning. Lay members belonged to the connection.[12] Clergy were members of a conference. If a preacher were to "locate" it meant becoming inactive. Congregations were gatherings of people for worship, but they were not self-governing local corporate entities.

Even in the United Methodist Church today, the clergy members of annual conferences are "traveling" preachers according to the Constitution[13] and the laws of the church.[14] Their authorizations go with them when they move. Bishops appoint clergy not to local churches but pastoral charges. As the denomination's Constitution says, "bishops shall appoint . . . ministers to the charges."[15] Their places of ministry are the communities, not congregations. At the local level, the authoritative unit of constitutional governance is called a "charge conference"[16] not a congregation. Officially, at least, the Methodist approach to order emphasizes the priority of the connection. As the Constitutions of the United Methodist Church and of the Methodist

---

11. *Doctrines and Discipline of the Methodist Church 1939*, ¶ 1361.

12. *Doctrines and Discipline of the Methodist Church 1939*, ¶¶ 132–33.

13. See the Constitution of the United Methodist Church, Division Two, Section IV, Article IV.6, and Section V, Article IV.7, in *The Book of Discipline 2016*, ¶¶ 27.6 and 31.7.

14. *Book of Discipline 2016*, ¶ 603.6.

15. See the Constitution, Division Three, Article X, in *The Book of Discipline 2016*, ¶ 54. Previously it was called a "quarterly conference."

16. See The Constitution, Division Two, Section IX, Article I, *The Book of Discipline 2016*, ¶ 43.

Church before it established, "The Annual Conference is the basic body in the Church."[17] Methodism is connectionally, not congregationally, defined.

Nevertheless, beginning in the 1920s, the General Conferences of the northern and of the southern Methodists began to use the phrase "local church" in church law.[18] In the 1930s, the phrase became a bit more visible as a sub-section heading for one portion of the denominational responsibility for Christian Education.[19] In 1944, the Methodist Church revised the format of its *Book of Discipline* and put all the "local church" legislation regarding membership, ministry, property, finances, or anything else into one section of fifty pages in the *Discipline*.[20]

The result was a thoroughgoing racial segregation of American Methodism achieved in principle and in practice. In principle, the largest Methodist denomination in the United States chose to order itself constitutionally in a way that separated Black and White laity and clergy in governing systems. In practice, most Methodist members expressed their faith and experienced their church life in racially separated local gatherings for worship and mission. The division of the church into White and Black was a combination of two factors: (*a*) deliberate contrivance; and (*b*) derivative consequence.

The deliberate contrivance was a constitutional scheme that created jurisdictions and set their boundaries. By allocating the basic bodies of the church—the annual conferences—to their jurisdictions and by assigning to each jurisdiction the responsibility for electing bishops and for setting annual conference boundaries, the Methodist Church in 1939 guaranteed that the church in America would be racially divided. The racial division was established in its Constitution.

Each annual conference would choose the clergy and lay delegates for its jurisdictional conference. At that assembly, bishops for the jurisdiction would be elected and assigned to the Episcopal Areas within that jurisdiction. Also at that assembly, the boundaries of the annual conferences within that jurisdiction would be set. Because of the way that annual conferences

---

17. See Division Two, Section VII, Article II, published as ¶ 22 in *Doctrines and Discipline of the Methodist Church 1939* and Division Two, Section VII, Article II, published as ¶ 37 in *The Book of Discipline of the United Methodist Church 1968*.

18. For example, it appears in *Doctrines and Discipline of the Methodist Episcopal Church 1924*, ¶ 110.

19. See *Doctrines and Discipline of the Methodist Episcopal Church, South*, ¶¶ 450–60.

20. *Doctrines and Discipline of the Methodist Church 1944*, ¶¶ 101–270. In 1988, the United Methodist Church gave legislative primacy to the local church, saying, "It is primarily at the level of the local church that the Church encounters the world" (cf. *Book of Discipline 1988*, ¶ 202).

were grouped into five regional and one racial jurisdiction, delegates to the Central Jurisdiction Conference would be overwhelmingly if not entirely Black Methodists and delegates to the five regional jurisdictional conferences would be overwhelmingly White Methodists. If any decision were made to redraw the boundaries of annual conferences, each jurisdictional conference only had authority to do so for its own jurisdiction. Central Jurisdiction delegates could redraw the boundaries of its annual conferences in the northeastern quadrant of the United States, but they could not touch the boundaries of the annual conferences in the Northeastern Jurisdiction.

Therefore, Black Methodists were certain to be elected as bishops but were effectively restricted to oversight of Black annual conferences, Black clergy, and Black lay members of Black congregations. White Methodists were certain to be elected as bishops but would only oversee White annual conferences, White clergy, and lay members of mostly White churches.

Because this deliberate contrivance was a constitutional scheme, any effort to change it would require a constitutional amendment. Black annual conferences elected delegates to the General Conference, where such a constitutional amendment would have to originate. But their numbers would be relatively few in comparison to the White delegates from the White annual conferences. The Constitution was set. The Methodist Church from 1939 forward would have six jurisdictions, five regional and one racial. This deliberately contrived, racially segregated, White supremacist system solidified segregation in principle and in practice.

The principle was further codified in the manner that the boundaries of the five regional jurisdictions were drawn. Together, two of those five—namely, the South Central Jurisdiction and the Southeastern Jurisdiction—nearly matched the territory of the Methodist Episcopal Church, South. They also nearly conformed to the area of what formerly was the Confederacy. They included the states in the South that had notoriously imposed Jim Crow laws beginning in the final decades of the nineteenth century. These states restricted Black voting rights, separated public accommodations, affirmed segregated businesses, and ran segregated public schools.

If those who drafted the Plan of Union for the Methodist Church in 1939 merely hoped to create jurisdictions just for administrative purposes, the boundaries could have been drawn in a variety of ways in the United States. For example, jurisdictions could have been created using America's time zones. But the way they were drawn was clear evidence the jurisdictional system was a deliberate contrivance to impose the principles of racial segregation and White supremacy.

The derivative consequence was the result of an increased emphasis on the local church in American Methodism. Most local churches had sharp racial demographics. Since the earliest decades of Methodism in America, Black members sought to be free from suppression by and subordination to White leadership. And White members preferred separation from Black ones. In practice, if not in principle, congregational segregation by race had become the norm. Thus, the Methodist Church drew support for its segregationist principle from segregated local practices.

The Methodist Church was a denomination with a racially segregated Constitution, which fit conveniently with racially segregated patterns in most places of worship. And segregated local churches took their cues from the segregated social order. Separation by race was woven into the fabric of both society and church. Worshipers attended local churches the way they patronized restaurants, used water fountains, and sent their children to school. Congregations derived their behaviors from the social order and echoed them.

American society and American Methodism determined by custom, if not by law, that Blacks and Whites would worship separately. As the local church became increasingly important in Methodist life and as a "congregationalization" of American Methodism became increasingly normative in the twentieth century, the segregation of Black and White congregations formed an ecclesiastical culture that reinforced constitutional principles and reflected social mores.

Polity Matters

The term "polity" refers to the systems by which churches are organized for making decisions. A church's polity determines whether a congregation operates alone or is controlled by a hierarchy on matters involving ministries, finances, property, ordination, and theological education. A church's polity determines how clergy will be ordained and assigned. Methodism has a "connectional" polity. All its entities link with one another. No entity has total authority.

Polity matters in the United States, where the Constitution gives churches the liberty to govern their operations. Religious groups make decisions based on their doctrines and rules, not based on civil laws. For example, laws in the United States prohibit discriminating by gender in employment. But the polity of the Roman Catholic Church, which prohibits the ordination of women as priests, cannot be overruled by civil laws. Even the criminal laws of states do not dictate church polity. An ordained or licensed minister might be arrested, tried, convicted, and imprisoned for something.

But only that minister's church, under its polity, can decide whether she or he remains a credentialed member of the clergy in good standing.

Each church uses its own procedures to select, ordain, and assign leaders. Episcopalians group their parishes in a diocese, and each diocese elects its bishop. Roman Catholics also have bishops and diocesan structures, but the pope chooses bishops. The African Methodist Episcopal Zion Church, African Methodist Episcopal Church, and Christian Methodist Episcopal Church elect bishops at their respective General Conferences. United Methodist bishops are elected by central conferences outside the United States, and by jurisdictional conferences inside it.[21]

The United Methodist Church today has both formal and informal approaches to polity. Any ordained elder can be elected as a United Methodist bishop. Yet, in practice, jurisdictional conferences in the United States pay close attention only to candidates from annual conferences in their own regions.[22] Those elected immediately become members of the Council of Bishops, a constitutional body that serves as the collective episcopacy for global United Methodism. But no individual bishop has authority over another. And there is no chief executive of the church.

While the bishops in a jurisdiction might choose to discuss matters of public importance for church mission in their region of the United States, United Methodists have neither a national office nor a national presiding bishop. When an issue arises in the United States, no individual or entity can speak with authority to the whole church in America, and no United Methodist can speak to the people of America on behalf of the whole church.[23]

So, polity can deprive the church and the nation of an authorized public voice in moments of crisis. No church entity exists as a national authority to act, though the country gives a church constitutional freedom to act. Polity, not public law, limits the church's capacity to act promptly. If the church woke, it would have a means for prophetic and immediate national action.

Twentieth-century decisions gave the Methodist Church a polity that institutionalized racism. It established principles of racial segregation and

---

21. See the Constitution, Division Three, Article II, published as ¶ 46 in *The Book of Discipline of the United Methodist Church 2016*.

22. A notable exception to this practice occurred in 1984. The Western Jurisdictional Conference elected Leontine T. C. Kelly, a Black clergy member of Virginia Annual Conference in the Southeast Jurisdiction. She had also been a candidate for election simultaneously in the Southeast, but when it became clear that the Southeastern Jurisdictional Conference delegates were not going to elect a Black woman to the office of bishop for the first time, the Western Jurisdictional Conference elected her.

23. The General Board of Church and Society can do so, but only within parameters the General Conference permits.

White supremacy. It used endorsement from practices in local churches. Polity can stifle the church. But nothing silences prophecy.

When the Church Woke and Witnessed

Prophets can show that the gospel is ashamed of the church. The church could hear, heed, and trust prophets who speak. But that requires courage, confession, and commitment by local churches, denominational authorities, and legislative processes of a denomination.

If the church woke, the clergy and the bishops who appoint them will make anti-racism a prominent point in proclaiming the gospel. If the church woke, local churches will demonstrate their determination to end segregated practices. If the church woke, preachers and parishioners in American Methodism will reclaim their constitutionally guaranteed religious liberty and confront public leaders on public policies. If the church woke, every entity in the connection will confess the heritage of White supremacy woven into Methodism and make reparations for it.

If the church woke, there will be prayerful liturgies and public events for confessing the White supremacist legacy, the inheritance of racist divisions and practices, and the unjust social systems that the church tolerates with unrighteous silence. If the church woke, people of faith will examine—rather than ignore—an ecclesial history of which the gospel is ashamed. If the church woke, prayers in sanctuaries and postings on social media will acknowledge what we have done, admit what we have left undone, and atone for ways that the gospel of love has been suppressed or set aside or buried in some secondary status beneath other agendas.

If the church woke, then promises of faith and pledges of finances will be commitments to fund programs, endow positions, and institute priorities that are intended to abolish the racist sentiments of society. As with some of our Methodist forebears who acted to abolish enslavement of other human beings, Methodism that woke will rediscover the inspiration to abolish practices that are unloving, even if they are not enslaving. If the church woke, then commitments to educate, rather than tolerate, ignorance about race will prevail. If the church woke, renewed spiritual disciplines will shape a Christlike rejection of injustice, as Jesus did in the temple.[24]

If the church woke, it will do such things even though they may not immediately succeed. If the church woke, it will be a witness to the future. At the 1936 northern General Conference of the Methodist Episcopal Church,

---

24. See Matt 21:12–13; Mark 11:15–18; Luke 19:45–46; and John 2:13–17.

as Methodists prepared to establish a jurisdiction system that would segregate the church, Dr. Mary McLeod Bethune addressed the plan.

> I wish that every woman in this audience and every man in this audience could turn black just for a season and come up against some of the problems that we have confronted for these years. . . . I have not been able to make my mind see it clearly enough to be willing to have the history of this General Conference written, and the Negro youths of fifty or a hundred years from today read and find, that Mary McLeod Bethune acquiesced to anything that looked like segregation to black people.[25]

The Archives of the United Methodist Church and its predecessor denominations are housed on the campus of Drew University. Among them are formal documents and informal memorabilia. There are minutes of actions taken by constitutional entities, official records of denominational agencies, histories of local churches, and random materials, which exhibit the experiences of American Methodists. One item is a baptism certificate. It is a routine record of an early twentieth-century day when an infant was baptized and received by the church.

But this specific certificate is significant in two key details. First, the individual whose baptism it certifies was later elected a bishop of the Methodist Church. Second, as written by the hand of the preacher who administered the baptism and signed the certificate, it verifies that the child baptized was "White."

The regulations no longer require recording baptisms separately for White and Black (or "Colored," as would have been noted at the time). However, their absence now is no cause for celebration. That they existed at all is cause for lament. Such practices inflicted a deep wound on the body of Christ. And the stigmata remain.

Methodists may have stopped inflicting some wounds. They woke. But the church must confess that such things were done, must educate new generations of Christians that such things were practiced, and must commit to overcoming all the residual pain that remains in the tissue memory of the body of Christ. If the church woke, it will bear witness to these things. If the church woke, it will act in ways that impact the world.

On Capitol Hill in Washington, DC, Methodists constructed a building that has stood as a witness for nearly a hundred years. Completed in 1923, it was intended to be a platform from which Methodists could speak to the nation and to the national government on matters of public policy that involve the care of God's creation and God's creatures.

---

25. *MEAS*, 551.

From offices in the building, one can look across the street and see the great institutions of the American people. To the west is the United States Capitol, where the houses of Congress meet. To the south is the Supreme Court building and, just past that, the Library of Congress. Its offices host ecumenical bodies, and its meeting rooms host discussions about matters of national importance for Christian mission. Within an easy walk are all the buildings where House and Senate members have their office suites. Methodists have a voice on Capitol Hill to inform Congress and to teach the entire church about official positions of the denomination on public topics such as immigration, education, health care, and the environment.

But, in its hundred years, the building has also offered another kind of witness. At one point, the building housed a cafeteria, where anyone could enter and buy lunch. What became known among Black Methodists was that the cafeteria in the Methodist Building, through the efforts of church leaders, became a desegregated space.[26]

Indeed, it became the only place on Capitol Hill where Black people could buy a meal.

Black families, who were driving from Alabama or Georgia or the Carolinas to visit relatives up north, knew they could leave home early in the morning, while it was still dark, and drive as far as Washington. They could stop at the Methodist Building for lunch. And then they could finish the journey to see their families at dinnertime.

In the days when it was not necessarily safe for Black families to be on the road, and in the days when it was never certain that they could find a place or eat or sleep on the trip, the Methodist Building on Capitol Hill was a witness that, when the church woke, the church acts. When the church woke, the hungry are fed. When the church woke, the homeless are housed. When the church woke, the lonely are visited. When the church woke, there is space for all.

From a building on Capitol Hill, a connectional church has a presence and provides a witness that proclaims the gospel of which the church is not ashamed. While no congregation could do that, all of the congregations and institutions in the body of Christ collectively and connectionally can do that. And polity could express prophecy when the church woke to act against the divisions in society and church.

---

26. *MEAH*, 391.

CHAPTER SIX

Beneath the Cross of Jesus

Confrontations in Context

The church woke in the middle of the twentieth century. At least in some places and in some ways, it did. In 1939, the Methodist Church was racially segregated at every level: annual conferences, local churches, and jurisdictions. Most institutions affiliated with, or controlled by, the church were racially segregated too. Anti-segregation efforts existed. And a desegregation process began, though it was slow and uncertain. Quite often, it was opposed by violence.

Methodists founded thirty-one colleges and universities for Black students. Two-thirds of them were created by the three leading Black denominations.[1] The need for Black colleges and universities existed because so many of the educational institutions established by, or affiliated with, the White churches were segregated. Duke, Emory, and Southern Methodist Universities were founded between 1911 and 1924 with admissions policies that prevented Black students from becoming candidates for academic degrees.

After 1950, the Methodist Church and its White universities began taking steps toward racial integration. Southern Methodist University started it. In 1952, five Black students were admitted to Perkins School of Theology as degree[2] candidates, and they graduated with divinity degrees

---

1. Seven of those higher education institutions have closed. Two became public universities in Maryland.

2. Cuninggim, *Perkins Led the Way*; Payne, *One Hundred Years*, 196–98.

three years later.[3] Other institutions dallied. Emory rejected the application of a Black candidate for admission to its medical school in 1959 with a letter from its admissions director who wrote, "we are not authorized to consider for admission a member of the Negro race."[4]

Duke admitted Black graduate students in 1961. Then the Trustees voted to admit Black undergraduates in 1963.[5] However, the vote by the Duke board was not unanimous.[6]

The academic institution of the church that woke to act first, namely Southern Methodist University in Dallas, was founded in 1911. Having Black students on campus and in classes for degree studies took courage in 1952. Dallas was considered "the most racist city in America."[7]

That label, which had been attached to Dallas early in the twentieth century, was one that the city earned. On March 3, 1910, a crowd of 5,000 people had gathered in downtown Dallas to witness a Black man being lynched.[8] Allen Brooks, who was sixty-five years old, was reported to have been seen in his employer's barn with the owner's two-and-one-half year-old daughter. Brooks was arrested and charged with attempted rape. During a hearing inside the Dallas County courthouse, a mob broke into the courtroom, overwhelmed the sheriff's deputies, and then tossed Brooks through a second-story window to the city street below. Whether he died from the fall or from being beaten by the crowd in the street is unknown. But his body was dragged a half mile through the city and hanged from a lighted arch that welcomed visitors to Dallas. Postcards with photos and accounts of the lynching were sold and sent as souvenirs.

3. The nomenclature for the graduate degree that most churches accepted as an educational credential for ordination was known as the bachelor of divinity degree. During the last quarter of the twentieth century, nomenclature changed to identify the graduate-level nature of the three-year program of studies. The most common designation has become "master of divinity" (or "MDiv") degree.

4. Asmelash, "Emory University School of Medicine," para. 7. Emory did not desegregate or offer admission to Black students until 1962.

5. Gillispie, "Let's Embrace Duke's Entire History," para. 7. Duke has been affiliated with, but not owned or controlled by the church, since its founding. Southern Methodist University and Emory University were founded by and, through electing the Boards of Trustees, controlled by the church. SMU admitted its first Black undergraduates in 1962. Emory did so in 1963.

6. See the June 2, 1962 entry at https://spotlight.duke.edu/50years/timeline-2/.

7. This label, which had been assigned to Dallas in the 1920s, was remembered forty years later in the context of events surrounding the Kennedy Assassination in November 1963. See Payne, "When Dallas Was the Most Racist," originally published in 1997 in *Legacies: A History Journal for Dallas and North Central Texas* by the Dallas County Heritage Society, the Dallas Historical Society, and the Sixth Floor Museum.

8. See Martinez and Holter, "Inside a Sickening Moment."

By the 1920s, Dallas was a center of the Ku Klux Klan. It controlled the politics of the city. Dallas had the largest chapter of the Ku Klux Klan in the world in the 1920s and the largest Klan membership per capita in the nation.

About a third of the men in Dallas were Klansmen.[9] During the State Fair of Texas each fall in Dallas, one day was designated as Ku Klux Klan Day.

On a Saturday night in 1921, a parade of Klansmen marched in the streets of downtown and carried the banner, "We Stand for White Supremacy." The next day, Charles C. Selecman, the pastor of First Methodist Church, told his congregation, "If the situation is such that a Ku Klux Klan is justified in Dallas, then it is a good thing." Two years later, in 1923, Selecman became president of Southern Methodist University. In 1938, he was elected to the office of bishop of the Methodist Episcopal Church, South.

Racist policies and White supremacist practices early in the twentieth century created an "era of racial terror"[10] in Dallas. Klan power in regional and state politics included Methodism.

Just north of the city, on May 31 and June 1, 1921, a massacre in Tulsa killed dozens of Black people, injured hundreds of Black people, displaced thousands of Black people, and also destroyed Black-owned homes and businesses, leaving the Greenwood section of the city in ruins. In 1922, a Tulsa preacher described his involvement with the Klan and the prevalence of Klan members in Methodism. In a letter to Bishop Edwin Mouzon, the Methodists' leader in Dallas and the first dean of the Southern Methodist University theological school, the preacher from Tulsa wrote of Methodists in the Klan,

> Some of your Bishops are members, all but two of the Presiding Elders in this state were, at least 75% of our preachers, and dozens of our churches have their entire official boards, or the large majority, within the organization.[11]

---

9. The "women, children, and minorities" were not eligible to join the Klan. See Payne, "When Dallas Was the Most Racist," para. 4.

10. Dillard, "In Downtown Dallas," para. 1. The population of Dallas in 1910 was about 92,000. So more than 5 percent of the city witnessed the lynching of Allen Brooks. With the population of Dallas at nearly 1.4 million in 2020, that would be proportional to a gathering of 74,600.

11. Letter from Harold G. Cooke to Bishop Edwin Mouzon, November 1922 (*MEAS*, 506–7). Mouzon was elected to the office of bishop in 1910. He remained in office while he simultaneously served as the first dean of the School of Theology at Southern Methodist University, when it opened for students in 1915.

The Ku Klux Klan organized and provoked incidents of racial violence. They also created a mighty mystique. With robes, rituals, and rhetoric, the Klan tapped into mythic images carrying medieval anti-Catholic and anti-Jewish sentiments. The Klan also adapted a terrorist technique from the Middle Ages. In Europe, as early as the twelfth century, cross burnings were used to intimidate adversaries, issue public statements, and declare war. In the twentieth century, the Ku Klux Klan burned crosses to make racist threats and to celebrate turning those threats into reality.

As a symbol, the burning cross appears twice in Thomas Dixon's 1905 novel called *The Clansman: A Historical Romance of the Ku Klux Klan*. In the 1915 film, "The Birth of a Nation," which D. W. Griffith based on Dixon's book, Klan members burn crosses before they lynch a Black man. Burning a cross became a distinguishing mark of racial and religious targeting.

On Thanksgiving night 1915, after lynching a Jewish man whose conviction had been reversed by the Georgia court, a cross was set afire in a ceremony on Stone Mountain. It quickly became a hallmark of the Klan, who lit crosses to terrorize Black people and their allies.[12]

In 1924, the Ku Klux Klan constructed a building in downtown Fort Worth, Texas, and used it for meetings as well as a staging area for "cross lightings," as the Klan called them.[13] That year, which was the "high water mark"[14] of the Klan, came two years after Texas elected a Ku Klux Klan member named Earle Bradford Mayfield to a seat in the United States Senate. His election happened, in part, because the Klan had formed a political alliance with some Protestant Prohibitionists that generated enough votes to secure Mayfield's election.

The size and influence of the Klan declined during the Depression years. And in 1933, when Prohibition ended, the Klan lost a political ally. But White supremacy did not diminish. It remained a force in Dallas and across the South.

When Southern Methodist University decided to desegregate, it had to confront White supremacist policies and racist practices in the city and the region. But it also had a new leader. President Selecman became a Methodist bishop in 1938. His successor was no ally of the Klan.

---

12. See Kirchner, "Cross Burning Is More Common." Kirchner writes, "The race of the intended victims is still the biggest motivating factor." See also Rian Dundon, "Why Does the Ku Klux Klan Burn Crosses?" Dundon writes, "Incorporating religious iconography can add a bit of mystery to the menace" (para. 4).

13. A 2003 Supreme Court decision (538 U.S. 343) known as *Virginia v. Black* says that states may ban cross burnings that are intended to intimidate but not cross lightings, which are forms of free speech.

14. Chalmers, "Ku Klux Klan in Politics," 234–47.

Umphrey Lee assumed the presidency of Southern Methodist University in 1939. He was well-known in Dallas. As an undergraduate at Southern Methodist University, he had been the president of the student association. As the pastor of Highland Park Methodist Church, he led the construction of its new building on the corner of the university campus. A scholar of Methodist history and of the theology of John Wesley, Lee earned a PhD from Columbia University. He was the dean of Vanderbilt Divinity School when he was offered, and accepted, the presidency of Southern Methodist University. A native of the Dallas area, he envisioned possibilities beyond its racist practices.

From 1939 until retiring in 1953, Lee led the university through the difficult years of World War II and the post-war era of rapid growth in the student population, when dormitory space was so insufficient that some students were housed in Quonset huts. He also guided some significant changes that transformed the university and its school of theology. Substantial gifts from Joe and Lois Perkins of Wichita Falls, Texas, led to creating an endowment, constructing new buildings in a new quad, and naming the theological school "Perkins School of Theology." In 1951, in another dramatic act, Lee hired a new Perkins School of Theology dean, to whom he said regarding the idea of desegregating the school, "The way is open now."[15]

Merrimon Cuninggim had raised the issue of ending racial segregation early in his discussions with Lee about accepting the position as dean. He knew that a few Black non-degree students had taken classes at Perkins. But admitting students to degree programs, having them in the dormitories, and giving them a public presence in the life of the theological school and the university would be revolutionary. Cuninggim recruited five Black men from various states who had earned undergraduate degrees at different historically Black colleges and universities:[16]

- John W. Elliott, Edenton, NC (Shaw University);
- James A. Hawkins, Jackson, TN (Lane College);
- James V. Lyles, Texarkana, AR (Philander Smith College);
- Negail R. Riley, Oklahoma City, OK (Howard University);
- A. Cecil Williams, Austin, TX (Huston-Tillotson College).

---

15. Allen, *Perkins School of Theology*, 113.

16. Allen, *Perkins School of Theology*, 114. At the time Cecil Williams received his undergraduate degree, his school was called Samuel Huston College. In a 1952 merger with Tillotson, a women's college, it became Huston-Tillotson.

Confession, Courage, Commitment

To achieve the admission of these students required an act of confession by the university that the policies and practices of racial segregation were wrong. But to achieve success with this "Experiment," as Cuninggim called it,[17] great courage and commitment would be needed on the part of the five Black students, the administration of the university, and the church.

The courage and commitment were tested multiple times in the early years. One of the major challenges occurred near the close of the Black students' first year. It almost ended the "Experiment," because the students' residence in the university dormitories went from quiet accommodations to public conversation. Cecil Williams let it be known that his roommate for the next year would be a White student, with whom he had formed a friendship. The rhetoric of "Experiment" shifted to a discussion of the "Negro Problem."

A university trustee, Joe Perkins, who was the key benefactor of the theological school, phoned the university provost. He said, "I want the Negroes out of the dormitory."[18]

Joe Perkins was an entrepreneur before people had begun to use that word as a term for a career path. He pursued business opportunities in a variety of fields including real estate, coal mining, banking, ranching, retail clothing, and oil drilling. In Texas, it was said, plenty of people drilled oil wells. Some grew rich, finding oil. Others went broke, finding nothing. But all of them needed drilling equipment, which he sold them. In 1909, he moved to Wichita Falls. In 1911, he joined First Methodist Church. A few years later, he met Lois Craddock, a young woman from China Springs, Texas, who happened to have found a job, almost by accident, in Wichita Falls. In 1918, they married.[19]

Lois and Joe Perkins were devout Methodists, social benefactors, philanthropists, and partners. They made major gifts to Southern Methodist University, and Joe joined its Board of Trustees in 1928. They worked closely with Methodist clergy including Bishops A. Frank Smith and Paul E. Martin. They created the Perkins Lectures at First Methodist Church of Wichita Falls, at Martin's suggestion, to bring national and international voices to their remote city. They provided their largest gift to the school of theology late in 1944 and announced it in February 1945, when the outcome of World War II in Europe and in the Pacific remained in doubt.

17. Allen, *Perkins School of Theology*, 115.

18. Allen, *Perkins School of Theology*, 117–18. Four of the five students actually lived in the dormitories. John Elliott was married and lived off campus.

19. Allen, *Perkins School of Theology*, 85–86.

Beneath the Cross of Jesus

The announcement expressed bigger hopes than the ones associated with enhancing the university and its theological school. The gift acknowledged it was a time for public awakening. It linked the mission of Methodism and the school of theology to the roles they would play in helping to shape "the future Peace of the World."[20]

Nevertheless, when it came to ending racial segregation by practicing racial inclusion, Joe Perkins could not stretch his vision that far. Bishop Paul Martin interceded with him to settle the situation. So did Lois Perkins, who said simply, "I don't agree with my husband on this particular matter."[21] Because of their courageous capacity to help Joe Perkins see beyond racial exclusion, the desegregation of the university continued.

Breaching Barriers with Acts of Ministry

So, a White institution of the Methodist Church ended its segregation officially in 1952. When Merrimon Cuninggim wrote a memoir of the event, he entitled it *Perkins Led the Way*.[22]

Yet even though one institution of the denomination woke with action, the denomination was still a racially segregated church under its Constitution and its laws. Racial segregation was still standard practice at the local church level. And Dallas was still a city where racial separation was culturally and religiously normative. The five Black students who enrolled at Perkins School of Theology in the fall of 1952 experienced it firsthand, face to face.

In those days, it was customary for the entering class of Perkins students to attend the 9:00 am service at Highland Park Methodist Church on the first Sunday morning of the academic year. The pastor and congregation would greet, recognize, and welcome the first-year students during worship. On the first Sunday of the academic year in September 1952, John W. Elliott, James A. Hawkins, James V. Lyles, Negail R. Riley, and A. Cecil Williams prepared to process into the sanctuary of Highland Park Methodist Church with the other members of their class.

The doorway to enrollment had opened, as Umphrey Lee had told Merrimon Cuninggim. The next step would test the welcome mat at a local church.

But getting inside the doors of the university did not mean the church was hospitable. When James Lyles returned to the campus sixty years later

20. Allen, *Perkins School of Theology*, 89.
21. Allen, *Perkins School of Theology*, 124.
22. Cuninggim, *Perkins Led the Way*.

to receive an honor, he recalled what the five Black men were told by the Highland Park staff: "You will be seated but not greeted."[23]

After the conclusion of the early service at Highland Park Methodist Church, the five Black students decided to attend worship for a second time at a different place. They went to downtown Dallas, to St. Paul Methodist Church, where they entered the sanctuary of a church that had been started by former slaves. At St. Paul, John Elliott, James Hawkins, James Lyles, Negail Riley, and Cecil Williams were both seated and greeted.

Following the service, some members of St. Paul asked the five young men if they had plans for lunch. By the time that they would get back to campus, the university food service for the midday meal on Sunday would be closed. One of the young men said they could find some place to eat in the neighborhood. A member of St. Paul smiled and said that opportunities for a Black person to buy Sunday dinner near Southern Methodist University may not exist. In a few minutes, all five young men had received invitations to the homes of St. Paul members.

The university had opened its doors to Black students, but Black people were not yet welcomed inside most institutions in Dallas. Still, desegregation of the campus had a formative impact on many people, who were inspired by the courage of the five students, the university president, and the theology school dean. Their commitment endured and prompted other types of action during the years that followed.

In 1958, a Black student at Perkins named Earl walked with five White students from Perkins to a restaurant near campus, and they sat at a table for lunch. A waiter approached. He pointed to Earl, and he said to the five White students, "I'm not serving him."

Then, turning to one of the five White students, the waiter asked, "What will you have?" The White student replied, "I'll have whatever Earl is having." The waiter looked at another White student and asked him, "What will you have?" Again, the White student's response was, "I'll have whatever Earl is having." And so it went, as a small group of theological students, who intended just to get some lunch, instead were inspired to stage a sit-in protest by making it clear that White folks will not eat until Black folks can be served.

Two years later, in 1960, a White graduate of Perkins was appointed to his first charge as a Methodist minister in a rural Louisiana community. A visitor approached him on behalf of a group wanting to start a new school in town. They thought that the Methodist church building might house the

---

23. This account and those that follow came in individual conversations between the principals and the author.

school. The visitor said his group would pay rent, so the revenue could help the church. He also mentioned that the group with whom he was involved had been distressed that the Supreme Court ordered their White children to attend public school with Black children. The new school they planned to open would be private. So, it would only admit the children whom he and his group wanted in attendance. In short, it would be a school for White children only.

Forty years later, as the minister recalled the incident at a Perkins alumni event, he said,

> Nobody at Perkins ever taught me how to address an issue like that. But Perkins gave me a place to stand. So, I just stood on that place, looked the man in the eye, and said, "NO you cannot have our church as a site for your new school." Perkins did that to me.[24]

What their theological education had done was to inspire a generation of ministers like him to resist injustice even when it is expressed by powerful people and potent forces. A church that woke will act to break barriers. It also will provoke confrontations.

What happened at lunch one day in Dallas and in a confrontation about a segregated school in Louisiana were actions by people who woke. Often, such actions can provoke hateful and hostile reactions. That is what occurred among the Methodists in Birmingham, Alabama.

Facing Ferocities

The Methodist Church in 1950 had three annual conferences in Alabama. Two White conferences, North Alabama and Alabama West Florida, were in the Southeastern Jurisdiction. One Black conference, the Central Alabama Conference, was part of the Central Jurisdiction.

At its 1950 session, the North Alabama Annual Conference approved a resolution that was drafted by a district superintendent named G. M. ("Mont") Davenport. It condemned the Methodist Federation for Social Action, calling the MFSA "a seedbed of Communism," and it committed the North Alabama Conference to "segregation in church and society."

In that era, a very effective political weapon for identifying an organization or individual as an evil threat was to allege communist connections. Another was to allege that some person or program was a threat to the segregated social order. The 1950 resolution by the North Alabama Annual

---

24. Interview with the author.

Conference blended both allegations in one bold statement. Four years later, after the Supreme Court found racial segregation in public schools unconstitutional, White Methodists in Alabama formed an Association of Ministers and Laymen to affirm again a commitment to racial segregation in the church.[25]

In 1956, following the Montgomery bus boycott that began when a Black Methodist woman named Rosa Parks kept her seat on a city bus, the Supreme Court ruled that segregated seating in public transportation was unconstitutional. A Black civil rights leader named Fred Shuttlesworth, who had been raised a Methodist but had later become a Baptist, created the "Alabama Christian Movement for Human Rights" to demand enforcement of the Supreme Court decision and to call for integration of the entirely White police force in Birmingham.

The person in charge of the police in Birmingham was the city Commissioner of Public Safety, T. Eugene ("Bull") Connor, who held that office for twenty-six years.[26] Connor was a member of Woodlawn Methodist Church in Birmingham. His pastor from 1953–62 was John Rutland, who opposed segregation and who made his position clear in his Sunday sermons and in his pastoral actions. With crude racist vulgarity, Connor publicly denounced the "N***** preaching" that his pastor offered in the Woodlawn pulpit. On occasions, Connor rose from his pew during the sermon to denounce his minister's messages.[27]

Opposition to Rutland's proclamation of the gospel was not limited to Connor's verbal outbursts in the sanctuary. Klan members made threatening telephone calls to Rutland's wife. Someone set fire to a cross on the lawn of the parsonage where the Rutland family lived. The bishop of the Birmingham Area, Bachman Gladstone Hodge, complained about the way Rutland kept preaching on "the race question" and lamented that he was unsuccessful at arranging some alternate appointment for Rutland in the North Alabama Conference or elsewhere. "I tried to move you," Bishop Hodge said, "but where could I put you?"[28]

White lay leaders in Alabama formed the Methodist Layman's Union. They said that the group was being "organized to prevent integrating the church."[29] A White Methodist minister named Bob Hughes, who led the bi-

---

25. Nicholas, *Go and Be Reconciled*, 15, 23.

26. Connor was first elected to the position in 1936 and was continuously re-elected until he left office to run for governor in 1954. After failing to win that election, he was elected again to lead the Birmingham police in 1957, and he held office until 1963.

27. Nicholas, *Go and Be Reconciled*, 16–17.

28. Nicholas, *Go and Be Reconciled*, 17.

29. Nicholas, *Go and Be Reconciled*, 27.

racial Alabama Council on Human Relations, deplored the ferocious forces of racism that were tearing the fabric of the church apart. Hughes wrote, "I'm sorry I'm a Methodist."[30] In Hughes's view, the gospel was ashamed of the church. But some saw overt racism as a political advantage.

One Methodist who was not sorry about the direction of his church was a circuit judge named George Corley Wallace. The fact that the most powerful Methodist laity in the state were defending segregation gave him a chance to be a successful gubernatorial candidate. He saw it as a platform on which to run and a political base on whose support he could count. Having been unsuccessful in the 1958 governor's race, Wallace vowed to run as a segregationist candidate in 1962. He did, and he was victorious. In campaign speeches and in an inaugural address, he took a position and made a promise: "segregation now, segregation tomorrow, segregation forever."

It was a violent era. On May 14, 1961, an integrated group of civil rights protestors had arrived by bus in Birmingham. The Birmingham police were asked to protect them. And John Rutland had begged Bull Connor to guard the security of the "freedom riders" aboard the bus. But Connor dismissed his pastor's pleas. He let his officers inform the Ku Klux Klan about the location of the bus. He withdrew Birmingham police from the site. He later explained that it was Mothers' Day, and the police were short-staffed because officers wanted to be home with their mothers. Klan members, apparently not being so preoccupied, assaulted the freedom riders.[31]

In the spring of 1963, Black students marched in Birmingham to advocate racial justice and to protest segregation. They faced ferocious police dogs. They felt the force of water from fire hoses that police used to flush marchers to the curb and off their feet.

It was a churchgoing Methodist named Bull Connor who had put White supremacy into such policies and authorized such brutality in the streets. It was another Methodist named George Wallace who promised to maintain segregation forever in Alabama and to stand in the door at the University of Alabama personally, blocking any Black student from enrolling in the school. The Methodist Church never woke to take action against their faithless ferocities.

Ending Constitutional Segregation

At the midpoint of the twentieth century, racial segregation was "constitutional" under the Constitution of the United States and the Constitution of

---

30. Nicholas, *Go and Be Reconciled*, 43.
31. Nicholas, *Go and Be Reconciled*, 48. See also Branch, *King Years*, 24.

the Methodist Church. And racial subordination of Black people was common practice in both the state and the church.

With the 1954 Supreme Court decision that ruled segregated public school systems to be unconstitutional in the states, Methodists had to face their segregationist and White supremacist practices in the churches. Fault lines that divided the church were exposed. One fault line was in the Council of Bishops of the Methodist Church, who issued a positive statement in response to the *Brown v. Board of Education* decision. But they had to overcome objections from bishops of the Southeastern Jurisdiction, who expressed fears that "the vast numbers of the people among whom we labor" and the "acute tensions" in their region would suffer adversely if the bishops said anything. When the Council of Bishops issued their statement, eight Southeastern bishops said for the record that they preferred "no statement be made at this time."[32]

Meanwhile, pressure was growing for the church to address racial divisions in American Methodism. Steps toward integration would require amending the denomination's constitutional system of racially segregating the Methodist Church by its jurisdictions in America.

In 1951, a Black annual conference petitioned the General Conference to set "a racially inclusive policy at all organizational levels in The Methodist Church where such policy is not in violation of civil laws." It proposed appointing a commission "to discover the most expeditious and sound ways and methods of establishing racial inclusiveness in The Methodist Church at all levels and in all geographical areas."[33]

During sessions in 1956 and 1960, the General Conference of the Methodist Church appointed committees to seek ways to end the Central Jurisdiction. The Women's Division proposed a plan for doing so. In 1962, the Bishops of the Central Jurisdiction published their perspective on plans for eliminating their jurisdiction.

While an end to the constitutional segregation of the Methodist Church was being discussed, other units of the church were taking action. In 1964, two Black annual conferences merged with White annual conferences in different regions. The new conference in each case became part of its geographic jurisdiction. Two Black bishops—Prince Albert Taylor, who was elected in 1956 by the Central Jurisdiction, and James S. Thomas, who was elected in 1964 by the Central Jurisdiction—were assigned to

---

32. *Minutes of the Council of Bishops of the Methodist Church*, November 1954 (*MEAS*, 588–89). These eight southeastern bishops were John Branscomb, Marvin A. Franklin, Paul N. Garber, Costen J. Harrell, Arthur J. Moore, Clare Purcell, Roy H. Short, and William T. Watkins.

33. *Lexington Conference Journal*, 1951 (*MEAS*, 575).

overwhelmingly White conferences in geographical jurisdictions.[34] In addition, some White annual conferences received Black local churches in their regions by transferring them from Black annual conferences.

Yet many Black leaders of the Methodist Church remained adamant that the deep issues of racism were not being faithfully addressed. Late in 1967, a few months before the Evangelical United Brethren and the Methodist Church merged to become the United Methodist Church, a thousand Black Methodists met in Cincinnati. The group held another meeting in February 1968, ten weeks before a "Uniting Conference" in Dallas marked the merger. Participants pushed the church to resolve divisions about race.

At the February session, former Methodist James Farmer (founder and director of CORE, or the Congress of Racial Equality) and former Methodist Stokely Carmichael (leader of SNCC, or Student Nonviolent Coordinating Committee, and messenger of "Black Power") sought dialog with church leaders. Both Farmer and Carmichael had left Methodism because of its racism.

The participants in the February conference, according to James Lawson, confessed that

> for too long we have played the game of being church-men in The Methodist Church; participated in the politics of seeking prestige and position without sacrifice and obedience; that, like our white brethren, we wore masks where too frequently we said what we thought others wanted to hear.[35]

They critiqued the denomination's failure to feed the hungry and serve the poor in Black neighborhoods, depending instead on local churches whose Black members do not "have money for day care centers, for poverty programs, and other efforts to make the city more human." They warned that ending the Central Jurisdiction at the 1968 General Conference would not end the racism in the church. Its official disappearance might be celebrated. However, "after Dallas the deadening game of racism will go on in less visible ways." Lawson added,

> Let me summarize the conference another way. The Methodist Church has never listened to responsible Negro leadership. In 1939 Negro Methodists rejected segregation. Yet union dictated the creation of the Central Jurisdiction. From that time on, Negroes agitated for the integrated church. Only Central

---

34. *MEAH*, 396–97. See also "Charter on Human Rights," January 1952 (*MEAS*, 577–78).

35. Lawson, "Black Churchmen Seek Methodist Renewal." See *MEAS*, 612.

Jurisdiction leaders made the effort to study, discuss, and define "The Inclusive Church and how racism could be ended at all levels of the church."[36]

Most of the White people in the Methodist Church did not know this history at the time. Many United Methodists still do not know it to this day and, in the twenty-first century, may not realize that major leaders in confronting racism and segregation in the nation were Methodists. Oliver Brown, whose name is part of the 1954 Supreme Court decision called *Brown v. Board of Education*, was an African Methodist Episcopal Zion Church pastor. Rosa Parks, who refused to vacate her seat on a bus in Montgomery, Alabama, was a deaconess in the African Methodist Episcopal Church. Jackie Robinson, who broke the color barrier in baseball, was a member of the Methodist Church, as was Branch Rickey, who hired him.[37]

Most of the White people in the Methodist Church and the Evangelical United Brethren, after they merged, did not engage in desegregating the church when constitutional segregation ended. Most did not know the harm that had happened during centuries of racial stratification, racial separation, and racial violence. Most had never felt threatened by a cross set afire.

"By This Sign . . ."

The United Methodist Church was established in 1968. It had a new Constitution. The Central Jurisdictional ended, and its shadow disappeared from the official denominational map. The new church had five regional jurisdictions. Its conferences, clergy, and congregations were in an officially desegregated denomination. But it inherited the racist realities of its predecessors.

Many traditions flowed into the new denominational institution. In the nation's capital, for instance, the Washington Area of the United Methodist Church included the ecclesial DNA of all forms of Methodism that were now "United Methodist." Within its bounds were Methodist Protestants and Evangelical United Brethren, as well as clergy and congregations from Methodist Episcopal Church South, Methodist Episcopal Church, and Central Jurisdiction constituencies.

Meanwhile, the new denomination developed a different profile globally. Autonomous Methodist churches formed in Peru, Singapore, and Malaysia, separating from their colonizing founders. Liberian Methodists,

---

36. See *MEAS*, 613.
37. *MEAH*, 391–94. See also Patterson, "Baseball Icon."

after considering autonomy, chose to be United Methodists, as did Methodists in other African nations who were missionally linked to American Methodism.

In America, congregational segregation remained the norm. The new Constitution in an overwhelmingly White denomination did not alter local racial practices of predecessor churches. Increasingly congregational, the denomination known as the United Methodist Church had little impact on—or showed little interest in—desegregating the racial divisions and practices in the local churches or their surrounding communities.

Moving to a new church identity was a slow process. Twenty years after its formation, the United Methodist Church finally adopted its own *Hymnal*.[38] Four years after that, it added a *Book of Worship*. But many local churches retained the hymnals and songbooks already in their pew racks. And most local churches never experienced any changes in their racial demographics or the racial identity of the clergy appointed to lead them.

One modification that happened rather quickly, however, was the development of a new denominational logo. Implemented in 1971, it has been the only official insignia established by the United Methodist Church. The "cross and flame" design is a registered mark that identifies and links United Methodism specifically to the terms of the 1968 merger,

> with the cross proclaiming Jesus Christ as its foundation, and the two flames descending to one point celebrating its origin when two denominations became one, and affirming its readiness to go forth to the ends of the earth to all people to make disciples of Jesus Christ for the transformation of the world, as the anointing of the Holy Spirit with "individual flames of fire" sent forth the apostles speaking the language of people wherever they went.[39]

There is no disputing the significance of the cross in the life of the church. It has served as a Christian symbol since the founding days of the faith. One of the earliest Christian hymns, quoted by the apostle Paul, refers to Jesus, "who humbled himself by becoming obedient to the point of death, even death on a cross."[40] The hymnody of the church has emphasized the brutal suffering that Jesus endured on the cross,[41] and the comfort and

---

38. *The Methodist Hymnal* (released in 1964) was repackaged with a new cover and title, as *The Book of Hymns*. But the contents between the covers remained the same.

39. *The Book of Discipline of the United Methodist Church 2016* ¶ 807.10.

40. Phil 2:8 CEB.

41. See Charles Wesley, "O Love Divine, What Hast Thou Done" (1742); Isaac Watts, "When I Survey the Wondrous Cross" and "Alas! And Did My Savior Bleed" (both in 1707); or Johann Heermann, "Ah, Holy Jesus" (1630).

courage that the cross gives.⁴² Indeed, "beneath the cross of Jesus," many Christians have committed themselves to the faith. And by the sign of the cross, many Christians have conducted their devotions or offered prayers.

A cross seems an eminently suitable symbol for a Christian individual or denomination. In two millennia, Christians have worn crosses as jewelry and sported crosses as tattoos. Some scholars focus their theological methods on it.⁴³ Military forces painted their hardware with it.⁴⁴

And, since 1915, it has served another purpose. Racist people have been setting fire to it.

The last of those—setting the cross on fire—became a powerful device to warn, threaten, intimidate, and endanger Black people in America. Thomas Dixon Jr. linked the burning of a cross with the lynching of a Black man in *The Clansman*. D. W. Griffith linked the torture of a Black man to a burning cross in *The Birth of a Nation*. Both helped the Ku Klux Klan and its allies to promote their "cross lightings" as rituals of fear. A burning cross has been associated with violence and terror directed at anyone who supports justice for Black people in America.

When United Methodism adopted the insignia of a "cross and flame," its White majority approved an explanation of it. But to Black Methodists in America, it has a different meaning.

The description of the insignia in the denomination's *Book of Discipline* celebrates its significance for the uniting of two overwhelmingly White denominations. But it demonstrates insensitivity to the emotional impact of a violent history that a burning cross signifies to Black Methodists, for whom the cross and flame marked brutality, violence, and murder. Having the cross and flame as a registered trademark on countless bulletin boards, letterheads, and church flags is one more sign of just how racially divided the United Methodist people are.

Some United Methodists woke and are acting to change that.⁴⁵ They insist that the official symbol of the denomination should not be a terroristic threat.

---

42. See Elizabeth C. Clephane, "Beneath the Cross of Jesus" (1872).

43. See, for example, McGrath, *Luther's Theology of the Cross* and von Loewenich, *Luther's Theology of the Cross*. Others, such as Augustine, Anselm, and Grotius have built interpretations of the doctrine of the atonement on a theology of the cross.

44. In 312, Constantine's legions used the symbol of the cross at the Battle of Milvian Bridge.

45. The North Texas Annual Conference of the United Methodist Church voted to send a petition to the General Conference that would mandate a change in the insignia no later than 2023.

PART TWO

When the Future Woke the Church

CHAPTER SEVEN

A Matter of Mission

Vision and Mission

In early November 2021, when the global Council of Bishops of the United Methodist Church was preparing to meet, the members of the Council received a letter signed by more than a thousand United Methodists. Their letter asked that the bishops support their "intention to shift our focus from legislative solutions that are dependent upon a General Conference to supporting strategies for a gracious exit that can be enacted at the annual conference, central conference, and jurisdictional levels."[1] It was a bold request—not about racist White supremacy, but sexuality.

Those who signed the letter apparently felt that a majority vote by, or a magisterial voice from, the bishops could authorize units of the church to leave the denomination. They seemed to assume that bishops can bypass church laws and constitutional provisions by joining "strategies" for seceding from the church. By inference, they wanted the bishops to end the church divisions regarding human sexuality by institutionalizing those divisions in a schism, even though most who signed the letter apparently agree with the positions currently codified in church law on human sexuality in general and homosexuality in particular.

When the president of the Council of Bishops delivered her message at the start of the meeting, she made no reference to the letter or its appeal. Instead, she offered her own appeal that United Methodists "stop speaking ill

---

1. "A Call to Grace," November 1, 2021 (obtained from Derrick Scott III, derrick.luruth@gmail.com).

of one another and creating even more confusion and more fear and more anxiety." Further, she urged United Methodists to "love the Lord your God with all your passion and prayer and intelligence and energy . . . and love others as well as you love yourself."[2] She expressed the hope for a church that "receives and honors the gifts of all of God's children . . . Black, Brown, White, Asian, straight, gay, transgendered."[3]

Their letter and her address offer two different visions for the future of the church. One sees a church satisfied only by separation. The other sees a church gratified only in unification.

Both envision what the church should do in the near future. One sees the next steps to be whatever will facilitate splitting the denomination. The other sees the next steps to be whatever will overcome divisions splitting the denomination. These conflicting visions compete to set the agenda for the church. Each vision seeks to control what the church will do soon.

According to Proverbs, "When there's no vision, the people get out of control."[4] But the church does not lack vision. On the contrary, it has many visions. And they are in conflict. The challenge is to discern which vision faithfully adheres to the gospel. To be unashamed of the gospel, the church needs a formula for pursuing the vision that fulfills the mission of the church.

According to Lovett Weems, "vision" needs "mission."[5] Vision shapes what the church will do in our time. Mission announces why the church exists for all time.

A vision sets goals, and it expresses them in realizable ways. A vision guides the actions to be taken and who will take them. A vision must be renewed, refreshed, revised, and rewritten on a regular basis. A vision can be cast by anyone in the church and compete with other visions.

Mission is given, not cast. Mission expresses the purpose for which the church comes to life. Mission is a gift of grace. Mission is not determined by legislative processes, by executive edicts, by congregational votes, by denominations, by persuasive pastors, or by church politics. Mission is a gift granted by the One who calls the church to life. Mission is the identity given to the church by the risen Christ.

Mission is why the church exists. Mission is creedal and credible.

2. Bishop Cynthia Fierro Harvey, quoted in Hahn, "Bishops Encouraged," para. 5.

3. Bishop Cynthia Fierro Harvey, quoted in Hahn, "Bishops Encouraged," para. 15. In a communique at the end of their meeting titled "A Narrative for the Continuing United Methodist Church," the bishops affirmed a vision of unity. See their news releases on November 3–4, 2021 (cf. Council of Bishops, "Narrative").

4. Prov 29:18 CEB.

5. Weems, *Church Leadership*.

The church is an article of faith according to the Creeds.[6] It "will be preserved until the end of time," according to the liturgy for baptizing, confirming, and receiving members.[7]

Vision is valuable. It can look five years ahead, see what the church can be, and design steps that can be taken to fulfill that image. Vision sees the future and shapes church programs. Yet vision has a limited horizon. It must be redrawn as technological developments, population demographics, and economic directions turn. A vision for the ministries of the church in mining communities, for example, must be revised as climate change forces shifts away from coal.

Mission is vital. Mission is given with the resurrection. It transforms death to life. It is the eschatological future that bursts into the present. It is a gift of God's grace, for the church both to receive and to embrace. It is the purpose for which the church exists. It is a sacred treasure and a saving summons. It is granted by the risen Christ whose resurrection is the powerful promise of the life to come.

In mission, the church participates in the life to come. In mission, the church is endowed with the gift of knowing and acting on the mystery of the resurrection. In mission, the church exists as a face, force, and voice of transformative life. In mission, the church receives the grace of discipleship that expresses love, not merely as a moral virtue but as the presence of holiness.

The church owns tangible assets, and its institutions form public alliances. But the church is not defined by its material resources nor is its existence based on such corporate connections. The church exists not because it has billions of members, popular festivals, mountains of money, grand buildings, or potent political allies. The church exists because it is a mission, which God has launched in the world, and on which God's people are sent.

Expressing the Mission

Back in 2020 BC (that is, "Before COVID"), I was in Pennsylvania to deliver two lectures and a sermon about the mission of the church in a divided denomination. In the sanctuary of the Elm Park United Methodist Church in Scranton on the first weekend in February, I began with what I considered a rhetorical question: "What is the mission of the United Methodist Church?"

---

6. Both the Nicene Creed and the Apostles Creed affirm belief in the church and link it to the Holy Spirit. See *United Methodist Hymnal*, nos. 880–81.

7. "The Baptismal Covenant III," in *United Methodist Hymnal*, 45, and in *United Methodist Book of Worship*, 106.

Somewhat to my surprise, a chorus responded: "To make disciples of Jesus Christ for the transformation of the world." I was pleased to hear numerous voices respond from the pews, and I was pleased to hear them quoting from the denomination's official statement about the church's mission. Moreover, I was pleased that they got it right!

Or, at least, they got it right according to the way the General Conference of the United Methodist Church describes the mission of the church. Ever since delegates to the 2008 General Conference session adopted that language,[8] it endures. But it is hardly permanent or perfect.

In truth, Methodists have expressed mission differently through the years. In 1771, when John Wesley sent Francis Asbury to organize Methodism in America, the mission was to reform the continent and spread scriptural holiness over the land. In 1968, The United Methodist Church formed as a new denomination, saying that the church "exists in and for the world."[9] In 2000, the General Conference said, "The mission of the church is to make disciples of Jesus Christ."[10] In 2008, General Conference kept those words and added others about transforming the world.

So, the people at Elm Park United Methodist Church in February 2020 correctly quoted the current denominational *Discipline* on the church's mission. But the question remains whether it accurately expresses the purpose of the church or the basis upon which the church exists.

The reality is that the mission statement of the United Methodist Church since 2008 has been, at best, incomplete in describing the purpose of the church. Its imperfection is, in part, a reliance on one Bible text among the many where the risen Christ commissions the church.

Beyond the cross of Jesus, the Bible bears witness to his resurrection. It says only a little about departing from the tomb but a lot about his presence with disciples after the resurrection. Multiple passages in the New Testament report that, after the resurrection, the risen Christ gives the church a purpose to live. In varied texts, the church has multiple messages about its mission. The Bible, in different ways, defines the purpose with which the risen Christ endows the church.

Texts reveal that the church receives life from within the realm of the resurrection. They emerge from its mystery and proclaim that the risen Christ commissions the church by endowing it with a purpose from the perspective of the life to come. They bear witness to the promise, from which the church receives an irresistible hope that no force on earth can defeat.

---

8. *Book of Discipline of the United Methodist Church 2008*, para. 120, 87.
9. *Book of Discipline of the United Methodist Church 1968*, para. 102, 67.
10. *Book of Discipline of the United Methodist Church 2000*, para. 120, 87.

A Matter of Mission

Any ecclesiastical entity—the Papacy, a Pentecostal community, or a United Methodist General Conference—can craft a vision and define a doctrine to teach in support of that vision. But authority for expressing the mission lies not with a voting majority or ecclesial decree. The risen Christ brings the church to existence as a mission. The Bible says so in more than one way.

Matthew 28:19-20 is prominent among passages that express the mission of the church. Labeled "the Great Commission," it is a source for the doctrine of the Trinity, for the ritual of baptism, and for the United Methodist mission statement since 2008. It reports that the risen Christ said, "go and make disciples of all nations, baptizing them in the name of the Father and of the Son and of the Holy Spirit, teaching them to obey everything that I've commanded you."[11]

But that is not the only New Testament text where the risen Christ gives the church its mission. Texts at the ends of the Gospels of Mark, Luke, and John, and in the opening of Acts, reveal the mission of the church. They testify that the resurrection provides the purpose of the church. They reveal that the church exists not by a human proposition but by a holy promise.

Together, these texts carry Christ's commission. Collectively, they convey the word that identifies the purpose of the church. In concert, they proclaim the promise that graciously gives the standard to which the church is held accountable. This gospel brings the church to life. This gospel is the measure that determines what it means to be the church.

The Generosity of Scripture

The Bible is generous with the message of God's grace. In Genesis, it offers two stories of creation, and they differ in many ways. In Matthew and Luke, it has two stories of Christmas, and they differ in all but a few details. Its testimonies to Jesus' miracles have varied versions that paint sacred mysteries in vivid and vibrant colors. Its stories, songs, sagas, and skirmishes reveal the power of hope and expose the limits of fear. Its creation stories are not foes of cosmology. Its nativity narratives are not enemies of biology. Science, art, and theology all ask questions. Their answers are complementary, not confrontational. Grace uses heart, soul, mind, and might.[12]

Each creation story and each nativity narrative points to the mystery of holiness. The Bible is unafraid to discuss sacred mysteries in multiple

---

11. Matt 28:19-20 CEB.

12. See Deut 6:5; Mark 12:30; and Luke 10:27-28, which declare this in different ways.

ways. One creation story emphasizes the place of humanity in the ecology of the natural world. Another emphasizes the responsibility of humanity to make moral decisions. One Christmas story puts emphasis on the birth of Christ in cosmic, interfaith, intercultural, political significance. Another puts emphasis on its importance for the poor and the powerless. To read them all is to hear infinite nuances of grace.

Elsewhere, the Bible presents Jesus as teacher and preacher in multiple messages. One is Matthew's famous Sermon on the Mount. Another is Luke's less famous Sermon on the Plain. The power of the gospel expands exponentially through their differences.[13] Matthew offers the familiar blessings or "Beatitudes." Luke also offers Jesus' blessings but adds Jesus' judgments. Matthew says, "Blessed are the poor in spirit." Luke says, "Blessed are the poor" and "woe to you who are rich." To be unashamed of the gospel is to be grasped by the grace of it all.

The church knows how to process multiple messages. Its Lenten sermons, Holy Week Bible studies, and Good Friday services may focus on the seven last words of Jesus on the cross. Yet, it is impossible to go to some specific place in the New Testament and find a single list of his last words. They are in scattered locations.[14] Matthew has one, Mark also has one, and they are the same—namely, a question from Psalm 22 about feeling forsaken by God. Luke has three words, but none of them repeats the saying in Matthew and Mark. John also has three, but none of them repeats any of the words in Matthew or Mark or Luke. Jesus' seven last words are strewn across different accounts of his crucifixion. The church combines them, creating a composite message to spread the word about Jesus' dying on a cross.

By a similar process with the texts that bear witness to the word of the risen Christ, the church can discover why it exists. The Bible generously offers multiple post-resurrection reports about the mission of the church. All of them are vital. They make clear the purpose for which the church exists. It is more than making individuals into disciples and then expecting individuals to transform the world, as the text in Matthew may be read or the United Methodist *Discipline* may be understood. In multiple expressions, the Bible witnesses to the power of life that overcomes death. Collectively, as a whole community, the church is a mission for all time in all the world.

---

13. See Matt 5:3–12 and Luke 6:20–26.
14. Matt 27:46; Mark 15:34; Luke 23:34, 43, 46; John 19:26–27; 19:28; 19:30.

A Matter of Mission

The First Words of New Life

The authors of the four Gospels present not only the last words of the dying Jesus on the cross but also the first words of the risen Christ after the resurrection. In Matthew, Mark, Luke, John, and Acts (that is, the second volume of the two biblical books by Luke)[15] are reported appearances and proclamations through which the risen Christ commissions his church.

All of them have lively forms. They are not gasps or phrases from a dying man. They are interactive and conversational words of a living person.

With imaginative narrative details, the Gospel writers present the risen Christ not as the victim of violence but as the voice of vitality. The witnesses to his resurrection—that is, those whom the Bible says he encounters—receive his authority and his spirit. They acquire his power, are granted the same authority he was given, and receive the same capacity for the care of others that he possessed.[16] They provide gifts from the life to come and directions for the life of the church now.

The risen Christ connects the mission of the church and its apostolic responsibilities for mission to the directives of Moses' law and to the judgments that come from the prophets.[17] The risen Christ chides the foolish who misunderstand his word and critiques those who are reluctant to trust his promise.[18] The risen Christ frees the frightened from fear and delivers the dubious from doubt.[19] The risen Christ invites the church to pursue questions and to seek answers.[20] The risen Christ empowers the church to forgive and to judge.[21]

In short, the biblical complement to the seven last words of Jesus are the first words of the risen one who sets his church loose in the world with mission and purpose. The resurrection transforms. The last gasps on a cross yield to the first words in conversation about the purpose and power of the living church.

They convey gifts of life to come. They continue the sacred story, come from the promise of the future, and confront the world. They offer the themes that define why the church exists.

---

15. See the introductory words of explanation in Luke 1:1–4 and Acts 1:1–2.
16. See Matt 28:18–20; Luke 24:48; John 20:21.
17. See Luke 24:26–27, 44–47.
18. See Luke 24:25 and John 20:29.
19. See Matt 28:10; Luke 24:38–39; and John 20:27. See also the disputed endings in manuscripts of Mark 16 that occur in the context of 16:8 (which is generally accepted) and appear in 16:17–18 (which is generally suspect).
20. See Luke 24:17–18 and John 21:17, 20.
21. See Luke 24:47–49; John 20:22–23; and Acts 1:5–8.

- The church continues the liberating message of Moses and the prophets.
- The church breaks boundaries that people create and overcomes barriers to love.
- The church exercises spiritual power to transform life.
- The church discerns the forgivable from the unforgivable and acts on both.

First, according to the New Testament, the words of the risen Christ say that the mission of the church is consistent with the whole story of salvation.[22] As the laws of Moses, the faith of Hannah,[23] and the warnings of Malachi[24] are in the background of the rest of the gospels, and as the church celebrates the laughter of Sarah[25] and sings the psalms of David the shepherd,[26] the story continues. The purpose of the church is not to supplant or replace that story. However, the church is accountable for all the Lord's sheep,[27] including those enfolded in other stories.[28]

The initial words of the risen Christ in the New Testament also show that the mission of the church, while consistent with the past, conveys the promise of the future. Transformative resurrection means life overcomes death. The church exists because new life overcomes deadly forces dividing God's people. Its purpose endures in time and space to the end of the earth.[29]

Second, the mission of the church confronts and overcomes what separates nations.[30] To the modern mind, the term "nations" may connote sovereign states. But "nations" also refers to clans, cultures, and communities of people who are identified by language or lore more than by borders or governments. Any Americans who drive on the interstate highway system in the northeast, upper Midwest, southwest, southeast, or southern plains, see highway signs announcing that they have entered Indian Nation territory.

---

22. Luke 24:44. In his Nativity narrative, Luke 1:46–55 reflects the song of Hannah (1 Sam 2:1–10) in canticles.

23. 1 Sam 2:1–10 and Luke 1:46–55.

24. Mal 3:1 and Mark 1:2.

25. Gen 18:12.

26. See, e.g., Pss 126; 134.

27. John 21:15–17.

28. See Isa 56:8 and John 10:16.

29. Acts 1:8.

30. Matt 28:19.

One may be in the state of New York, Oklahoma, or North Dakota, and yet be in another "nation."

The initial words of the risen Christ in the New Testament show that the purpose of the church does not impose one culture on other "nations" or tolerate animosity between "nations." The mission of the church honors differences but overcomes divisions, whether the divisions are matters of geography, ethnicity, ideology, language, or culture.[31] So, the church is inclusive and comprehensive. No one is beyond its purpose, nor is any "nation" superior to another "nation." Therefore, the church exists to overcome racial superiority and pretensions of White supremacy.

Third, according to the New Testament testimonies about the initial words of the risen Christ, the mission of the church has transformative power. While the texts acknowledge some reluctance by the church to exercise that power,[32] they testify that the mission of the church is given the same power that the risen Christ has. Matthew[33] refers to it as "all authority in heaven and on earth." John[34] refers to it as peace that comes with the power of the Holy Spirit. Luke indicates that it is power to understand instruction, obey rules of conduct, and recognize sacred mysteries in simple rituals like breaking bread.[35]

And, with the gift of the Holy Spirit that is both promised and presented, according to Luke and Acts,[36] the mission of the church enables "nations" to keep their own languages as it empowers them to hear one another and to overcome divisions.[37] For the church in America, therefore, Black and White Methodists have the power to hear one another.

Fourth, according to the New Testament testimonies about the initial words of the risen Christ, the mission of the church includes knowing the distinction between truth and falsehood, knowing the distinction between the forgivable and the unforgivable, and acting in accord with that knowledge.[38] To teach and preach forgiveness is clearly within the scope of the purpose of the church. But judging sins and acting in accord with such judgments is also within that scope.

---

31. See Matt 28:19; Mark 16:15; Luke 24:47; John 21:10–11; Acts 1:8; 2:8–12.
32. See Mark 16:8 and Luke 24:11, 22.
33. Matt 28:18, 20 CEB.
34. John 20:21–22.
35. Luke 24:25, 38, 44.
36. Luke 24:49 and Acts 1:5; 2:4; 2:33.
37. Acts 2:8.
38. Luke 24:25, 47; John 20:23.

Sins identified by the church as unforgivable are unforgiven. Thus, collaboration by the church with the Nazi regime must not be forgotten and may not be forgiven. Collaboration with the Ku Klux Klan in America must not be forgotten and may not be forgiven. And the emotional, spiritual, and intellectual resources of human life are capacities within the mission of the church for forgiving and for judging.[39]

These four themes testify that the church has the promise, purpose, prophetic legacy, and the power to deal with deadly forces through transformative life.[40] Such forces exist in the world and in the church. They may exercise financial leverage, influence ideas, and deceive by lures of prestige or status. Such temptations are persistent and prevalent.[41] The church exists to oppose them.

Mission and Discipleship

The authors of the four Gospels testify differently to the purpose of the church in varied witnesses to the resurrection. Collectively, they are crucial to any church statement of mission.

For example, the passage in Matthew 28 alone could be heard (and often has been heard) as evidence that the mission of the church is to recruit individuals. But read in combination, not in isolation, the Gospel writers show the church exists to teach correctly, to distinguish sins that are forgivable from those that are unforgivable, to hear other nations speak, to feed the hungry, and to make disciples. Thus, growing the church means making disciples for knowing and acting in these ways. The church exists for this mission. And the church is accountable for the nature of discipleship, regardless of the numbers of disciples.

That may be difficult for the United Methodist Church or other mainline denominations to appreciate, given their data-driven fears. Numerical growth led them to link statistical success with spiritual power. Then decades of decline followed. The church felt its power diminishing and dying. Postmortems blamed poor recruiting, leftist politics, lazy theology, and loss of vision. Such critiques could be correct yet miss the point. The power of the church comes from holy gifts not human assets or efforts. The vitality of the church wanes when commitment to mission weakens. Loss of purpose, not lower numbers, causes loss of life.

---

39. Luke 24:25.
40. Luke 24:16, 31.
41. Thomas and Dobson, *Blinded by Might*, 23.

The future of the church will be determined by attending in the present to all dimensions of discipleship. Being unashamed of the gospel is knowing that the church has sacred power for hearing all cultures, for loving as the core of what the law commands, for honoring God's prophets, for feeding hungers, for confronting falsehoods, for lifting the fears of the frightened, and for forgiving and judging sins. This is how the church brings hope to the world as a face and voice of resurrection. The promised future arrives through present discipleship.

When authors of the New Testament gospels report encounters where the risen Christ gives the church its mission and purpose, references to "disciples" appear in multiple accounts. The term is used broadly about those who are his followers, not narrowly as if it meant an elite few like those called "the Twelve." Matthew 28 mentions making disciples. Mark 16 mentions meeting the disciples. Luke 24 mentions a group, besides the eleven and their companions. And John 20 tells of an event late on the day the resurrection was first reported. According to John, some disciples had gathered behind locked doors. Without noting the names or numbers of the persons present, John just refers to them as "the disciples." They could have been any group of any size. Whoever they were, they were simply Jesus' followers. Wherever they were, they had assembled behind locked doors.

It is a revealing report about why the church exists. Its word is not about individuals but about community. Those gathered are unknown numbers of unnamed persons collectively called disciples. They could have been people of any class or status. The risen Christ commissions them as a community for discipleship and entrusts power to them for mission as the church. There are no elites. Thomas, who in the next passage is named one of "the Twelve,"[42] was notably absent. Individuals are neither named, numbered, nor notable. The church is given a mission as a whole community. To be in the church is to bear the mission and be accountable for discipleship.

John's report also explains why the group gathered. They were "afraid." But the text must be read closely. Some translations say, "they were afraid of the Jewish authorities." Others say, "for fear of the Jews."[43] Such turns of phrase, when taken out of the context in which they were written, have led to gross misinterpretations of the gospel and have provoked antipathy to Jews. Antisemitism is an evil that has marked the history of the church. And it is not the only one.

---

42. John 20:24.

43. Cf., respectively, the Common English Bible and the "King James Version" of John 20:19.

John's Gospel was written fifty or more years after the crucifixion, when a schism was threatening to part the Christian community from Jewish leaders. It is a malevolent misreading of this text to use it as a basis for anti-Jewish sentiments or anti-Semitic politics. To take these first words of the risen Christ as a justification for hate is to mistake the mission of the church. The passage does not authorize hatred. But it does acknowledge fear. And it shows that the power of the resurrection transforms fear into faith. That is the loving purpose for which the church exists.

But fear can draw an audience—on the internet, on television, in writing, or in person. It can prompt people to gather. It can provoke intense emotional reactions and divisions.

On September 16, 2001—the first Sunday after the 9/11 attacks—worship spaces were gathering places for regular attendees, as well as infrequent churchgoers and marginal members. Many Americans went to church in fear for a few weeks in the fall of 2001.

On Sunday, November 24, 1963, two days after the Kennedy assassination, Americans went to church and prayed for the widowed first lady, for the wounded Texas governor, and for the city where protests had greeted the Catholic president who favored racial desegregation. At Northaven Methodist Church in Dallas, the preacher mentioned the fear and its hold on the city. He said a teacher witnessed some students applauding the news of Kennedy's death. His words went public. Some people in Dallas expressed outrage, not that the students applauded but that the preacher discussed it. He and his family received death threats from those who feared the truth. They were moved out of their parsonage under police protection. Fear was fierce in 1963.

On December 14, 1941, a week after the attack on Pearl Harbor, Americans were afraid when they went to worship. Since the bombing seven days earlier, Congress declared war. Pews were filled with people who feared another attack, including those between seventeen and thirty-five who were likely to be drafted. The fear was palpable and personal just before Christmas in 1941.

On the first evening of the first Easter, fear prompted an unknown number of disciples to assemble. The frightened group gathered behind locked doors. To their amazement, the fear was overcome as a gift of life transformed them and gave them a new identity. The church received a life-giving purpose and a power to fulfill that purpose. The church exists as the face and voice of resurrection, with a mission to conquer the fear that fractures a community and imprisons the soul.

A Matter of Mission

The word of the risen Christ initially is "Peace be with you."[44] It is an ordinary greeting. Yet, as the gospel, it is a unique gift. It conveys multiple messages simultaneously to the church across the ages. One is a word to the group gathered in fear on the first Easter. Another is a word to the divided community receiving John's report fifty or more years later. Another is the church now split into factions and threatened by schism. The "peace" of Christ is a gift that comes from the resurrection to give new life, carrying many meanings for many circumstances in many ages.

It is possible to process multiple forms of meaning to serve one purpose.

I have been wearing corrective lenses since second grade. I started with glasses and now wear monovision lenses. They enable each eye to see different things and trust the brain to unite various bits of information into one body of knowledge for one action. The lens in my right eye sees distant things. The lens in my left eye sees nearby things. When I drive, my brain processes different information from multiple sources and directs my hands and feet to act as one body.

The peace of Christ, as the gospel reports it, creates the capacity to receive multiple gifts that serve one mission. A frightened group of disciples becomes the church. A group facing a crisis recognizes the mission again and overcomes the fractures of fighting factions. A divided church, which ponders problems of monumental proportions, woke to recognize that its mission is an offer of new life in discipleship that brings transformative hope to the world.

Sent into Mission

In every age and every crisis, the peace of Christ comes with one mission, empowering the church to cope with dangerous division, debilitating fear, and foolish teaching. It comes as a greeting of peace, which has a broad biblical context, including a text to which the church often turns: "Peace I leave with you. My peace I give to you. . . . Don't be troubled or afraid."[45]

Those words in many translations have been part of the rituals for funerals and memorial services for a long time, including years since the formation of the Methodist Church in 1939. They typically are read to calm the anguish of the grieving and to comfort all who fear death.

---

44. Luke 24:36 has the same greeting, but the veracity of the text is disputed. The text in John 20:19 is not disputed.

45. John 14:27 CEB.

The risen Christ's greeting of peace to the fearful, however, is not only to comfort but also to confront. It is a gift of grace that challenges whatever provokes fear and overcomes it. Disciples gather initially behind locked doors. The peace of Christ, rather than being the security of a lock, is a mission to abandon false security and to face the world with sacred power.

A locked door, from the perspective of the resurrection, is powerless to prevent the risen Christ from entering or to keep the church from being sent into the world in mission. That is why the church exists. When Black students are locked from entering a university or from receiving a greeting in a sanctuary, patterns of discipleship break barriers and open doors.

The mission that endures in the church is a life of discipleship. In the cascading crises of the twenty-first century, the church faces a troubled world—afraid, divided by racism, dominated by a political ethos that finds votes by fostering fear. There is plenty to fear.

Yet, the risen Christ offers peace and bestows power so the church can overcome fear and fulfill its purpose. As the texts from the writers of the four Gospels make clear, the church comes to life and is sent into the world.

The root word in Greek for being sent is "apostle." Jesus greets disciples with "peace," gives the church purpose, and sends the church into the world.[46] In the Gospels, peace is not an absence of war or a secure feeling. The peace of Christ is an apostolic mission, offering not a pause from problems but power to overcome problems. The church exists not to feel comfortably safe in the world but rather to confront the world. The church is sent to speak and act with power in the world. Discipleship is the way of life that is unafraid to embrace this mission.

In preaching, the church exists to confront falsehood with truth. However, reactions to the truth can be harsh. They may even tempt the church to seek security elsewhere than in the peace of Christ. Pulpits are places for proclaiming truth, for instance, but they can be places where the liberating word of the gospel takes refuge in homely platitudes that substitute for holy promises. A preacher can fear telling the truth about racist iniquities and ethnic inequities. Yet the church is sent into the world both to know the truth and to be free to proclaim it.

The peace the church offers through the gospel is let loose in the world: "As the Father sent me, so I am sending you,"[47] the risen Christ said. It is like a breath of fresh air.

John 20:22 says the risen Christ breathed on the assembled disciples. "Breath" is biblical language for the gift of the Holy Spirit. The second of

---

46. See Matt 28:19; Mark 16:20; John 21:15–17; Acts 1:8.

47. John 20:21.

A Matter of Mission

the two creation stories in Genesis reports that God gives life to humanity by breathing.[48] The prophet Ezekiel hears noise from a valley of dry bones that are transformed by life when they receive breath as a gift of the wind.[49] Pentecost in Acts[50] describes the breath of God as a fierce wind that gives life to the church.

Texts speak in many ways about gifts of new life. But they all point to the breath of God.

In multiple metaphors that speak of the spirit as the wind and breath that bestows the gift of life to the church, the Scriptures point to the transformative power of the mission. Sent with the authority that includes power to forgive and retain sins, the church is an agent of prophetic judgment. Some sins are forgiven. Other sins, which are beyond being forgiven, are retained. The church has the authoritative power to know the difference.

But, as with other texts bearing witness to the gift of the risen Christ creating the church, this one must be read with care. It is important to be clear what the gospel of John means by sins.

Its reference is not to a moral code. Instead, it is a model creed. In the words of one New Testament scholar, the late Gail O'Day, when the Gospel of John refers to sin, it is "a theological failing, not a moral or behavioral transgression."[51] When Jesus met Pilate, they debated the nature of truth. When Jesus discussed discipleship, he said faithful discipleship expresses truth, which sets people free. Sins are forces that confine. Truth liberates.[52]

Hence, when the risen Christ empowers the church to determine which "sins" are to be forgiven and which "sins" are to remain unforgiven, the authority granted to the church is unlike an assignment to prepare a catalogue of bad behaviors. Rather, it is authority to draw theological distinctions between falsehood and truth, between what imprisons the world and what sets the world free. The mission of the church is to overcome barriers between neighbors. The mission of the church is to proclaim life by feeding the hungry. The mission of the church is to preach and to practice forgiveness that repairs brokenness. The mission of the church is to discern and judge the difference between lies and truth. The mission of the church is discipleship that makes the difference between separation and reconciliation. It is the difference between death and life.

---

48. Gen 2:7.
49. Ezek 37:7–10.
50. Acts 2:2–4.
51. O'Day, "Gospel of John," 727.
52. See John 8:32; 18:37–38a.

Collectively, the writers of the four Gospels craft the mission and purpose of the church with a multi-layered pattern of discipleship. Combined with the commissioning for teaching that appears in Matt 28 and the mind-opening understanding that appears in Luke 24, the text in John 20 reveals that teaching, questioning, judging, and distinguishing falsehood from truth are ways the church exercises sacred power to forgive sins or leave them unforgiven.

In the critical situation facing the church in the third decade of the twenty-first century, it is time the church woke to be the face and voice of the resurrection. It is time for discipleship that knows the truth and demonstrates in practice how to live when the church is set free.

CHAPTER EIGHT

The 8:46 Lectionary

The Primacy of Scripture

When the church woke, it read the Bible with refreshed eyes in new light. Martin Luther launched the Protestant Reformation based on studying Scripture. Wesley emphasized "searching the scriptures" as one of the General Rules for all Methodists because the practice puts us in touch with God's Spirit, who "writes on truly awakened hearts."[1] When United Methodists search the Scriptures, they "require a constant effort to integrate authentic experience, rational thought, and purposeful action with theological integrity"[2] in the process of salvation.

On May 25, 2020, and thereafter, data emerged about the death of George Floyd. Video evidence showed that he died after a police officer applied physical pressure with a knee to his neck for eight minutes and forty-six seconds.[3] The initial expressions of outrage at this murder were soon linked to the video taken by a bystander. Its eight minutes and forty-six seconds made "8:46" a sign of the public violence by police and others that threatens Black Americans.

---

1. *The Book of Discipline of the United Methodist Church 2016*, "The General Rules," ¶ 104.
2. *The Book of Discipline of the United Methodist Church 2016*, "Our Theological Task," ¶ 104.
3. Other video evidence at the trial of the police officer convicted of his murder showed an even longer period of pressure was fatally applied to Mr. Floyd's neck.

The entertainer Dave Chappelle performed a monologue titled "8:46" that looked at the violence faced by Black victims. And "8:46" is a way to read the Scriptures with fresh eyes.

People read the Bible in various ways. Some start with Gen 1:1 and try reading until Rev 22:21, though they often lose momentum before they finish Leviticus. Others study Bible passages by themes, by focusing on topics and finding relevant texts in random passages, or by literary genres in pondering apostles' letters or Jesus' parables. One practice that regained popularity in the twentieth century is following a lectionary, which lists passages from books of the Bible for reading in an orderly manner driven by the sequence of the church calendar or the cycles of Christian experiences.

An "8:46 Lectionary" is a provocative possibility. The symbol of a White police officer kneeling on the neck of a Black person for 8:46, causing his death, offers a new way to honor the victim and the Scripture. An "8:46 Lectionary" can call attention to specific passages.[4]

There are only three places in the Bible where one can find chapter eight, verse forty-six. Many biblical books lack eight chapters. In those with an eighth chapter, not all of them have forty-six verses. Thus, "searching the scriptures" yields only three verses—in 1 Kings, Luke, and John—that form the core of an "8:46 Lectionary."

- First Kings 8:46 says there is no one who does not sin. It is in a context that calls for confession and repentance to heal broken relationships.

- Luke 8:46 contains Jesus' reference to his "power" in a context that focuses on two people who feel utterly powerless, overwhelmed by suffering, death, and discrimination. Jesus recognizes and overcomes their powerlessness, as he links faith and belief to the gift of empowering life.

- John 8:46 is at the core of a confrontation between Jesus and those who try to dismiss him with a label instead of dealing with him as the bearer of truth. He confronts them, clarifies that he speaks with God's authority, condemns them as liars, and claims that his word is more powerful than death.

These verses must be viewed with great care. As the official United Methodist statements of doctrine make clear,[5] such biblical passages should be studied critically and constructively.

---

4. Coincidentally, at 8:46 am, the first plane hit the World Trade Center in New York on September 11, 2001.

5. The "doctrinal statements" of the church must be distinguished from the "Doctrinal Standards" of the United Methodist Church. Briefly, the "Doctrinal Standards" are

> Scripture is primary, revealing the Word of God "so far as it is necessary for our salvation." Therefore, our theological task, in both its critical and constructive aspects, focuses on disciplined study of the Bible.[6]

United Methodist doctrinal statements also make clear that the Wesleyan method for studying Scripture requires recognizing that texts of the Bible are to be "illumined by tradition, vivified in personal experience, and confirmed by reason." According to the United Methodist doctrine, studying the Scriptures cannot be disconnected from tradition, experience, and reason.

> What matters most is that all four guidelines be brought to bear in faithful, serious, theological consideration. . . . While we acknowledge the primacy of Scripture in theological reflection, our attempts to grasp its meaning always involve tradition, experience, and reason. . . . In recognizing the interrelationship and inseparability of the four basic resources for theological understanding, we are following a model that is present in the biblical text itself.[7]

If the church woke with a lively determination to apply the United Methodist doctrinal understandings for studying the "8:46 Lectionary," it will know the gospel, and it will be sent into action by these three texts. If the church woke and if these texts are illumined by tradition, experience, and reason, they will reveal the truth of God's word for discipleship.

John Wesley's "Articles of Religion," which the Methodist Church brought to the 1968 merger creating the United Methodist Church, and the "Confession of Faith" that the Evangelical United Brethren brought to the merger. Upon these "Doctrinal Standards" the denomination bases its proclamation of the gospel, programs of mission, and polity for the ordering of the church. "Doctrinal Standards" precede the authority of the church Constitution and church laws, and they are protected by the special Restrictive Rules of the Constitution (Division Two, Section III, Articles I-II, ¶¶ 17–18). To change the "Doctrinal Standards" would require amending the Restrictive Rules in a process starting with a two-thirds vote of the General Conference and ending with three-fourths of the aggregate votes of all the annual conferences in the world. After that process had been completed, then the "Doctrinal Standards" could be modified. The "doctrinal statements" are enacted by a simple majority of the General Conference and are published in *The Book of Discipline of the United Methodist Church 2016* (¶ 105). See Lawrence, "Question of Doctrine."

6. *Book of Discipline of the United Methodist Church 2016*, para. 104, p. 82.
7. *Book of Discipline of the United Methodist Church 2016*, para. 104, pp. 82, 83, 85.

Confessing and Correcting Broken Relationships in 1 Kgs 8:46

The words in 1 Kgs 8:46 come from a majestic moment in biblical history. It was a ceremony to dedicate the temple in Jerusalem—the first temple in the history of Israel, the one that David did not get to build. His son Solomon presided.[8] In the eighth chapter of 1 Kings, Solomon's remarks make clear what sort of building this is. According to one commentator,

> The Temple is neither God's residence nor the place where the petitioner personally encounters the deity. Rather it is a place at which the needs of the petitioner coincide with the willingness of the deity to respond. The Temple is not the place where the very person of God is; rather, it is merely the place where God's presence may be known, where the authority of God is proclaimed.[9]

Solomon begins the portion of the rite that is the prayer of dedication in 1 Kgs 8:22. His prayer includes seven circumstances in which the people of God will find a need for God to act with authority in response to their petitions. Each of the seven is an extended plea. Together, the seven petitions serve as a complete prayer. Solomon's seven sections of prayer cover all human situations in which people find hope through trust in God.

The seventh one—the final and, therefore, most important one—begins in 8:46 and says reconciliation is possible, even after a hateful and anger-filled separation, if confession and true repentance happen. It covers forgiveness from God and forgiveness from others, so it is both a holy reconciliation and a human reconciliation. Hope of forgiveness rests "in a change of heart, or repentance."[10] First Kings 8:46 concerns confessing and correcting what is broken. It requires knowing the harm that has been done and the hurt that has been inflicted to divide the "heritage" of God's people. It requires that the heirs and descendants of those who broke relationships be as accountable as the offenders and, the next verse says, that "they come to their senses."

First Kings 8:46 initiates a promise that God can heal such fractures if "eyes be open" and God can grant "compassion" to those who "plea" for reconciliation. But such awakening requires courage, both to repent and to repair the damage. It requires both confessing and correcting what has

---

8. David intended, and expected, to build a temple as a house for the Lord (2 Sam 7:27). But this privilege was denied him, because of his violent conduct (1 Chr 28:3). So, the honor of being the temple builder went to David's son Solomon (1 Kgs 6:1).

9. Seow, "First and Second Books of Kings," 2:678.

10. Seow, "First and Second Books of Kings," 2:679.

been divisive. So, this text in "the 8:46 Lectionary" prays for repentance and reparation.

That will challenge many churches today, where confession is not a priority. A worship hour presents scheduling constraints. One element often redacted is confession of sin. It may be reduced to a few pious platitudes, put into general prayers, or removed entirely. Loss of a prayer of confession is compounded by declines in Lenten observances and small-group class meetings for spiritual discipline. Thus, 1 Kgs 8:46 can correct failures of faithful discipleship.

The United Methodist Church has conducted public services of repentance for previous misdeeds. Formal liturgies have been crafted to confess enslavement of Africans, slaughter of Native Americans, and other egregious behaviors. But such services rarely occur outside of the major denominational meetings and tend to be absent from local churches.

Besides, the need for confession and repentance about racism is not readily apparent to many White Methodists. They have seen "Black Lives Matter" marches and signs condemning "White Supremacy" but wondered why they are targets of protests. "I never owned slaves" and "I never lynched anybody" are often heard as justifications for feeling that there is nothing to confess. But an encounter with Scripture through the "8:46 Lectionary" with 1 Kgs 8:46 is a means to awaken awareness that confession is not something one does on the basis of feeling a need to do so but as a disciplined spiritual practice. Confession and repentance are practices that put us in the realm of grace. As 1 Kgs 8:46 shows, heirs on opposing sides of a division must accept God's grace as the gift that forgives and reconciles. The descendants of offenders must confess their legacy of sin. Embracing a tradition of grace shows that the church woke.

Yet tradition is a tough term for many United Methodists and other Christians. We use the word in a variety of ways. Some traditions are benign. Some are beloved. Some are boring. But, when the church woke, traditions of faith can be adapted to become reconciling blessings.

Most churches have candlelit Christmas Eve services. A traditional practice at the end is singing "Silent Night" quietly with a candle in hand. Eighty years ago, one Methodist minister altered the tradition. He used "Angels We Have Heard on High" as the final hymn, and he asked the congregation to lift lighted candles each time they sing the refrain, "*Gloria, in excelsis Deo!*" It made Christmas Eve illuminating. It liberated the church from darkness and drew worshipers closer to the joy of shepherds who woke in Luke 2:20. When the church woke, joy happens.

But adapting tradition is another challenge, especially for United Methodists who are giving "tradition" another connotation and using it to justify church laws about human sexuality. The General Conference, at a special session in February 2019, added restrictions to its existing legislation, which already prohibited same-sex marriage in United Methodist churches, banned same-sex weddings conducted by United Methodist ministers, prevented homosexual persons from getting credentials to be clergy, and proscribed funding for organizations that advocate acceptance of homosexuality. The delegates acted, in part, as a nod to their idea of tradition.

The February 2019 General Conference called these laws the "Traditional Plan" for the church. It divided the denomination rather than reconciled it, as 1 Kgs 8:46 proposed. A slim majority of the delegates imposed its political will without offering a confession of its own faults and without repairing the damage its legislative agenda caused.

First Kings 8:46 shows that everybody needs forgiveness, and everybody needs to practice traditions of confession and repentance. They are disciplines of grace. Though Solomon prayed at the temple dedication three thousand years ago, his words are poignant in the present. "There is no one who doesn't sin," Solomon said. There is also forgiveness, as he prayed, if they are

> changing their lives and begging for your mercy, saying, "We have sinned, we have done wrong, we have acted wickedly!" and if they return to you with all their heart and all their being . . . then listen to their prayer and their request from your heavenly dwelling place. Do what is right for them, and forgive your people who have sinned against you.[11]

Such acts of confession open the way to receive forgiveness from God and from one another. The wisdom of Solomon, exhibited in prayer in 1 Kgs 8:46, offers healing for what is broken. The broken relationships in United Methodism need confessing and correcting by all people for God to heal the brokenness. We could hear that from a text in "The 8:46 Lectionary."

Coping with Powerlessness in Luke 8:46

Luke 8:46 comes amid a complex section in the gospel. It is a story within a story, framed in a larger set of stories—one of the literary devices Luke uses

---

11. 1 Kgs 8:46–50 CEB.

to narrate the good news of Jesus.[12] It emphasizes "power," a topic that also appears elsewhere in the writings of Luke.[13]

What frames Luke 8:46 and the story that contains it is a series of events demonstrating Jesus' power over nature, demons, death, hunger, and religious practices.[14] There are separate reports of a dying girl and a hemorrhaging woman, both of whom may have been considered ritually unclean. But even rigid religious rules bend to Jesus' power.[15] So do reigning monarchs, as the next portion of Luke's narrative shows, where Herod is in awe of Jesus.[16]

The stories in 8:40–56 feature two people who seem to be at different spots on a spectrum of power. One is a religious leader, with institutional status in the world. The other ranks near the lowest levels of the social order, in bondage to her medical condition. Yet both are powerless.

The first is a man named Jairus. He and his wife have a daughter, who is seriously ill. Luke reports that Jairus is "a leader of the synagogue," so he is clearly a man of high religious rank. But, in this case, he is powerless to deal with a dying daughter. He begs Jesus to visit the family home and to deliver his dying daughter from her terminal illness. He kneels at Jesus' feet, demonstrating the desperation that would overtake any parent of a suffering child. His daughter is seriously ill, and he is powerless to do anything about it, regardless of his lofty status in the society and the synagogue.

The second featured character is a woman. She has a medical condition that no physician could treat. She has exhausted her financial resources. She is so powerless that she is nameless. Like many women mentioned in Scripture, she is known by her ailment, not by her identity. She is voiceless also, so she cannot speak in the crowd. She tries to reach Jesus without being seen. She approaches him from behind. She barely touches the bottom of Jesus' garment.

Luke 8:46 is not a parable. It presents a narrative about a problem Jesus faces. These two people intrude on him. They make desperate pleas for powerful help. They are powerless.

---

12. See, for example, the description of the hostility between two brothers, and the reconciliation between the father and the older of his two sons, woven within Jesus' parable of the prodigal son (Luke 15:11–32). The same technique appears in Mark 5:21–43, and in other Markan passages.

13. See Luke 5:17; 9:1; 24:49; and Acts 1:8.

14. Luke describes calming a storm in 8:22–25, exorcising demons in 8:26–33, raising a dead or dying child in 8:40–42 and 49–56, and feeding five thousand in 9:12–17.

15. Culpepper, "Gospel of Luke," 8:157.

16. Luke 9:7–9.

All of us know what it means to reach the limits of power. We want our children to get an education, but we cannot get them into the school that is best for them. We want to live in a safe neighborhood, but we cannot afford to move to one. We want to pursue a desirable career, but the demands of the day force us to pause our dreams. Our power hits its limits.

It happens to the most accomplished among us, as well as to the lowest achievers and the least gifted. Athletes reach limits when they cannot run as swiftly, or turn as sharply, or see as precisely, or dominate as effectively. A surgeon at the peak of her career must stow her scalpel because she can no longer trust her hands to do exacting work. A singer can no longer reach or hold familiar notes. A parent who has tried every tactic to detoxify her son from his addiction to a dangerous drug reaches the limit of patience and is powerless to get through to the child she loves but can no longer help.

We reach such limits. We realize that we are without power to define our own lives. Even those of us holding positions of power are perplexed about how to use it. We defer, since power will end when life ends. We despair, feeling powerless now. A pandemic deprives a worker of a job. A government decides not to extend unemployment benefits. A landlord sends eviction notices to tenants. A physician informs a family that there is nothing further to do.

Powerlessness can be brutally impersonal. The climate on this planet may have already suffered permanent damage. Human beings—having contributed to climate troubles—may now be powerless to reverse a process that will lead to an inevitable and inhospitable conclusion. If so, then the socially and politically powerless will be the first to experience the consequences, though they made the least contribution to the conditions.

Another kind of powerlessness exists in social systems that create vulnerability based on race. Several years ago, in a large southern city, a Black professor at a university found a route to campus that used local streets and that avoided crowded highways. The route took her through an upper-class White neighborhood. One day, a police car signaled her to pull over. The officer said she exceeded the school zone speed limit, which is twenty miles per hour. She asked him what her speed was. He said she was driving twenty-one miles per hour. When he issued the ticket, he told her she could file an appeal with the municipal office and seek a hearing.

Several weeks after filing the appeal, she received a notice from a municipal officer, who gave her the date of her hearing. She realized that she would be out of the country attending an academic meeting and asked to reschedule the hearing. The officer responded that no alternate date was possible. If she did not appear on that date for the hearing, her only alternative was to pay the fine. She was powerless—not because of those rules, but because racial profiling trapped a Black victim who dared to drive through a wealthy White neighborhood on a public street.

Luke 8:46 and the narrative that surrounds the verse concern coping with powerlessness and overcoming it. Whether one feels powerless in the face of climatic forces, social structures, medical conditions, or anything else that breeds deprivation or death, there is nothing that can separate us from God's power. A powerless woman found power at the hem of a garment, and a powerless father found power in a word of promise in Luke 8:46. The gospel is empowering.

Claiming the Authority of Truth in John 8:46

The words in John 8:46 flow from a lively debate, in which bigotry confronts reason. At the climax of the discussion, Jesus poses a theological challenge to his adversaries. He tells them that he speaks the truth, yet they accuse him of being a liar. He tells them that he is innocent of evil, yet they insist that he is guilty. Then Jesus asks, "Who among you can show I'm guilty of sin?"[17] Jesus wants them to prove, through evidence and logic, that he is a fraud. He tells them to assemble facts and construct a rational argument to demonstrate his guilt. A mere allegation that he is a sinner will not suffice. He demands coherent reasons to reach an objective conclusion and prove he lacks the truth to set people free.

In its context, John 8:46 is a passage about the importance of reason in making decisions about truth, evil, and freedom. To read John 8:46, we must use the insights of reason, as Jesus did in this debate.[18]

First, the use of reason is a means to move the manner of the debate from bigotry, which irrationally fuels emotions of hatred and suspicion, to fidelity through rational argument. This enables the disputing parties who disagree with one another to focus on what they know not on whom they fear. Jesus' opponents condemned him based on their bias. Some used frightening labels and said that he was a Samaritan possessed by a demon.[19] Both characterizations could arouse emotional reactions. In that environment, calling a person demon-possessed evoked fear of terroristic force, and calling someone a Samaritan invoked religious and cultural prejudice. To call Jesus a demon-possessed Samaritan was to make him appear as a threat to be feared. But he resisted the fear and demanded reasonable discussion.

---

17. John 8:46 CEB
18. O'Day, "Gospel of John," 8:540.
19. John 8:48. See O'Day, "Gospel of John," 8:547.

The accusations against him drew upon bigotry. It was a debater's device for diverting the discussion from rational consideration to emotional reaction.

People in the first century, at the time of Jesus, were just as effective at this as partisans today. Code words like "the Left" or "religious Right" can be used to silence serious discussions by provoking visceral responses.

Second, the use of reason is a means to recognize and respect what is at stake. Jesus faced foes who insisted that, as heirs of Abraham, they enjoyed all the blessings of Abraham. But Jesus distinguished being a child of Abraham as an inherited legacy from being a child of Abraham by believing as Abraham did.[20] What made Abraham and Moses both patriarchs of faith was their trust in the promises that God provided them, with the imagination they needed to go where God beckoned them and the courage to do as God called them. Abraham heard the word of the Lord, who said "Go!" He "went."[21] Moses heard the word of the Lord promising to liberate Israel from slavery. He went, after being initially reluctant, and told Pharaoh, "Let the Israelites go!"[22]

Having Abraham's lineage and knowing Moses' law are not enough. Faithfully following the promises to Abraham and courageously maintaining the covenant crafted through Moses are vital. Fidelity is not a legacy we inherit. It requires using the intellect, acquiring understanding, trusting reason, and then taking action in boldly believing ways.

Third, reason is the logic of liberty. It offers freedom from bigotry. It is the capacity to reach objective judgments about very complex matters. It is the ability to collect, compile, and critique information to escape emotional bondage. It exposes the ironies and hypocrisies of life. It is a means to find freedom from self-importance and to stay humble.

Reason is a vital resource for reading Scripture, for engaging in theological debate, and for understanding what it means to act upon all of the information available—not just data that support prejudged conclusions. Reason is a gift for interpreting Scriptures that bear witness to Jesus as Lord. Reason is a process for challenging the prejudice that provokes reactions based on hate rather than responses based on faith. Reason is a means for the church, when it woke, to act faithfully. And reason is one of the resources among others, according to the official doctrine of the United Methodist Church, that enable the church when it woke to tell the truth. Reason is an

---

20. John 8:39.
21. Gen 12:1; 13:1.
22. Exod 6:6, 11.

important resource for salvation because, as Jesus said, only the truth will set us free.[23]

John 8:46 is part of a reasonable argument in which Jesus demands that his opponents show him to be wrong. It requires facing facts that one might prefer not to know and listening to truth one might prefer not to hear. And it links to other texts of truth.

In the book of Amos, the prophet confronts a priest named Amaziah, an ally of King Jeroboam. Amaziah has informed Amos that his prophecies are unwelcome because the king does not want to hear them. Amos says the king's preference to avoid hearing God's truth will not stop him from telling it.[24] Such ancient prophecies compel us to know the truth now.

In the summer of 2020, Duke University Archivist Valerie Gillispie described Duke as "a place of extraordinary scholarship and research, as well as beauty and wonder." But she added it "has parts of its past that are disturbing and ugly." Among the "disturbing and ugly" details are things that some people would rather not know or prefer not to have anyone tell. To love Duke is to understand that "it's a more complicated love" than they might like, as the Archivist wrote and demonstrated with photographic and documentary evidence.[25]

During the nineteenth century, before the Duke family created an endowment and then provided support that led the university to be known by the family name, Trinity College used enslaved labor. And the president of the college personally owned slaves. While enslavement ended in North Carolina with Emancipation and passage of the Thirteenth Amendment to the Constitution, racial segregation and White supremacist subordination of Black people endured in the institution. It existed when the Duke family gift arrived, and it lasted long afterward.

In 1919, eleven Black janitors signed a letter to the president of the school, pleading for an increase in pay. Seven months later, they signed another letter, making the same request. No evidence has been found that President William Preston Few ever acknowledged or answered either letter.

In 1946, Duke University hosted a party for the staff to celebrate the holiday season. A photograph of the event shows that it was racially segregated. Black and White employees were in separate sections of the same dining hall. The photograph reveals what most were unwilling to discuss about segregated racial patterns at the institution.

---

23. John 8:32.
24. Amos 7:10–17.
25. Gillispie, "Let's Embrace Duke's Entire History," para. 9.

In 1966 Duke hired Samuel Dubois Cook as its first Black faculty member. Until 1966, all the members of the university were White. Dr. Cook came three years after Duke enrolled the first Black undergraduates as degree candidates. Between the arrival of Black undergraduates and a Black professor, the first Black preacher occupied the pulpit of Duke Chapel.

That building, which remains the iconic structure on campus, was constructed according to the west campus design developed by Julian Abele, a Black architect from Philadelphia. He had the imagination to draw what was to be built. From time to time, he visited the site when it was under construction. But when he visited, he was not allowed to stay in one of the local hotels. They had no accommodations for Black guests.

The design of the chapel includes an undercroft. Beneath the pulpit is a crypt, where the remains of the deceased presidents of the university have been placed.

The remains of the longest serving president, William Preston Few, are among them. He assumed office when it was just Trinity College and before it was Duke University. Few worked with the Duke family to secure the philanthropic gifts that led to the new name of the institution. He stayed in the position until his death in 1940. He was once asked if a Black minister might preach in Duke Chapel, and he reportedly responded with the words, "Over my dead body."

On Sunday, April 12, 1964, Samuel DeWitt Proctor prepared to preach at Duke Chapel. He was a person of immense distinction. As the first Black preacher in that pulpit, he brought a word. At the time of the sermon at Duke Chapel, he was in the midst of an exceptional career. He had earned his doctorate at Boston University in 1950, the same year that he delivered a lecture at the Crozer Theological Seminary, where he met a student named Martin Luther King Jr. Later in the 1950s, he had been president of Virginia Union University. When he entered the pulpit at Duke Chapel, he was the president of the National Council of Churches.

At Dr. King's invitation, he had delivered lectures during the Montgomery bus boycott. He also had visited the White House, at the invitation of President Eisenhower, for discussions about impacts of the Supreme Court decision in *Brown v. Board of Education*. At that meeting, when Eisenhower asked the Black leaders to ease their demands for civil rights, Proctor and others refused to comply with the president's request.

In 1960, Proctor became president of North Carolina A&T. He took a leave of absence in 1963, at President Kennedy's request, to direct the work of the Peace Corps in Africa. Later, he was a distinguished professor at Rutgers, while serving simultaneously as the senior pastor of Abyssinian Baptist Church in New York.

So, on April 12, 1964, when Dr. Samuel Proctor stood in the pulpit of Duke Chapel as the first Black person to preach there, he was already an accomplished intellectual, religious, and political leader. On that Sunday morning, he began his sermon with an unusual word. It woke Duke Chapel.

In the pulpit, looking down toward the crypt, he told truth that amazed those in the pews and would have amazed those who lay in repose beneath him. He stood over the remains of the former Duke presidents. Then, over their dead bodies, he said, "Well, President Few, here I am."

From Preaching to Exhorting

There are many ways to preach the gospel and many resources to use in preparing to preach it. Taking a passage from Scripture by following the "8:46 Lectionary" is one way to find an appropriate biblical text for preaching.

It embraces both Old and New Testaments and draws from two of the Gospels. It affirms the tradition that includes the wisdom of Solomon, embraces a call to confession, proclaims the good news of repentance, exercises prophetic voices of judgment, and acknowledges the realities of privilege and powerlessness. It respects the experience of Black people who have been victims of violence and endured patterns of prejudice. And it prepares the church for preaching so they can hear the Lord who shows that reasoned arguments, not bigoted beliefs, are means to salvation.

The term "preaching" has a lot of definitions. For Martin Luther, it is the weapon "by which Christ will slay the antichrist," while for John Calvin it was "the exposition of the Word of God to the people assembled for worship."[26] For John Wesley, preaching both announces the gospel declaring salvation and instructs in the discipline that is integral to salvation.[27]

The Methodists in America developed an office in the ministry of the church for the purpose of implementing this approach to preaching. In addition to the steps of taking a text and applying it, as a preacher would, American Methodists exhorted the people to act on it. So, the licensed "exhorter" was a standard office in the nineteenth-century Methodist churches.

To make a difference in the world, the exhortations from a leader in the church would propel the church into the streets and fields, into their recreational spaces and workplaces, into public areas and political arenas. When the future woke the church, it acts in all the world.

The licensed "Exhorter" remained in the *Discipline* of the Methodist Episcopal Church and the Methodist Episcopal Church, South, until the

---

26. Edwards, *History of Preaching*, 287, 320.
27. Heitzenrater, *Wesley and the People*, 20, 185.

1939 reunion of the northern and southern Methodists with the Methodist Protestants. Then it was removed. But the African Methodist Episcopal Church, which was not included in the reunion of Methodist bodies that year, kept the office of "Exhorter" and, with it, the tradition that a complete commitment to the gospel includes encouragement to implementing it in private and public spheres.[28]

If the church woke to the substance of the Scriptures in the "8:46 Lectionary" with the resources of tradition, experience, and reason, the texts will arouse the church to action. The gift of freedom liberates the church to go into the world. The church, which was born by the word breathed by the risen Christ and by the breath of a mighty wind at Pentecost, becomes the church that lives again. When the future woke the church, new things happen.

---

28. *Doctrine and Discipline of the African Methodist Episcopal Church*, ¶ 129.

CHAPTER NINE

Miraculous Gifts and Messianic Commissions for a Messy World

Waking while It Is Still Dark

The cascading crises of 2020 inflicted incalculable harm on religious institutions and cast shadows of uncertainty over their futures in mission. Congregations faced unknown numbers of months until they could conduct public worship with people gathered in person. Denominations could not convene meetings to define doctrines, adopt regulations, elect officers, appoint boards, name committees, develop programs, set public policies, or run the national and international activities that connect their organizations together. Church leaders deferred ambitious goals, shelved plans, reduced staff, and slashed budgets. Church-affiliated universities, colleges, and schools wondered how they would survive declines in enrollments, delays in tuition payments, and drops in donor support.

Major logistical challenges confronted churches' basic activities. They suspended Sunday schools, Bible study groups, confirmation classes, and pre-schools. They closed food pantries, meal services, health clinics, and tutoring to prevent spreading the coronavirus. Stopping such activities was necessary, in part, because the volunteers needed to run them were unwilling or unable to continue serving. Meanwhile, churches lost revenue from offerings, which were not being collected, and from renting spaces for public events, which did not happen. Weddings were cancelled or conducted quietly. Church dinners were suspended. And memorial services were held at gravesides, where mourners tried to comfort one another from physical distances.

No one knew if patterns of church worship and programmatic participation had been permanently disrupted. No one knew if habits like sending children to Sunday School, having youth retreats, or holding adult Bible studies would ever resume. No one knew how long this would last, how low attendance would fall, how high budget deficits would rise, or how many local churches might never reopen.

Meanwhile, besides fearing the consequences of the current crises, America's religious groups were facing unfavorable long-term trends. Since 1960, they had been declining.

During the fifteen years immediately after World War II, Americans had dramatically increased their religious participation. And American culture had honored religious prerogatives. What people knew as church life tended to define public priorities. Secular groups would plan their events—like athletic programs for children and youth—using schedules that did not conflict with religious rites. Methodist churches, like other religious organizations, assumed they had big influence in America with bright futures. They planted new churches, expanded church-related institutions, and opened new theological schools to educate more ministers.

In the period after the end of World War II, as religious participation increased, weekly worship attendance rose to unprecedentedly high rates. Whereas pre-war patterns showed less than one-third of Americans were in houses of worship each week, post-war practices showed 42 percent of Americans attending worship each week—almost a one-third increase. It seemed to be a trend likely to continue. As late as the 1970s, 38 percent of Americans still said that they attended worship every week.[1] If one includes the Americans who participated in public worship only slightly less often, perhaps once or twice each month, then clearly a majority of the nation found religion to be an essential resource in the years following the end of the Second World War.

Many read these data as signs of a new normal. Those perceptions were wrong.

---

1. See "In U.S., Decline of Christianity," para. 24 and fig. 11. Beginning in 1972, the General Social Survey offered data that provided a single source for such analyses. Prior to that, various studies produced differing results. These estimates are based on reporting of a sermon by Harry Emerson Fosdick, "Fosdick Condemns Temple Tramplers" (21) and on books that include Sydney Ahlstrom's *A Religious History of the American People* (952) and *Sundays in New York* by William B. Lawrence (186–89). Pew reports that, by the end of the second decade of the twenty-first century, the portion of the American people who attend weekly worship dropped to 28 percent ("Pew Research Center," fig. 11).

All these positive statistics peaked around 1960. In 1968, when the Methodist Church and the Evangelical Brethren merged, the United Methodist Church had its largest membership on its first day. Ever since then, the numbers have been declining. Any local churches showing statistical growth are anomalies in a national trend away from religion.

According to the Pew Research Center, "The religious landscape of the United States continues to change at a rapid clip," and the change is relentlessly moving in negative directions. A majority of Americans identified themselves as Protestant in 2009. Only slightly more than 40 percent do now. Differences between generations are especially stark. Of all Americans, 84 percent born before 1945 and 76 percent born between 1946 and 1964 identify as Christians. But fewer than 50 percent of the nation's Millennials (that is, those born between 1981 and 1996) identify themselves as Christians. Additionally, 40 percent of the Millennials claim no religious affiliation and rarely attend a religious service.[2]

So, the future of the church will require reaching people who are less religiously active and less interested in religious affiliation than the age cohorts that control most leadership and decision-making authority in churches. The future of the church will also mean engaging people with different social views. Almost half of Millennials and Generation Z (born between 1997 and 2010) think same-sex marriage is a good thing for society. And two-thirds of the Millennials and of Generation Z think that Black people are treated with less justice than White people. The gap is huge between younger and older generations in their social views.[3]

If the future woke the church, it will deal with unprecedented problems. Its mission will address what it has not faced for a long time, namely the doubt that its mission matters.

Diminished by Division

Envisioning the future of American religion is truly a daunting task. On the horizon are generations with less interest in organized faith groups and less interest in institutions that put unwelcome policies in place. To put it another way, the freedom of religion in the twenty-first century means that people have spiritual options, not just constitutional protections. They are at liberty to ignore religion or to pursue it, without being limited to religious organizations.

---

2. "In the U.S., Decline of Christianity," figs. 10, 5.
3. Parker and Igielnik, "On the Cusp of Adulthood," figs. 7, 6.

Younger cohorts, for example, tend to favor the full inclusion of all persons without any restrictions regarding sexual identity. They also tend to favor equal justice for racially identified persons who have been deprived of liberty. But church politics, policies, and practices restrict sexuality and tolerate segregated patterns based on race—explicitly in laws, and implicitly in local practices. Denominationally, the United Methodist Church sets boundaries by sexuality. Locally, the church separates races rather than reconciles them. The church is deeply divided.

Fault lines and fractures appeared as the United Methodist Church formed. A faction calling itself "orthodox" or "evangelical" declared it would no longer be "a silent minority" treated with indifference by denominational leaders.[4] One caucus warned of "the impending death of the United Methodist ministry among Spanish-Americans."[5] Black women felt that academic and ecclesial systems skipped over them.[6]

These issues were well-known in the founding stages of United Methodism. The new denomination tried to address them. It created commissions and boards to focus on them. It elected women and persons of color to be episcopal leaders. It encouraged making cross-racial appointments of clergy. It gave caucuses a voice.

But the church divided into camps. Seeking means for reconciling differences gave way to securing electoral majorities. The church chose the power of politics to write rules restricting sexuality and chose intolerance for homosexual practices. However, the church also chose not to write rules rejecting racial segregation or White supremacy and chose tolerance for patterns of racial segregation as they were practiced locally. The absence of action on race diminished the church. The presence of action on homosexuality diminished it further.

The 1972 General Conference amended the denomination's Social Principles and added the statement, "we do not condone the practice of homosexuality and consider this practice incompatible with Christian teaching."[7] With that, a new, antagonizing phrase entered United Methodist vocabulary. Later, it was codified in church laws. And United Methodism entered a more deeply divided phase, which appears likely to cause a formal schism.

---

4. See Charles W. Keysor, "Methodism's Silent Minority," in *MEAS*, 598.

5. See *Daily Christian Advocate*, in *MEAS*, 620.

6. See Theressa Hoover, "Black Women and the Churches: Triple Jeopardy," in *MEAS*, 635–40.

7. *Book of Discipline of the United Methodist Church 1972*, ¶ 72C.

Meanwhile, the denomination muted its prophetic voice. The declaration that "racism is sin" in the Social Principles is a "call to faithfulness" and "to a prayerful, studied dialogue."[8] But it is not a church law requiring accountability or action. So, anti-racism is a rare witness.

If the church splits, it will do so as a significantly weakened institution. Its membership numbers and financial resources are declining. It has not established a public profile that insists on addressing the "sin" of racism. It has chosen to tolerate non-inclusive practices at local levels. It has neglected to communicate clearly why it exists and what it intends to achieve. It has failed to promote its mission as a spiritually lively institution in an age of anti-institutional spirituality. Its connectional system, constitutional order, and ecclesiastical practices are not in sync. Various centrifugal forces are pulling it apart.

Finding a Future

If the church is to have a future, it is now time to wake from sleep. The church has God-given ability to know the truth, the freedom to confess its failures, and the authority to fulfill the mission that is its purpose. If the church woke, it will have power to act.

A Lutheran preacher and homiletics professor named Edmund Steimle defined the power during a preaching class. Reflecting about sermons on Pentecost, Steimle mentioned an insight he received while studying the second chapter of the book of Acts. The gift of Pentecost is often interpreted as a miracle of speaking in many tongues, he said, but the mysterious gift at Pentecost is not talking but listening. It is a capacity to hear one another beyond boundaries of ethnicity, race, religion, and region. The miracle of Pentecost, amid all the noise, is a gift of hearing.

It is not a matter of audibility. The throngs gathered for Pentecost heard sound. But they belonged to ethnic groups from different regions and communicated in diverse languages. What makes Pentecost transformative is understanding one another. Pentecost overcomes a reluctance, refusal, inability, or unwillingness to hear others. The gift to hear is the grace of reconciliation.

In Isaiah 6, the opening verses report the call of Isaiah to prophesy. His first word was a harsh message that people would not understand because their minds would be dull, and their senses would be blocked. It is a blunt

---

8. *Book of Discipline of the United Methodist Church 2016*, Part V, "Social Principles," ¶ 162A.

word of judgment about sins of resistance to truth. Refusal to repent and to change impede grace. God summoned Isaiah to

> Make the minds of this people dull
> Make their ears deaf and their eyes blind,
> So they can't see with their eyes
> Or hear with their ears,
> Or understand with their minds,
> And turn and be healed.[9]

The unwillingness to hear is prophetic. According to the New Testament, Jesus taught in parables because it was difficult for people to hear his message, and human beings with hard hearts find "hearing" undesirable.[10] But the good news of Pentecost is an unwillingness to hear is a correctable condition. At Pentecost, the power of God overcomes it. People can hear each other, despite differences and diversities. The miracle of Pentecost is understanding others who are ethnically, socially, culturally, and linguistically separated: "We hear them."[11]

Its mystery overcomes divisions. In Wesleyan theology and United Methodist doctrine, reconciliation occurs when God's grace and human actions collaborate. Freedom from division and estrangement is not magically imposed. But it is mysteriously experienced in a process of salvation that binds the generosity of a gracious God with the justice of grateful humanity. God's gift of hearing works when it is embraced by a willingness to hear. If the church woke to the miracle of Pentecost, barriers to reconciliation will be breached.

Christians' Pentecost, which transliterates the Greek word *Pentekostes* (πεντηκοστῆς), occurs fifty days after Easter. Jews' *Shavuot* (שָׁבוּעוֹת) occurs fifty days after the second night of Passover. The words illuminate each other. Christians on Pentecost celebrate the gift of life to the church by the power of the Holy Spirit. Jews on Shavuot celebrate the gift of the Torah to the people who had been liberated from enslavement in Egypt. A crowd, gathered in Jerusalem for Shavuot, provided a context for the account in the book of Acts that became the story Christians tell of Pentecost.[12] Shavuot and Pentecost are associated with gifts that enable a community to be born with the power to fulfill their purpose in active religious living. For

---

9. Isa 6:10 CEB. A similar prophecy appears in Ezek 12:2, which says that the rebellious house does not hear.

10. Matt 13:10–17; Mark 4:11–12; Luke 8:9–10; John 12:39–40; Acts 28:25–27; Rom 11:8.

11. Acts 2:11.

12. See Winston, "'Gifts' of Pentecost and Shavuot."

Christians, Pentecost begins a future filled with hope.[13] It is a day when the future woke the church.

Becoming the Church of the Future

Discipleship after the resurrection does not rely on listening to Jesus speak in parables,[14] watching him weep at a friend's graveside,[15] or questioning him about some failures to solve an urgent problem.[16] It involves new relationships and new configurations of authority in faith. The gift of spiritual power is described differently in Acts 2 and John 20. The people in Acts 2 felt a mighty wind, saw fiery signs, heard noise, and asked one another, "How then can each of us hear them . . . ? What does this mean?"[17] The people in John 20 felt a fresh breath of life, heard of their new authority, and were freed from locked doors to be sent everywhere.

The purpose and power of the church are gifts of a great future beyond a grim present. The church woke. The report in Acts 2 is the only place in the Bible where this specific incident is described. Nevertheless, it is one of many New Testament stories that continue the narrative in Luke's Gospel about the experiences of disciples, after they faced Jesus' death and when they try to fathom the resurrection. The Gospel of Luke concludes with the risen Christ opening the minds of the disciples to understand things that perplexed them and telling them to wait for the power to pursue all that he taught. The book of Acts begins with the arrival of that power. The future woke the church. And the church woke, empowered to fulfill its mission.

It is risky to embrace the future. It is uncertain what can happen if we hear one another. Yet it is a holy gift. One would think that the church would welcome a chance to hear. But a woke church in a divided culture might face resistance. A secular entertainer faced that in 1968 when he tried to help Americans hear and "much of white America rebuffed" the opportunity.[18]

One of the top-rated television shows in the country that year was "The Tonight Show." Host Johnny Carson was one of the best-known comedians, emcees, and celebrity interviewers in America. For a week in 1968, the popular White host ceded his desk to a Black singer and actor, Harry Belafonte. On five nights, for ninety minutes each night, Belafonte was the

13. Acts 2:16–21.
14. Matt 13:10.
15. John 11:35.
16. Mark 9:14–29.
17. Acts 2:8, 12 CEB.
18. Walsh, "49 Years Ago," para. 38.

host while an array of twenty-five guests, fifteen of them Black, sat beside him as guests. The huge late-night television audience experienced what later was described as a "sit-in," when they heard what the Black leaders in America wanted to say.

A musician and journalist known as Questlove, who was born three years after Belafonte hosted the programs, says that it "was probably the most revolutionary move that mainstream television could have done at the time." Harvard scholar Henry Louis Gates, who as a child watched it with his father, considers it "history in the making." Belafonte thought it was an event of "defiance."[19] Only three television networks existed then. There was no live streaming or cable. So, that week of conversation reached a massive audience. It was one of the few times that ordinary White Americans heard prominent Black Americans speak of their experiences.

But getting tens of thousands of local churches to hear might be impossible. When the church has shown the courage to compel its Black and White members to hear one another, the occasions have been few and the results at best only fair. What United Methodists call "cross racial" appointments—Black clergy to White congregations, and White clergy to Black local churches—have tended to be occasional experiments rather than routine practices. When they did happen, both clergy and laity recognized the difficulties of trying to "hear" one another.

A White preacher in a Black church in the north struggled to understand the generational and the gendered customs of a congregation whose culture he did not know. A Black preacher in a White church in the South found that Black styles of preaching and music were "acceptable," but sermons that put a positive focus on "Black Lives Matter" were not.

The spirit of Pentecost loses much of its mystery and miracle if people are only willing to hear the parts of its powerful message that feel familiar or comfortable. Yet the church has been commissioned to speak about matters that are unfamiliar and act in ways that conflict with the comfortable. To be the church that fulfills its mission will require hearing one another say what many of us prefer to have nobody mention.

---

19. Kennedy, "Documentary Recalls," 2D. Among the guests that Belafonte hosted during the week were singer Aretha Franklin (whose father C. L. Franklin was a prominent preacher), Martin Luther King Jr. (who would be assassinated a few months afterward), actor Sidney Poitier, and singer Dionne Warwick. An NBC Peacock documentary titled "The Sit-In" was produced in 2020; see https://www.peacocktv.com/watch-online/movies/documentary/the-sit-in-harry-belafonte-hosts-the-tonight-show/0f4b9046-408f-33ac-a1ce-dd2099ee4a35.

Commissioned for Action

After the crucifixion and the burial of Jesus, varied accounts in the Bible say the disciples were in despair, dispirited and divided. Several men, according to Luke, were "stunned" by word from women in the group that Jesus was alive.[20] Mark says the women did not report anything to anybody: "Overcome with terror and dread" is how he describes them.[21] John says some of the disciples took refuge in a locked area, fearing danger, while others went fishing.[22]

Each Gospel writer has a different way of reporting what happened next.[23] Mark alone has multiple accounts, ranging from descriptions of the disciples as so afraid they maintained silence to descriptions of disciples as so unafraid that they healed the sick and raised the dead. Matthew, Luke, and John end differently, but all three have stories of the risen Christ meeting disciples and then sending them into mission.

Today, the church affirms that "Christ has died. Christ is risen. Christ will come again" in celebrating Holy Communion[24] and that Christ will come in judgment.[25] Creeds and prayers of the church rely on the future and engage in a mission of hope. If the future woke the church, the divisions of the present will not define the church. The intrusive promises of the future will. So, discipleship will be driven by the promises that the church knows and the actions that the church has authority to take. If the future woke the church, the life to come will come to life in its faith and work. The identity of the church will be determined not by the problems that divide but by the power that unites, not by private fears but by public purpose.

In all four Gospels, evidence for the resurrection is not an empty tomb but a full mission. A "cult legend"[26] about the tomb might provide a shrine but not a unifying hope. The good news is not a vacant grave but a vital mission on which disciples are sent.

All four Gospels mention meeting the risen Christ. Matthew and Mark refer to a meeting in Galilee. Luke reports meetings on the road to Emmaus

---

20. Luke 24:22–24 CEB.
21. Mark 16:8 CEB.
22. John 20:19; 21:3.
23. See, for example: Matt 28:16-20; John 20:19-23, 26-31; 21:15-19; Luke 24:45-49; Acts 1:8.
24. See "A Service of Word and Table" in *The United Methodist Hymnal*, 10, 14, 16, etc.
25. See "The Nicene Creed" and "The Apostles' Creed" in *The United Methodist Hymnal*, nos. 880, 881.
26. Perkins, "Gospel of Mark," 7:553.

and in a room with a meal. John reports meetings behind locked doors in a house in Jerusalem and at the Sea of Galilee, adding that those who see and believe are no more blessed than those who do not see and yet believe.[27]

In each meeting, disciples are empowered to act. The mission is what unifies them, and their actions will be the evidence of their power. While the Gospel writers' accounts differ in the details, what matters is the unity of the mission. It involves teaching, forgiving, and transforming life. The Gospels emphasize being sent by the risen Christ with power. Other texts cite mission in action.[28] The life to come thus comes to life in the mission of the church.

Going Public

Methodists in America, like adherents of all religions, are arbiters of their own choices. No civil law can mandate or prohibit religious activities. No person can be deprived of public office on the basis of religion. No president can demand that citizens pray in a certain way or order the arrest of a citizen who fails to pray. Politicians can question rival candidates, who might be Muslim or Mormon or Methodist, about applying the tenets of religion to the tasks of the office being sought. But no person can be constitutionally barred from candidacy for any public office based on adherence to a religion or lack of it. No religious community can be denied its constitutional freedom to function, privately or publicly.

Religious organizations, with whom Americans choose to affiliate, enjoy freedom for exercising public voices and for keeping silent. Amish are as welcome to express no opinions on matters of public policy as Catholics are to advocate for public policies.

Methodist churches have often called for governments to act and have insisted that their members should actively seek specific types of government action. In the early days of American Methodism, church leaders told members to lobby for an end to slavery. In the nineteenth and twentieth centuries, Methodists urged America to support workers' collective bargaining rights and to prohibit the sale and distribution of beverage alcohol.

The United Methodist Church now urges "changes in economic, political, social and technological lifestyles" to protect the earth. The United Methodist Church today believes "it is a governmental responsibility to

---

27. The location called the Sea of Galilee is also known as the Sea of Tiberias.
28. See, for example, Acts 1:8; Rom 1:4–5; Eph 1:17–23; Heb 12:14; and Jas 1:22.

provide all citizens with health care." The official statement of the United Methodist Social Principles says, "Health care is a basic human right."[29]

The church has a public voice. If the church woke, it would use that voice vigorously.

The church is an instrument for mission. The church exists to reform the continent and to transform the landscape, as Wesley said.[30] If the church woke, it will exercise a public voice to fulfill the purpose for which it exists. The sound of that voice might be, to some persons in the world, a source of discomfort. But others will hear and see signs of discipleship that overcome division as gifts of grace and sources of hope.

The world is a messy place. If the church woke, it will not accommodate itself to the messiness of the world but accept the commission of the risen Christ to overcome the world.

As the author of the New Testament letter to Titus wrote,[31] it is true that many places to which the mission sends the church offer complications and challenges. But, as Titus was told, that is why the church—with its mission and power—has been sent to the world.

The mission is to transform, not to be comfortable with the current form. The mission is to reconcile separations, not be accommodating with them. The mission is to judge sins and to name the sins that are unforgivable, not tolerate them. The mission has a capacity to hear one another and listen actively to one another. If the future woke the church, its commission and its power will awaken again.

---

29. *Book of Discipline of the United Methodist Church 2016*, Part V, "The Social Principles," ¶ 162V.

30. Wesley, *Works of John Wesley*, 10:845.

31. Titus 1:5.

CHAPTER TEN

When the Future Builds the Church

A Relationship with the Future

One value that most religions offer—and that many secular forces seek—is a hope for the future of the world. It can be a vision to achieve, a promise to receive, or a dream to cherish. It can be personal or communal or both. In the case of religion, it can involve this life, or the life to come, or both. If there is no hope, then every tomorrow is just another fleeting episode labeled "today," which will soon become another yesterday that is piled atop other yesterdays in a mass of meaningless existence. So says Macbeth.

> Life's but a walking shadow, a poor player
> That struts and frets his hour upon the stage,
> And then is heard no more. It is a tale
> Told by an idiot, full of sound and fury,
> Signifying nothing.[1]

Religion interrupts such meaningless despair with the prospect of a future based not in a sentimental optimism but a vibrant promise. Its promise can break the chains of enslaved people and offer liberation to entrapped people, who are confined by conditions they cannot personally change. It can allow those with wealth to see beyond owning more things. It can

---

1. Shakespeare, *Macbeth*, 5.5.24–28.

help those with power to see the pointlessness of trying to control more privileges.

For Christians, hope is not merely an antidote to despair in the present. It is an active link to the future. When believers affirm the faith by reciting the Nicene Creed, they "look for the resurrection of the dead, and the life of the world to come."[2] When United Methodists share the sacrament of Holy Communion, they believe that they are connected "to all the world, until Christ comes in final victory and we feast at his heavenly banquet."[3] Thus, the life to come has come to life in the church.

Religion is not the only resource for imagining a relationship with the future. Great discoveries in the sciences pursue a future when the air is clean, disease is controlled, and the cosmos is a destination to explore with joy. Political ideologies develop around the prospect of building an ideal future—whether they prefer democracy, theocracy, oligarchy, royalty, or some other alternative to anarchy.

One sign of enthusiasm for the capacity of human actions to create a great future was a decision by Benjamin Franklin in 1785. He had read a French mathematician's critique of his personal and political views, which the critic mocked for their appalling optimism. Indeed, the critic sarcastically suggested that a true optimist would leave some money in his estate that could only be used after it had collected interest for five hundred years. Franklin turned the tables on the critic, sent him a letter thanking him for the idea, made modifications in it, and created what has been called a "bicentennial endowment" with a bequest that would generate benefits for two hundred years. He took the critic's bait. And he took part in building the future.

In 1785, the American republic had barely begun to exist. It had a governmental system based on Articles of Confederation, which would soon prove to be unworkable. Victory in a war with England had been achieved, but it was no guarantee that independence would endure. And Franklin was seventy-nine, so he was unlikely to live long enough to know whether his optimism was fruitful or fraudulent. Yet he participated in building the future that he would not live to see.

In 1787, he was a delegate to the Constitutional Convention in Philadelphia that wrote the document creating a new structure for the American government. In 1789, the new Constitution went into effect. The nation had a functioning government with the inauguration of a president and the first meetings of the Congress and the Supreme Court. That same year, Franklin

---

2. See "The Nicene Creed" in *United Methodist Hymnal*, no. 880.
3. See "A Service of Word and Table I" in *United Methodist Hymnal*, 10.

wrote a codicil to his will, creating bicentennial endowments for Boston and Philadelphia.

With bequests of one thousand pounds to each city, he specified that the money was to be invested. Revenues that the endowments generated were to benefit apprentices and "artificers." Franklin died in 1790, the year after he changed his will. His endowments and their beneficiaries prospered. Since 1793, Philadelphia and Boston have been spending funds from the endowments for apprenticeships, scholarships, public works, and technical training schools. And thousands of students have been receiving Franklin Legacy Prize medals for nearly two hundred thirty years, as enduring evidence of his hope for the future by helping young people build it.[4]

Debating the Future

But there is a difference between building a future and believing in a future that is coming toward us. Christians believe in both but have long debated how current actions and future realities are connected. Their disagreements have aroused emotions, ranging from bold enthusiasm to morbid fear.

Some Christians insist there is discontinuity between life in the here and the hereafter. In a discontinuous view, people who suffer terrors in this life will find relief in the life to come, and those who behave unjustly or abusively in this life will face judgment with severe punishment in the life to come. In a discontinuous view, being poor on earth can mean riches in heaven or being in bondage on earth can mean freedom in heaven, so it can be used to justify oppressing others in this life while they await joy to come. Judgment may be given to the oppressors when they reach the life to come. But the coming future and current present are disconnected.

Other Christians insist that there is continuity between life on earth and life in heaven. In a continuous view, "Jesus Christ is the same yesterday, today, and forever!"[5] God's justice is the same here as it is in the hereafter. The word of the Lord does not differ in the present from the future. God's judgment and God's mercy are the same on earth as in heaven. Christian life on earth now is not merely temporal but eternal.

---

4. Thompson, "Optimism: Ben Franklin." The amount of Franklin's bequests is impressive. His total gifts of two thousand pounds would, in 2020, be worth almost fifty million dollars. And he inspired other such endowments. In 2006, Roy Huffington of Houston, Texas, established two Bicentennial Endowments with a gift of ten million dollars to Southern Methodist University. One endowment funds student scholarships, and the other endowment funds faculty positions. Huffington died in 2008.

5. Heb 13:8 CEB.

Besides these differences, Christians disagree about whether the relationship with the future is individual or communal. Some Christians emphasize an individual hope for personal peace after leaving the world at the time of death. Others emphasize communal hope for public peace and social equity in this life before joining the community of saints in heaven. Some, who have included renowned religious leaders like Harry Emerson Fosdick and John Shelby Spong, were skeptical about personal existence beyond death, believing that life now is God's sufficient gift for the joy of experiencing peace and love in human history.

Christians also disagree about how to imagine a relationship with a future intruding into the present. They debate a second coming of Christ, for example. In the early days of the church, speculation was intense about Christ's imminent return. A text in 1 Thess 4:15 suggests that Jesus would return during current believers' lives. A parable in Matt 25:1–13, however, suggests that Christians should prepare for a long delay in his return. Since those texts were written decades apart, the experience of the church had plenty of data to verify the delay.

In the decades following the first reports of Jesus' resurrection, the perspectives about his return changed. Centuries of debates among various pre-millennialists, millennialists, and post-millennialists followed. Conflicting voices said Christ was about to return, had already returned, or was not going to return because he already provided believers with what they need to live.

What became clear, to all but the few who still predict the Lord's return to end the world imminently, is that the church is empowered in the present to act in relationship with the future. The life to come has come to life in the church. Authority to forgive or retain sins is granted by sacred power.[6] Trusting the will of God "on earth as in heaven" is a petition the church offers constantly in the Lord's Prayer.[7] The promise made present at Pentecost is given to the church in real time for all time, because the word of the Lord endures forever.[8]

An Eschatological Intrusion

Since the dawn of the nuclear age in the middle of the twentieth century, humans have faced the fact that we have created a technology with the capacity to ruin the planet and make it uninhabitable for hundreds of thousands

---

6. John 20:23.
7. See "The Lord's Prayer" in *United Methodist Hymnal*, no. 894.
8. Isa 40:8 and 1 Pet 1:25.

of years. And, since the final decade of the twentieth century, nations of the world have begun to accept that earth's climate is being harmed by rising temperatures, toxic air, polluted water, and changes in amounts and availability of arable land. All these things endanger life on earth now and threaten its habitability in the future. Hopes mix with fears for a planet that could have a catastrophic future caused by human failures.

The 2008 film *WALL-E* imagines earth as a place from which humanity fled because of the ecological disaster it created. But it also imagines that a life force will intrude itself through the mysteries of love and offer a basis for hope. Art, philosophy, and science imagine the future as an end toward which history is moving.

The church knows the future as a promise moving toward us. For the church, this is more than awaiting it, building it, or being threatened by it. The church lives as the future intrudes into our midst. That is the importance of the Greek word *eschaton* (ἔσχατον).

That word, along with various forms of it, is very common in the New Testament. In its many occurrences, it refers to the "last" in a sequence of things. In that way, it appears in Jesus' parable of the laborers in the vineyard,[9] where workers are hired at various times until some are hired last. But it can also mean the most remote or most extreme, as in 1 Cor 15:8 where Paul lists himself as the last person—the least likely person—to have an encounter with the risen Christ. It is an ordinary word with multiple uses. However, Christians have given it a specialized meaning. As a result, *eschaton* (ἔσχατον) refers to a theological discussion about the last or the most extreme things. It has led to a sub-specialty of theology called eschatology.

Eschatological matters are not necessarily at the end of a chronological sequence. They can intrude into present matters by coming from an extreme, or least likely, source. And these eschatological interruptions can belong simultaneously to the future and to the present.

"Here comes the kingdom of heaven!" said John the Baptist as Jesus approached him in the desert of Judea.[10] It was right there, as the people gathered around him in the wilderness, at a remote location, according to the witness of Scripture, for heaven to be on earth.

A persistent theme in Jesus' message was, "The kingdom of heaven has come near."[11] In the gospel of John, present and future are synchronous. Regarding worship practices, Jesus told a Samaritan woman "the time is

---

9. Matt 20:1–16.
10. Matt 3:2 CEB.
11. Matt 4:17; 10:7; Mark 6:10–12; Luke 9:2; 10:9 CEB.

coming—and is here!—when true worshippers will worship in spirit and truth."[12] Regarding beliefs about eternal life or passing from death to life, Jesus said "the time is coming—and is here!—when the dead will hear the voice of God's Son, and those who hear it will live."[13] The life to come has come to life in the church.

As Gail O'Day wrote, "The ordinary present has been transformed into the eschatological present."[14] The future intrudes into life now. Its intrusion becomes the standard of judgment for the present. It puts everything about the life of the church into an eschatological perspective. Divisions have ended, even if their end is not yet fully practiced or experienced. As Paul wrote to the Galatians.

> You are all God's children through faith in Christ Jesus. All of you who were baptized into Christ have clothed yourselves with Christ. There is neither Jew nor Greek; there is neither slave nor free; nor is there male and female, for you are all one in Christ Jesus.[15]

When the Future Invades the Present

One of Jesus' eschatological messages is his parable of the last judgment.[16] It imagines an assembly of all nations and of all angels. As New Testament scholar M. Eugene Boring put it, "These are the last words of Jesus' last discourse, a climactic point to which Matthew has carefully built."[17] So, everything in the cosmos is drawn into this parable of present and future.

If one thinks chronologically, the parable pictures the end of time. However, if one thinks eschatologically, this parable preaches about the present so completely infused with the future that there is no separation between a human act and a holy power. The simplest act—or the most careless failure to act—has eternal consequences involving ultimate judgments. Delivering food to the hungry, offering a drink to the thirsty, providing a coat to the unclothed, and making a visit to the incarcerated are eschatological events. Such actions are the difference between life and death. Human interactions are inseparable from holy ones.

12. John 4:23 CEB.
13. John 5:24–25 CEB.
14. O'Day, "Gospel of John," 8:483.
15. Gal 3:26–29 CEB.
16. Matt 25:31–46.
17. Boring, "Gospel of Matthew," 7:337.

Thus, when the future woke the church, knowledge of what it means to live in the realm of eternity has occurred. Present practices are seen in permanent perspective. A glass of water, a plate of food, an article of clothing, a conversation with a prisoner, or a similar act may or may not satisfy all the hunger, slake all the thirst, cover all the unclothed, or comfort all the confined. The focus of the parable is not to measure improvement of one who is helped but to measure the church on the faithfulness of its acts. Eschatological consequences involve joy and judgment.

In this light, ordinary things have incalculable meaning. Finite encounters have infinite importance. If the future woke the church, the church will know that truth and live by that light.

The Eternal Significance of the Ephemeral

Several decades ago, when bishops were given their assignments to episcopal areas, a Black bishop was sent to an annual conference whose clergy and laity were overwhelmingly White. Church law at the time required annual conferences to have an Episcopal Residence for a bishop and the bishop's household, with a residence committee to care for the property. The committee chair in this conference had experience in construction and in managing properties. He also had professional relationships with contractors and suppliers in the area. So, he was an ideal chair.

One day, a grease fire occurred in the kitchen of the Episcopal Residence. Nobody was hurt. However, the blaze did enough damage to require repairing the kitchen and replacing the range. The committee chair contacted the insurance provider, hired a local contractor to make the repairs, and arranged to purchase a new appliance for the kitchen. He scheduled an appointment to take the bishop's wife to a local appliance dealer, so she could select a range. The committee chair and the bishop's wife drove to the store, where they met the manager. The chair explained that they would be discussing a new kitchen range for the residence of the bishop. He introduced "Mrs. ___" to the store manager, who welcomed her.

Then the store manager asked, "How long have you been with the bishop?" She replied, "I beg your pardon?" He repeated the words, "How long have you been with the bishop?"

With the repetition of the question, the chair realized what was happening, though the bishop's wife immediately understood. The woman who was choosing an appliance for a bishop's kitchen was Black. The White manager assumed the Black woman had to be the bishop's maid.

Deeply embarrassed, the committee chair tried to correct the store manager and get him to apologize for this racist error. Tragically, this was not the first time—nor would it be the last in this Episcopal Area—when the bishop or his wife had to cope with bigotry. Racism runs deep. It arises in routine encounters as eschatological moments. It must face eschatological judgment.

To excuse or pardon the store manager for such a lapse might be merciful. But it would be eschatologically inappropriate unless some acts of confession, reparation, and reconciliation occurred. The manager had instinctively drawn upon the resources of racism and assumed that, in an overwhelmingly White context, any Black person was a subordinate servant. In this case, a woman was presumed to occupy a position as servant in society because she was Black.

A mundane matter of buying a kitchen appliance became an eschatological event. Every act in the routine business of human transactions occurs in the presence of heaven and is judged by the extreme truth of the *eschaton*. Accountability exists on earth as it does in heaven. If the church woke, it will confront, confess, and overcome the trouble it too often tolerates.

Thus, church leaders in South Africa created a Commission on Truth and Reconciliation after the end of apartheid. And church leaders of the Methodist Conference in Britain created a "Truth and Reconciliation process . . . to ensure that all the various memories and experiences are listened to and heard."[18] Such systems of accountability are vital in the church and elsewhere.

When the Future Transforms the Present

Cities and counties have enacted ordinances declaring racism a public health crisis. Data demand such actions. Black women are four times more likely to die from complications in their pregnancies than are White women. Black men are twice as likely to be killed by police officers as are White men.[19] Black people are nearly twice as likely to die of COVID-19.[20] If the church woke, its public voice will insist on overcoming such injustices, which leave a long legacy.

---

18. Agenda 56, Strategy for Justice, Dignity, and Solidarity, the Methodist Conference, June 30, 2021.

19. Vestal, "Racism Is a Public Health Crisis," para. 4. See also Bellware, "Calls to Declare Racism."

20. "Risk for COVID-19 Infection," fig. 1.

In Texas, a hundred and ten years after Allen Brooks had been lynched while a crowd of thousands watched, the Dallas County Board of Commissioners adopted a resolution declaring racism to be a public health emergency. It demanded programs and policies that will quantify improvements in the lives of people of color. That act did not inspire every municipality in the region, however. In the Dallas suburb of McKinney, a member of city council said there was a "Black State of Emergency" in the town. Citizens launched a petition initiative to recall her.[21]

But a United Methodist church in a small town to the northeast of McKinney decided to acknowledge and confess the sins of racism. It began when the pastor of First United Methodist Church in Paris, Texas, was preparing a Sunday sermon several years ago. During his research, he discovered a tragedy that involved the community and the congregation. A lynching in 1920 was one of many in a history of violence directed by White people against Black residents in Paris. When the pastor delivered his sermon and included information about that episode, it was the first time most White people in town ever heard the story. And there was more truth to tell.

Paris is the county seat of Lamar County, where Texas has borders with Arkansas and Oklahoma. In 1893, on the Lamar County fairground, a Black teenager named Henry Smith was lynched by a mob after he had been accused of raping a three-year-old White girl. And that was neither the first nor last occasion when the fairground served as the location for crowds to watch a White mob beat, burn, hang, torture, and kill a Black person. Such events were periodic public spectacles. The fairground was the preferred place for them.

On July 6, 1920, an argument in Paris led to the deaths of two White men, John Hodges and William Hodges. Later that day, two Black brothers named Herman and Irving Arthur were arrested for killing the White men. A mob grabbed the Arthur brothers from the county jail and took them to the fairgrounds. They killed Irving Arthur and his brother Herman, a veteran of World War I, by burning them while they were still alive. The lynching was the twelfth incident of its kind in Paris between 1892 and 1920. But it was not the last act of injustice in the county.

In 2008, a Black pedestrian was struck by a vehicle and dragged to his death. Charges were filed against a White driver. However, some eyewitnesses changed their testimony. As a result, no investigation was ever conducted to identify people who may have been involved, and the persons responsible for the death of the Black man were never brought to trial.[22]

21. Garcia, "Dallas County Becomes One."
22. Witt, "Evidence Frays in Murder Case."

Additionally, recent actions of racial injustice occurred in the county that did not involve torture or death but were nevertheless inequitable. In 2007, a fourteen-year-old White girl was convicted of arson.[23] The county judge sentenced her to probation. Then, three months later, a fourteen-year-old Black girl was in court for shoving a hall monitor at Paris High School. She was sentenced to prison for seven years.[24] Only a public outcry in response to the unjust ruling by the judge provoked a reduction of her sentence.

In the research for his sermon at First United Methodist Church of Paris, the Rev. Rob Spencer learned all this history. He learned details about his congregation's role, too. A member of the mob that seized Herman and Irving Arthur and burned them alive in July 1920 belonged to First Methodist Church. The minister of the congregation in 1920 had tried to intervene with the mob at the Lamar County jail. Evidence shows he tried to discourage them when they grabbed the Arthur brothers and dragged them to the county fairgrounds.

Rev. Spencer also learned, however, that this same preacher believed that the burden of responsibility to end lynching rests not with the White community that forms or tolerates a lynch mob but with those who are victims of it. In Paris, Texas, in 1920, in the view of that Methodist preacher, responsibility for preventing lynching belongs to the Black community.

> If the Negro race will show its appreciation by living as these good men desire them to live, much of the errors of the past will be removed from the path of their race. We can never save the Negro until he decides to become an honest, tireless, faithful helper of the white man who desires to defend him.[25]

On July 12, 2020, almost a hundred years to the day after Herman and Irving Arthur were murdered at the Lamar County fairground, Rev. Spencer and two of the Black pastors from the community gathered with members of the Arthur family and members of the Hodges family for a service at the Red River Valley Veterans Memorial Park in Paris. Melinda Watters, a descendant of John Hodges—whose death had initially led to the allegation that the Arthur brothers killed him—first suggested holding such a service. As a White woman, she confessed the role of her family and others in the White community in this dreadful violence. She addressed the public and the descendants of Herman and Irving Arthur.

23. Witt, "To Some in Paris."
24. Witt, "Racial Tensions."
25. Madewell, "Apology 100 Years," para. 11. See also https://www.facebook.com/communityremembrancecoalitionparistx.

> I lament the monstrous lynching and murder of Herman and Irving Arthur. I am saddened that your family had to flee the Paris community and start over. I am sorry for the way the white community and my family and myself have been complacent in both my bias against Black people and in accordance with a system that continues to disproportionately allow violence upon their bodies.

A descendant of the Arthur family, Janese Walton-Roberts, spoke at the service, also. She did not live in Texas. Surviving members of the family had fled Paris in September 1920 and had resettled in Chicago. In her remarks, Ms. Walton-Roberts referred to the death of George Floyd and to the rise of Black Lives Matter as evidence of why this service was so important.

> I didn't think I would ever be in this place; it's not a place any of our family ever wanted to come back to. [But] the time has come for forgiveness, and this is a perfect time.

It took a hundred years after the lynching of the Arthur brothers at the Lamar County fairground to confess the truth. Such eschatological judgment should never be delayed. If the church woke, it will not wait. United Methodists today need not shove the responsibility to the victims of violence or to future generations. The church is free to act right now.

The Power of an Intrusive Future

In an Encyclical titled *Fratelli Tutti*, released on the eve of the Feast of Saint Francis in Assisi, Pope Francis calls attention to the divisions that exist in the world. He laments the rise of "huge economic interests" that create fortresses of privilege for the extremely wealthy without creating "diversified work opportunities" to enhance the lives of others. He laments the rise of attitudes "where hostility and conflict would burn all bridges." He makes clear that the dividing issues involve personal and public virtues. And he shows that both public and personal actions must be done with "esteem and respect for others."[26]

Chapter 1 confronts the politics of "despair and discouragement" in the world.

> Today, in many countries, hyperbole, extremism and polarization have become political tools. Employing a strategy of

---

26. Francis, *Fratelli Tutti*, 45, 123, 224. See also Reese, "Five Things to Look For," and Harlan and Petrelli, "Pope Francis's New Encyclical." The date of the encyclical was October 3, 2020.

ridicule, suspicion and relentless criticism, in a variety of ways one denies the right of others to exist or to have an opinion. Their share of the truth and their values are rejected and, as a result, the life of society is impoverished and subjected to the hubris of the powerful. Political life no longer has to do with healthy debates about long-term plans to improve people's lives and to advance the common good, but only with slick marketing techniques primarily aimed at discrediting others. In this craven exchange of charges and counter-charges, debate degenerates into a permanent state of disagreement and confrontation.[27]

Chapter 4 affirms the gifts immigrants bring "for enrichment and the integral human development of all" and laments that some people in their countries of origin lack liberty.

It is important to apply the concept of "citizenship," which "is based on the equality of rights and duties, under which all enjoy justice. It is therefore crucial to establish in our societies the concept of *full citizenship* and to reject the discriminatory use of the term *minorities*, which engenders feelings of isolation and inferiority. Its misuse paves the way for hostility and discord; it undoes any successes and takes away the religious and civil rights of some citizens who are thus discriminated against.[28]

Chapter 5 acknowledges the need for governments and institutions to aid the welfare of all persons. Virtues are not merely matters for individuals, as the Encyclical says. "Even the Good Samaritan, for example, needed to have a nearby inn that could provide the help that he was personally unable to offer," according to Pope Francis. "Love of neighbor is concrete."[29]

This Encyclical is one that all ecumenical Christians—including American Methodists generally and the United Methodist Church specifically—should take seriously. It points to the importance of institutions, including churches and social organizations that provide education, health care, and other services for the well-being of the public. The Encyclical also testifies to Christian commitments for the full inclusion of persons as matters of justice.

The *eschaton* (ἔσχατον) invades the present, calling the church to act. It turns ordinary and routine actions into matters of extreme, ultimate importance. It confronts current conditions, demanding confession and repentance as steps toward reconciliation. It summons us to define behavior

---

27. Francis, *Fratelli Tutti*, 15.
28. Francis, *Fratelli Tutti*, 131.
29. Francis, *Fratelli Tutti*, 165.

by the good news of love that Jesus proclaimed. It is a living witness from the mystery of the resurrection. And it is calling all nations to accept the opportunity to hear one another.

Among the post-resurrection texts in the New Testament is one about an appearance of the risen Christ to some disciples who had gone fishing. Although they had fished for a living in the days before Jesus called them and knew the ways of the water, they accomplished nothing on this night. But when they saw the risen Christ early in the morning and listened to his word, they accomplished everything. When they hauled their net on shore and saw what they had achieved, their net "was full of large fish, one hundred fifty-three of them." Even under immense pressure from such an enormous responsibility, their net did not break or split.[30]

The detail about the number of fish has perplexed biblical scholars and commentators for a long time. There is no broad agreement about the significance of that specific number. Some ancient scholars suggested that it might be an expression of *gematria*, in which numerical values are assigned to letters of the alphabet, making it a coded Greek message. Others say that ancient ichthyologists had identified one hundred fifty-three species of fish, so the curious detail might be a symbol of complete inclusion.

The detail about the unbroken net is another oddity. In ordinary experiences of fishing with nets, broken places in a net are part of the work. But when the church heeds the risen Christ, this witness seems to say, nets do not break regardless of the burdens they carry.[31]

These details connect the post-resurrection experiences of the disciples to Jesus' farewell discourse in John 14–17. They proclaim that he is still with the community of faith, though in a new way. When the church woke to know that the mission of the risen Christ is inseparable from the message to which the Gospels bear witness about his words and deeds before his death, their responsibilities for discipleship and their obligations for acting will never leave them broken.[32]

When the church woke, its recognition of the Lord in the light of the morning means his word is still present. The *eschaton* (ἔσχατον) is intruding into our systems and circumstances as power and as judge. Its witness excludes nothing, accomplishes everything, and will not break.

Texts in the other Gospels adapt an eschatological figure that appears in Dan 7:13–14, with "everlasting" and "indestructible" authority over "all

---

30. John 21:1–11 CEB.

31. See a list of interpretive possibilities for the witness to the fish and net in Gail R. O'Day, "Gospel of John," 736–37.

32. See John 17:18–21, where Jesus' Farewell Discourse includes reference to the apostolic mission of being sent and to the unity of the church.

peoples, nations, and languages." The figure is "like a human being" or "a Son of Man," and therefore has human attributes. The Son of Man is the presence of "heaven is claiming its right to rule."[33]

The church clearly attached the vision of the eschatological "Son of Man" to Jesus. At least sixty-nine passages in Mark, Luke, and Matthew refer to "the Son of Man," forty of them in Matthew. The figure appears elsewhere in decisive and critical moments in the New Testament, such as the martyrdom of Stephen in Acts 7:56[34] and Jesus' overheard contemplation of his death in John 12:34.[35] Both associate the coming of the Son of Man with the power of God. And both demonstrate that the authorities on earth feel threatened by the authority that comes with this eschatological Son of Man.

In Acts, when Stephen says he sees the Son of Man, the authorities "shrieked and covered their ears," as if they could deny eschatological truth by trying not to hear about it.[36] In the book of Revelation, when words of judgment must be delivered to churches, the Son of Man dictates the letters.[37] The Gospel of John says Jesus calls himself the Son of Man, who has "come into the world to exercise judgment."[38] There is no doubt that a central theme in Scripture is judgment, including the judgment of the church.

Some Christians prefer not to hear this eschatological message, having been persuaded that faith is merely a private relationship with Jesus, a friend who "walks with me, and he talks with me, and he tells me I am his own."[39] But that is unbiblical—or, at least, it is insufficiently biblical. It overlooks the Scriptures that define Jesus as the Son of Man, the eschatological judge, the authority who invades our social systems, the word that critiques our patterns of life, the force that is superior to earthly powers, the redeemer who delivers oppressed victims of injustice from the might of their oppressor, and the one who comes to awaken the church.

---

33. Smith-Christopher, "Book of Daniel," 6:778–79.

34. Acts 7:56 echoes Dan 7:13.

35. John 12:27–36 is a remarkable scene in which Jesus prays, confesses that his soul is troubled, and has a spiritual conversation with a voice from heaven as well as with voices from the crowd around him.

36. Acts 8:57.

37. Rev 1:10–20.

38. John 9:35–37 CEB.

39. See C. Austin Miles, "In the Garden," in *United Methodist Hymnal*, no. 314.

CHAPTER ELEVEN

Sacred Treasure

Shaped by the Future in Faith

When the future woke the church, the awakening means fulfilling a relationship with the future by acting on it. The eschatological future is coming. Yet it is also already here. It is what the people of faith are building. Yet it is also building the people of faith. It commissions and empowers the church for mission. The life to come has come to life in the church, living through liberation in which the church engages because bondage in any form—including bondage to sin and death—is condemned and corrected by the one who is coming and has come to be our judge and our redeemer. With the authority of mission, the church proclaims truth, which sets us free.

The church is the body of Christ. The church is a living organism, created with power and commissioned for the purpose of active eschatological practices, not just for ecclesiastical ones. "Christ has set us free for freedom," Paul wrote to the Galatians.[1] One facet of this freedom is to function in relationship with a future that is already present, not in chronological time but in the time that God fills with promise.

For American Methodists, in a republic that constitutionally guarantees religious liberty, there need be no delay in having the future shape the church now. The gifts and power of the spirit are treasures already present in the mission of the church. Every facet of worship, every system of church governance, and every decision to act occurs in an eschatological context.

---

1. Gal 5:1 CEB.

This means receiving the redeemer as our judge and revealing redemption by judging like a prophet in his name. The awakened church defines justice on earth the same way that justice is defined in heaven. When the future woke the church with eschatological power and authority, ordinary things become extraordinary means for the church to offer healing and reconciling actions in the world. To be shaped by the future is to be set free for the work of freedom.

Relationship with the Future in Worship

When the future woke the church, it overcomes a reluctance to be judged and to judge. That happens, even though some forms of resistance are remarkably subtle.

One of the most widely heard, watched, and shared religious services in the world is "A Festival of Nine Lessons and Carols" on Christmas Eve at King's College Chapel in Cambridge. Begun in 1918, the service has been broadcast annually since 1928 to listeners who now number in the hundreds of millions.[2] Though new anthems are regularly written and added, the order of service has remained unchanged since it was prepared by Eric Milner-White, who became dean of the chapel after serving as an army chaplain during World War I.

The first spoken words in the liturgy are those of the Bidding Prayer, offered by the dean of the chapel. The final spoken words in the liturgy, also offered by the dean, are those of the Collect and Blessing. In the Collect at the conclusion of the service, the dean prays,

> O God, who makest us glad with the yearly remembrance of the birth of thy only son, Jesus Christ: grant that as we joyfully receive him for our redeemer, so we may with sure confidence behold him, when he shall come to be our judge; who liveth and reigneth with thee and the Holy Spirit, one God, world without end.[3]

When *The United Methodist Book of Worship* appeared in 1992, the authorized liturgies, prayers, and resources in it included an order for "A

---

2. The only exception to the broadcast was 1930. Otherwise, the services continued through the years of World War II, when the stained glass had been removed from the chapel windows, which had then been covered with tar paper. The BBC estimates its current audience is 370 million and other additional broadcasters around the world carry it.

3. "Festival of Nine Lessons and Carols," https://www.kings.cam.ac.uk/pdfviewer/44242.

Festival of Nine Lessons and Carols." It was adapted from the service at King's. But at least one important item is missing. In the rubric that states its connection to the service at King's College Chapel, there is a specific reference to the Bidding Prayer and to the closing Blessing, when all participants in the congregation have joined in the Lord's Prayer.

But the rubric makes no reference to the Collect. Rather, the rubric simply ends with the following note: "The service has been edited for United Methodist congregations."[4] The editing process understandably altered some words in the Bidding Prayer. The United Methodist version omits praying for the Queen and her "dominions," and it omits prayers for "royal and religious" educational institutions established by King Henry VI. The liturgist uses the word "sin" rather than the term "disobedience," when the leader invites the people to acknowledge

> in Holy Scripture the tale of the loving purposes of God from the first days of our sin until the glorious redemption brought by this Holy Child[5]

However, it is in the Collect at the end that the United Methodist version reveals its most substantive editorial change. Any United Methodists who follow this service on Christmas Eve when it is broadcast from King's College Chapel in Cambridge hear the dean pray for people to "receive" the Lord Jesus, "when he shall come to be our judge." But the service in the *Book of Worship* says nothing about Christ as "judge." Indeed, the Collect for United Methodists is quite different in spirit and emphasis.

> May the Christ who by his Incarnation gathered into One things earthly and heavenly, fill you with the sweetness of inward peace and goodwill; and the blessing of God Almighty, the Father, the Son, and the Holy Spirit, be upon you and remain with you always.[6]

There is a considerable difference between praying that the people will be filled with an inward "sweetness"[7] and praying that they will welcome a

---

4. "Festival of Nine Lessons and Carols," no. 284.

5. "Festival of Nine Lessons and Carols," no. 285. (This portion of the Bidding Prayer also Americanizes the text, by using the word "until" rather than the Anglicized preposition "unto" in the original.)

6. "Festival of Nine Lessons and Carols," nos. 287–88.

7. Charles Wesley's hymn "God Our Portion" begins stanza 7 with the words "Abundant Sweetness." References to "sweetness" appear in other Charles Wesley hymns including "Subjection to Christ" (where it refers to the "taste" of "sacred warmth" on a "frozen breast") and "Employment" (as a "fragrance" that is diffused by God's "gracious skill").

"redeemer" as our "judge." It is not just a matter of rhetorical difference but a matter of eschatological indifference.

Some might deem it unimportant, since it involves only one service a year with a liturgy that many United Methodist churches never use. But the problem is vastly more widespread than a single service, and it is far more insidious. It ignores the tension in the church between an intrusive future and a resistant present. It resists the role of the risen Christ as judge.

Among the persistent challenges facing every worship leader is to say what must be said when worshipers may prefer not to have it heard. In the eighth century BCE, Amaziah the priest of Israel did not what to hear what the prophet Amos had to say. In 1744, the vice chancellor at Oxford did not want to hear what John Wesley had to say. Today, it is one thing to have a Bible teacher or preacher quote Amos: "Let justice roll down like waters, and righteousness like an ever-flowing stream."[8] It is another thing for the leader to say that those ancient words of Amos are akin to the words "Black Lives Matter" in the present.

The church may hear Amos' ancient prophecy as an artifact of the distant past. But that misses their meaning. For Amos' words in the sanctuary at Bethel provoked huge reactions from political and religious authorities, namely King Jeroboam and the priest Amaziah.[9] In fact, their reaction was so intense that Amaziah delivered a message to Amos, apparently on behalf of the king, telling Amos that he was never again to speak there about such things.[10]

Some worshipers today insist that statements like "Black Lives Matter" not be said or heard in a sanctuary. Other worshipers believe connecting "Black Lives Matter" to the Scripture helps clarify what the ancient text means and how Christians can navigate conflicts and proclaim sacred truth now. A preacher or teacher can only convey accurately the substance of what Amos said by getting the emotional response Amos received when his words first were heard.

Speaking clearly and controversially may be the only way to convey the message of a biblical prophet. But many members, ministers, and bishops of the church prefer soft silence or cautious ambiguity to preaching or teaching about controversies and conflicts. They forget that silence is also controversial—if it ignores or mutes the eschatological message of judgment.

Churches can feel fragile, especially in crises. Silence about some subjects may seem to be a way to stay safe. But such silence is a fear of freedom.

---

8. Amos 5:24 CEB.
9. Amos 7:10–17.
10. Amos 7:13.

To be free is to act faithfully. To stay silent may show a preference for remaining in the bondage of unfaithfulness.

Local churches that remain culturally homogenous, racially segregated, ideologically differentiated, or ethically rigid might minimize controversies. It is simpler to be a congregation that is nearly all White, or nearly all Black, or nearly all upper-middle class, or nearly all poor, or nearly of one mind in moral matters. It is easier to conduct the kind of service that worshipers find familiar, that lasts a comfortable amount of time, that uses language everybody knows, that reads texts people are willing to grasp. But such churches are not free if they are deprived of rich resources for understanding Scriptures, if they only hear Bible passages read through experiences with which they resonate, if creeds are explained in ways that fit their preferred interpretations, or if the only traditions they practice are the ones with which they are personally acquainted.

Reaching All the Nations

But if the future woke the church to hear the eschatological Son of Man speak, the church receives the Holy Spirit as a divine presence and sees faith emerging from the future rather than from the familiar. At the conclusions of Matthew and Luke, the risen Christ commissions his disciples. In Matthew, he sends them to make disciples, baptize, and teach in all nations. In Luke, he sends them to preach a change of heart and life to all nations. In both the church is sent to "all nations." As noted earlier, the word has had different meanings in different contexts.

In the twenty-first century, sovereign states called "nations" determine citizenship, issue passports, collect taxes, exchange ambassadors, defend borders, certify vaccines, authorize teams of athletes for international competitions, and determine what religions—if any—can be allowed to practice inside their boundaries. When the United Nations General Assembly meets, it has 193 member nations.[11]

In the New Testament, the Greek word translated "nations" is *ethne* (ἔθνη), from which come English words such as ethnic and ethnicity. Jesus sends the church in mission to embrace peoples, tribes, ethnic groups, and language groups, who may be migrants or homeless persons or stateless persons. They may be undocumented and be without citizenship. Wherever they are or from wherever they have come could be territories without physical boundaries. They may be identified best by ethnicity, not by nationality.

---

11. Two other "nations" have "observer" status, namely Palestine and the Holy See (the Vatican).

When people gathered for Pentecost, according to Acts 2:7–11, they had a variety of political, linguistic, regional, and racial designations. And they are "better understood as groups rather than nations," as Free Methodist scholar Robert W. Wall has written. He says the identity is "theological" and inclusive, not jurisdictional or political.[12]

A mission to all nations is ethnically inclusive. To emphasize it might get the church into trouble. It got Jesus into trouble. He outraged authorities by embracing Samaritans, for example.

In eras of American history, Methodists (among others) launched mission initiatives to take the gospel to other countries. In the nineteenth and twentieth centuries, missionaries went to nations outside of the United States. But the mission to the nations on which the church is sent by the risen Christ is to ethnically and racially separated groups, to immigrants and citizens, to people who differ in identifiable ways. To reconcile ethnic and racial divisions is its mission.

Feeling the Freedom of the Future

To some people in the United States, including some American Methodists, an emphasis on inclusiveness, on overcoming racial and ethnic boundaries, or on hearing a word of judgment about racist church practices is a political issue, not a spiritual one. Interpreting the Scriptures in this way is critiqued as being "politically correct," when in truth it is theologically correct.

In the Wesleyan theological community, salvation is not derisive or dismissive of some. It is available to all. Faith hopes in what is promised and is now present. Faith involves private piety and public responsibility. Faith finds justification through the grace of the risen Christ and seeks justice through the grace of the risen Christ. Faith pursues personal and social holiness in a sanctifying process that moves toward the goal of Christian perfection.[13]

Unlike other theological methods, which discuss salvation by emphasizing participation in a sacramental system or by insisting upon an individual's accepting Jesus Christ as a personal savior, Methodism emphasizes the gift of God's grace in a process toward being made perfect in love in this life.[14] The doctrine of Christian perfection is a crucial component of Methodist teaching as well as practice. In most Methodist denominations, including the United Methodist Church, a person who seeks election to full

12. Wall, "Book of Acts," 9:42n98.
13. Heitzenrater, *Wesley and the People*, 48.
14. Wesley, *Works of John Wesley*, 2:152–69.

clergy membership and ordination must answer these traditional Wesleyan questions:[15]

- Are you going on to perfection?
- Do you expect to be made perfect in love in this life?
- Are you earnestly striving after perfection in love?

But, in the Wesleyan movement, this was not simply a matter for the clergy or for those who work professionally as theologians. It infused all of the practices and structural systems of Methodism. As Richard Heitzenrater wrote,

> The possibility of perfection in love through grace was the distinctive and defining message in Wesley's revival, and the very organization of the movement itself, as a network of disciplined small groups, was designed to nurture the hope of perfection in the lives of the Methodists.[16]

For Methodists, salvation is not based on an event in the past when an individual accepts Jesus as a personal savior, nor is it based on conditions in the present defined by one's status as a communicant in good standing. It is based on an eschatological future moving graciously into the present, offering the gift of saving grace, transforming lives through the ecclesiastical disciplines that determine how individuals shall live and how churches shall arrange their systems of living, including their governance.

This relationship with the future is eschatologically liberating. It gives heft to hope. It grants freedom from social patterns that separate and stratify people by race, wealth, language, ethnicity, or personal traits. It grants freedom to experience grace within the faith community and to share grace beyond the faith community without insisting on any preconditions for receiving the gift. It grants freedom to accept judgment as a corrective in the process of salvation, and to offer judgment as a prophetic voice to correct the public order. Where justice is promised by the life to come it will prevail in the church that has come to life, if the church woke. Where justice is promised by the word of the Lord, it will overcome the world—where the church is sent.

Not all Methodist leaders feel as free as this promise permits. Some feel constrained by competing forces in their region. Some fear that speaking like a prophet may limit their capacity for functioning as a pastor among politically divided constituencies.

---

15. *Book of Discipline of the United Methodist Church 2016* (¶¶ 330.5d, 336).
16. Heitzenrater, *Wesley and the People*, 242.

But other leaders know that there may never be another opportunity. If now is the time to awake from sleep, now is the time for the church to act. The future is intruding into the present. The eschatological moment is here.

In the fall of 2020, during a tense presidential campaign in the United States, the Council of Bishops of the African Methodist Episcopal Church issued a public statement to

> decry and denounce an advertisement from the campaign committee of Donald J. Trump linking an African Methodist Episcopal Church to violence and implying that those who gathered there are "thugs."[17]

The statement from the Council of Bishops came within one day after the pastor of a local AME church called attention to the advertisement. He condemned it as a racist act, and he demanded an apology.[18]

The political advertisement appeared on September 9, 2020. It used a photo taken at Bethel AME Church in Wilmington, Delaware, on June 1, 2020, a few days after the killing of George Floyd, when candidate Joseph R. Biden spoke to a group of Black clergy and community leaders. As part of the event, Biden knelt in front of a group of participants for a photograph.

The partisan ad began with video clips from protests in the summer of 2020. Protesters marched, condemned, and deplored the killing of Black people by White police. The video clips were edited to emphasize images of violence between protestors and police. Then the partisan, political commercial showed candidate Biden kneeling in front of the persons at Bethel AME Church and displayed the words, "Stop Joe Biden and his rioters." The ad ended with audio of the voice of Vice President Mike Pence saying, "You won't be safe in Joe Biden's America."

In their statement, the Council of Bishops of the African Methodist Episcopal Church responded to the politically partisan advertisement by calling it an effort that

> subtly incites white terrorism against people of color and attacks the Black Church and Black people for refusing to bow down to the idol called white supremacy. . . . We are deeply concerned that the white supremacist lynchings, murders, and

---

17. Jeffrey Cooper, AME General Secretary, Council of Bishops, African Methodist Episcopal Church, released the bishops' statement on September 14, 2020. See Anderson, "AME Bishops Decry Trump Ad," and Cooper, "Response to Trump Campaign Ad," para. 4.

18. Jenkins, "Black Church Leaders Demand Apology."

assassinations of Black men and women, boys and girls in the past, is the plan for the present and the future.[19]

The AME Bishops sent four specific demands to those responsible for the campaign ad. First, apologize to Bethel AME Church and the pastor, Silvester Beaman. Second, remove the advertisement from distribution and use. Third, provide federal protection for the Bethel AME Church members, staff, and persons using the building. Fourth, have the Department of Justice, the Department of Homeland Security, or both, investigate the legality of infringing upon the religious liberty of that church and the legality of language in the advertisement "that might incite violence" against people of color.

With their statement, the Council of Bishops and the other African Methodist Episcopal Church leaders acted prophetically. They also demonstrated what it means to act promptly with the freedom to judge. That freedom is what a relationship with the future provides.

Not all church leaders have the capacity to act that quickly or the determination to act that directly. And not all church leaders feel free to act as the eschatologically empowered judge of the present into which the future intrudes. Some feel constrained by the politics of the present. For the church to be faithful in a relationship with the future, its clergy and lay leaders must decide whether to remain bound by the present and avoid action, or to be liberated by the future and act. "Great leaders," Fareed Zakaria wrote, "read polls to understand the nature of their challenge, not as an excuse for inaction."[20]

At the Pivot of the Present and the Future

When the future woke the church, one of its contributions is building a system of order and governance that is shaped by the future, not just by the ecclesial politics of the present. For example, the Wesleyan theological emphasis upon moving toward to perfection and being made perfect in love in this life is an important facet of the process toward clergy membership and ordination in the United Methodist Church. Most Methodist denominations include these and other historic questions in a ritual, which the church corporately or liturgically celebrates when commissioning or ordaining persons for ministry. However, apart from historic and dramatic

---

19. "Response to Trump Campaign Ad," paras. 5, 11.
20. Zakaria, "Pandemic Upended the Present," para. 10.

moments in denominations, questions about Christian perfection are rarely asked or answered.

Clergy are generally not held accountable for any reports on their journeys to holiness by God's sanctifying grace after they give formal responses in their ordination processes. Laity are generally almost never called to account by their clergy, or by one another, about their spiritual disciplines in moving toward being made perfect in love in this life.

Laity and clergy—including bishops—live in a pattern of indifference to any progress toward perfection until some outrageous or egregious imperfection is alleged to have occurred. So instead of a continuing spiritual discipline driven by the future and a process toward being made perfect in love, the prevailing practice is to ignore the moments missed for eschatological action. The church just waits for something catastrophic to occur. Then it uses judicial processes.

Amid the twenty-first-century crises cascading in and around the church, American Methodists in general and United Methodists in particular have an opportunity to welcome the intrusions of the future. With the United Methodist Church on the verge of some schism over sexuality and with congregations functioning as racially, ethnically, socially, and economically separated entities, it is time for restructuring the denomination.

But any new organizational system should respond to the priorities of the future, not the politics of the present. Structures for determining the mission of the church should be based on the multiple commissions of the risen Christ—not only the one at the end of Matthew, but also the ones offered by Luke and John. Procedures for selecting leaders should follow the principle in Acts—the gift of being able to "hear" one another—rather than a political practice of having enough votes to control one another. Organizing principles should emphasize the discipline of going on to perfection, knowing that none has reached the perfection eschatologically promised. Systems should show all of us need one another if we are to be made perfect in love in this life.

Among the institutional goals should be the end of congregational segregation by race. That is essential in welcoming the eschatological judgment on centuries of White supremacism and racial stratification in American Methodism.

Bearing the Treasure

In 2 Cor 4:7, the apostle Paul has left to the church a text that could aid its full awakening. One standard translation of it refers to the treasure that we have in earthen vessels, and common interpretations connect this verse to the ensuing ones that mention the death of the body. This views an earthen vessel as a synonym for physical flesh. *The Common English Bible* captions this section of Paul's letter, advising readers that it refers to "Physical bodies and eternal glory." Two lectionaries put this verse with one from the Gospel of Mark about removing grain from their husks.[21]

So, a standard view of this word in 2 Cor 4:7 is that earthenware vessels and clay pots are references to physical, ephemeral, unimportant things in comparison to the essential treasure of the gospel. From the perspective of this interpretation, physical forms do not matter.

That is certainly the sense given by New Testament scholar J. Paul Sampley as his understanding of the passage.

> So grand a treasure borne in such a menial, frail, seemingly inept container makes it unmistakable that the power enabling the whole enterprise is "from God and not from us."[22]

But an alternate interpretation of the text is possible. The treasure is a sacred mystery that requires a container. It is not a solid object that creates its own space. Nor is it a feeling that flits or floats uncontained, like gas. The treasure is like a fluid that will be spilled and lost unless it is borne in a vessel of some kind. Moreover, like a liquid, it takes the shape of the container. What bears the treasure is vital to the availability of the treasure and to those who are ready to taste it.

With this interpretation, what holds sacred treasure is the system of the church, including its polities and its practices. Both the container and the contents are vital to the mystery of grace. If the treasure is housed in an institutional structure that is built on supremacist principles, then the sacred message is indistinguishable from what contains it. When medieval Crusaders slaughtered Muslims, when colonizing conquistadors killed Incas, when Puritan men hanged women, when slave owners claimed to be saved at Methodist revivals while retaining property rights over those they enslaved, when the church either silently tolerated or loudly affirmed lynching, and when the church remains structured by race, the container is inconsistent with its sacred contents.

There are places in Scripture where containers are the core of the text. In Luke 5, Jesus builds a parable around types of containers that are suitable for wine, emphasizing that new wine must be in new wineskins. In John 2, Jesus delivers the finest wine that anyone ever tasted in six huge containers

---

21. Mark 2:23—3:6 (Year B, the Ninth Sunday after Epiphany; Proper 4 [9] the season of Pentecost).

22. Sampley, "Second Letter to the Corinthians," 9:929.

at Cana, emphasizing that the immensity of the sacred treasure is greater than a need we have for it. And the vessel is vital to contain the mystery that brings such joy.

The treasure is a fluid that must be housed, or it will be lost. If the gospel were a slab of stone, it would have its own shape and occupy its own space. But the treasure of the gospel is like a fluid that flows into—and takes the shape of—whatever container is provided for it. The container is essential. If it is allowed to become unbalanced, the treasure spills. If it breaks, the treasure is lost. If it shatters or splinters, the treasure is wasted. If it is flawed, the treasure is tainted. If it is not carried into the world, the treasure will go unnoticed.

When the future woke the church, the gospel is carried to the world in a container that is appropriate to the contents. It will have the shape that the treasured contents can suitably take to be available in the world. The proper container will not explode when pressure builds. And the container will never confuse itself with the sacred mystery of the contents it bears.

When the church celebrates the sacrament of Holy Communion, we give thanks over a cup as we prepare to receive its mysterious and life-giving contents. Without the cup, the holy element spills on the ground. When the disciples discovered that Jesus had mysteriously turned the hunger of a crowd into an abundance of gifts through a surplus of grace, they needed some baskets to carry the treasure that remained.[23] Good containers are necessary for gifts of grace.

Christians have created many kinds of institutional containers. Methodists in Malaysia redefined the office of bishop as a pastoral, liturgical, spiritual one, rather than as a corporate executive. Methodists in Singapore make pastoral appointments as multi-year assignments based on needs for effective leadership unconnected to a congregation's capacity for compensation. The Methodist Conference in Britain welcomes LGBTQ+ persons whom the spirit of God calls into marriage. The African Methodist Episcopal Church expects bishops to be prophetic voices of eschatological judgments about justice on earth, as it is in heaven.

Finding Methods in the Midst of Crises

Multiple crises are challenging the church. There is a crisis in Methodism that involves racial separation and racially based supremacy. There is a crisis in United Methodism involving sexual identity. There are crises affecting the United Methodist Church that involve missional identity, connectional

---

23. See Mark 6:43 and Luke 9:17.

polity, doctrinal authority, financial viability, constitutional complexity, and other crises besides these.

United Methodism does not have a single crisis. It has many. The one that currently poses the greatest threat to institutional unity is the dispute about homosexuality. It gets most notice. But the one that has done the deepest damage is the earthen vessel of White supremacy.

Race and sexuality are not the same crises. They are not even analogous as crises. But they both are products of self-righteous values, self-serving rationalizations, and self-centered structures imposed by political powers and by parliamentary majorities.

None of these forces is an expression of love. Love is humbling oneself to the needs of a neighbor, not humiliating a neighbor to satisfy the needs of oneself. Love is hearing the voices of others, not limiting those voices to the ones we prefer to hear. Love is learning truth, not fearing knowledge. Love speaks of justice, without silently tolerating injustice. Love has the courage to judge, just as the prophets did with the word of the Lord. And love has the humility to be judged, just as the risen Christ corrected the disciples' misunderstandings.

When the future woke the church, its structures center on meeting the needs of neighbors of the church as aggressively as they respond to the needs of the church. When the future woke the church, its systems show that they are honoring the sacred mysteries they contain. When the future woke the church, its members hold leaders accountable for judging the difference between forgivable and unforgivable sins and for making it publicly clear.

CHAPTER TWELVE

Creating the Church of the Future

Defining the Church

When John Wesley was leading the movement called Methodism during the eighteenth century, he was careful to distinguish his *connexion* as he called it from what he understood to be "the church." He viewed Methodism as an initiative within the established Church of England, in which he was a priest. He resisted pleas and pressures to take steps that might be understood as acts of separating from the church, such as conducting or authorizing the ordinations of persons for ministry. He built "chapels" and arranged their administrative oversight, but he did not call those buildings "churches." And he maintained that approach until circumstances compelled him to conclude that he could no longer cling to it.

The outcome of the revolution in America was a major factor. He authorized the creation of a church in America that he designated as Methodist. He authorized ordinations of ministers. And, while he made specific recommendations regarding ministerial leadership, he said that the Methodist Church in America was free to devise its own systems of polity for governance.

As this Methodist story illustrates, one way to define the word "church" is to speak of a self-governing institution engaged in religious activities from a Christian perspective. But that is a rather flimsy definition, for it does not take into account all the different patterns of church life in the world and it substitutes institutional language for theological understanding of the church. There are sovereign states that prohibit religion or control religious activities as they control all other human activities. There are sovereign states that have established some specific religion, such as Islam in Turkey and Judaism in Israel, where the central government determines if other religions may be practiced under state supervision. There are sovereign states with an established national church and varying tolerance or support for any church not in the establishment. Then there is the American model, where "church" is defined by whoever uses the term as they wish.

In one community where I served as a United Methodist pastor decades ago, a man earned his livelihood by selling and installing home repair materials. He stored his equipment and sold his wares in a building where he conducted prayer meetings and preaching services, calling it a church. He sought a property tax exemption from the county, claiming that he had exactly the same rights under the law as the Catholics, Presbyterians, Baptists, and Methodists, all of whose churches had property tax exemptions. He said he led a group of people who came to pray and to hear him preach, and that combination of praying and preaching among people satisfied the legal definition of church.

All states in the United States have their own legal definitions of "church." A group of people who assemble for praying and preaching may, or may not, be sufficient for some states. Criteria typically include adherence to beliefs that are codified in a way (e.g., a creed) and are affirmed by group members, plus practices such as gatherings for activities that are consistent with those beliefs. Though their practices are constitutionally protected, those protections are not absolute. A church cannot engage in cruelty, abuse, or threatening conduct, though a group that claims to take the Bible literally and considers the dubious ending of Mark to be valid might still practice snake handling or drink suspicious liquids from questionable containers.[1] Some groups have resisted mandates for wearing masks during the pandemic, claiming religious liberty.

In provisions of state law and the precedents of case law, two definitions of church types exist. One is congregational. The other is hierarchical. In the first, each local unit is independent and self-governing in the way it determines its body of beliefs, acceptable practices, and choices of leaders. In the second, local units are part of larger associations that determine the acceptable beliefs, practices, and qualifications for leadership.

Civil courts have settled church disputes when they are considered matters of property rather than piety. Richard Allen's group in Philadelphia became independent of the Methodist Church under such a decision, which led to forming the African Methodist Episcopal Church.

---

1. See Mark 16:18.

Yet the definition of church is beyond the limits of law. Defining church is a theological, rather than a legal, matter. The witness of Scripture, the affirmations of creeds, and the practices of believers who have trusted the promises of faith through persecution and war and famine and injustice have forged a determination to define church in the language of theology transcending the languages of jurisprudence and other disciplines.

Two classic theological definitions emerged. One defines the church by the word of God being faithfully preached and the sacraments duly administered. The other defines the church by the word of God being faithfully preached, the sacraments duly administered, and discipleship spiritually ordered. Lutherans, for example, have defined the church according to the former, and Methodists have defined the church according to the latter.

Maintaining order and discipline is an essential mark of the church within the Wesleyan theological tradition. It is a theme that comes to Methodism from Calvinism, which John Wesley believed was distinguishable from the truth of the gospel, but only in the narrowest way.[2] Thus, the theological definition of the church for Methodists is the basis of emphases on preaching, on celebrating the sacraments of Baptism and Holy Communion, and on spiritual disciplines for laity as well as clergy. It is particularly clear in an agenda item at annual conferences that ask, "Are all the clergy members of the conference blameless in their life and official administration (¶¶ 604.4, 605.6)?"[3] The answer assumes an annual conference system of accountability exists.

From the Future to the Present

Just as the church is defined by its theology, the church is also a reflection of its history. But, because the church has continuity with the past as well as with the promise of the future, its history is the memory of what has occurred, the knowledge of what is occurring, and the hope of what is to come. History is an ongoing process that includes, without being limited to, the past.

The history of the church includes what is revealed but is not yet real. The life to come has come to life in the church. However, it is far from evident in all the facets of church life. The promise of Pentecost, that all have the capacity to hear one another, is unfulfilled in the practices of the church

---

2. See the "Minutes" of the Methodist Conference in Bristol, August 1–3, 1745, in Wesley, *Works of John Wesley*, 10:153. See also Heitzenrater, *Wesley and the People*, 241.

3. The journal of an annual conference session records minutes in question/answer format. This is Question 17.

where members fail to hear one another discussing deep differences. The promises given by the risen Christ, as they are published in the post resurrection witnesses in Scripture, are that the church has authority to forgive sins, retain sins, and judge the difference between sins. It is not yet structured into all systems of church governance. The power given by the risen Christ for the church to achieve what is promised is not visible within all the institutions of the church, either congregationally or connectionally. Whatever power or authority the church exercises is an imperfect reflection of the mission upon which the risen Christ sends the church.

Faithfulness requires that the church live from the future to the present. So, its preaching will be the eschatological word of what is coming from beyond the periphery of our experiences, its sacraments will celebrate the community of saints that is in the process of being formed, and its structures will be ordered by acting on the promises it knows rather than on the basis of the problems it faces. Living from the future is continuous with the past and present, but it embraces the power and authority of the truth that sets us free from the limits of brokenness and failure. Living from the future is relying on freedom from sin and death rather than relying on the sins we can expose in others or the weapons that can be used against us.

It will require a lot of power to break the church out of the bondage of racism and White supremacy that remain in place. Forces of the past that are the residual remains of centuries in America have deep roots with a strong grip. They thrived during enslavement, ruled through an era of separate but equal policies that justified segregation in society and in the church, and still demonstrate their strength in the politics of the country and the polity of the church. In Congress and in many state legislatures, voting rights are treated as privileges to be exercised differently according to the race of those who register or try to do so. In congregations, patterns of worship and pastoral appointments are separated by race rather than united by the spirit.

But, if the future woke the church, a new power and authority will address the sins of the past and the circumstances of the present. If the life to come does come to life in the church, the current crises can be viewed from an eschatological perspective. If the community of faith allows its ears to hear what the spirit is saying to the church, then people who are extremely distant from one another in terms of economy and nationality and ethnicity and theology will discover their capacity to hear one another and overcome what divides them.

What is clear for the present is that the church is still in bondage to its own brokenness. It is evident in disordered practices that are unrelated to denominational differences. In the Roman Catholic Church, some bishops (notably some American bishops) listen to the voice of the pope for what they want to hear, rather than for a prophetic truth. In the United Methodist Church, clergy and laity listen to allies who already agree with them rather than to the enemies that all disciples are under orders to love. These are signs that the structures and the systems of order in the church, unlike the net in John 21, are broken by the stress of the burdens for which they are responsible. Recent developments in the United Methodist Church show that the church needs new life. If the church woke, it will do much more than mend a few threads.

When the pandemic erupted, it exposed the structural flaws in the governance systems of the United Methodist Church. For example, both the Constitution and the laws of the church in *The Book of Discipline* lack a means for maintaining connectional operations in an emergency.

The General Conference, which has declared itself to be the only entity with "authority to speak officially" for the denomination,[4] did not meet as scheduled in May 2020. The delegates could not assemble in person because of travel limitations. The commission[5] that has authority for setting the time and place of General Conference sessions chose not to gather delegates by using electronic technology, because of inequitable access to the internet in all locations. Hence, the legislative business of the General Conference—including the proposed protocol for splitting the denomination, some elections for church leadership positions that are assigned to the General Conference, and adoption of a denominational budget—has been held hostage by an unrelenting virus. And General Conference is not the only constitutional unit immobilized by the emergency.

The Judicial Council has met a few times via the internet, but conflicting church laws are creating questions about whether it has enough members and alternates to function.[6] Bishops, who are elected and retired

---

4. *The Book of Discipline 2016*, ¶ 509.1.

5. See the Constitution, Division Two, Section II, Article II, published as ¶ 14 in the 2016 *Discipline*.

6. Paragraph 2602 in the *Discipline* provides that a member's term of office "shall be eight years." Paragraph 2603 provides that an alternate's term of office "shall be for four years." Paragraph 2605 provides that the terms of both members and alternates "shall expire upon the adjournment of the General Conference at which their successors are elected." In the spring of 2020, the Judicial Council announced through the office of its secretary that its members and alternates would assume that they were to remain in office until the elections of their successors, but that only generated more questions because the Judicial Council has not been assigned jurisdiction to make announcements that are tantamount to decisions and because its jurisdiction extends only to matters brought before it by authorized church entities. Paragraph 2608.2 in the *Discipline* specifies that a quorum of seven members or alternates must be present in order to act on matters, except for matters involving "the constitutionality of acts of General

by jurisdictional or central conference actions, began making their individual announcements about their plans to retire when it became uncertain whether their governing jurisdictional or central conferences could meet.

While such flaws were being exposed, other forces seized initiatives in the denomination. Two are illustrative. One has been destructive. The other is at least potentially redemptive.

The former came to light when an *ad hoc* group began meeting in 2019, following the disastrous outcome of the special General Conference session that year. In January 2020, they produced the protocol that proposes splitting the denomination and providing tens of millions of dollars to help those who leave the United Methodist Church to form new denominations. They seized control of the momentum in the denomination by casting a vision for United Methodism based on objections to the sexual practices of LGBTQ+ persons.

The latter is another *ad hoc* group that began meeting in the autumn of 2021, focusing on issues related to the civil court bankruptcy case of the Boy Scouts of America. Many of the local churches in United Methodism have chartered and hosted Scout groups, whose organization has proposed to settle all civil claims of sexual abuse that Scouting personnel may have committed by offering nearly two billion dollars for payments to claimants. While the proposed settlement is controversial on its own merits,[7] the *ad hoc* group of United Methodists mobilized bishops and their cabinets across the United States to call special sessions of every charge conference for every local church that has hosted a chartered Boy Scout unit. The *ad hoc* group, claiming that its recommendations were based on sound legal advice, arranged to put documents and directions for voting before every identified charge conference on an accelerated timetable for urgent action in the early weeks of Advent 2021. What makes this endeavor potentially redemptive is that it could protect the rights and assets of the chartering churches as well as respect the rights and the needs of those victimized by abusers who used the cloak of church and Scouts for dreadful acts. What makes it problematic is a possibility that could expose the church to more litigation.

These developments illustrate that the United Methodist Church has a constitutionally established and legislatively ordered structure that seems incapable of fulfilling the mission of the church in a time of crisis. They also illustrate that neither the regular order of the church nor any *ad hoc* effort by

---

Conference," for which the quorum is nine. Following the death of one member who had been elected to a new eight-year term in 2016, the Judicial Council either has four duly elected members and no alternates, or eight duly elected members and twelve alternates, depending on how the conflicting paragraphs in the *Discipline* are interpreted.

7. See Levitin, "Boy Scouts Are Abusing."

some self-appointed leaders within the church has bothered to mobilize the United Methodist Church to address the realities of racism that have been part of the American Methodist community for hundreds of years and that remain in the church for the present.

After the denomination was formed in 1968, agencies and commissions were created by the General Conference with programmatic mandates to address matters of religion and race. A denominational effort called "Dismantling Racism: Pressing on to Freedom" is underway.[8] On June 19, 2020, the effort began. Five days later, some bishops led an online service of lament for the death of George Floyd and asked to pray daily for eight minutes and forty-six seconds in the ensuing month for an end to racism.

But such actions engage relatively few United Methodists. Conferences and cabinets are not mobilizing every charge conference to meet in special sessions to define the specific actions they will take to dismantle racism. Discipleship pamphlets are not printed and placed in pews or posted electronically on web sites to declare what United Methodists are expected to do as acts for overcoming White supremacy. Clergy are not held accountable for preaching in pulpits and for being prophetic in public on the topic. Bishops are not making appointments with it as a vital priority. And there is no protocol to direct tens of millions of United Methodist dollars to Black Methodist denominations, to Black Methodist local churches, or to descendants of Black persons lynched with the silent consent or with the loud approval of White Methodists as reparations for evil. The present church will not change the future until the future changes the present church.

If the future woke the church, it will not allow the urgency of the present to supplant the purpose for which the church exists. If the future woke the church, it will set the agenda based on the mission given by the risen Christ rather than have some current agenda drive the mission. If the future woke the church, then the life to come will come to life in the church, and the power of the risen Christ will be made known in actions that are unashamed of the gospel.

The MVP of the Church

The name Methodist began as an epithet for those who used a method to study the Bible and engage in acts of discipleship. Methodists in the

---

8. See https://www.umc.org/en/how-we-serve/advocating-for-justice/racial-justice/united-against-racism, including a statement drafted by the "Ebony Bishops" of the United Methodist Church about the resurgence of racism in the United States that the Council of Bishops adopted on November 6, 2018.

twenty-first century could adopt a method for coming to life in the future. One such method could be an MVP approach, which begins by expressing the Mission of the church, casts a Vision that imagines how the church will look in a few years of discipleship, and devises Practices needed to realize the vision for the mission.

What happened in the United Methodist Church soon after it was formed in 1968 was a tragic method in reverse of that. The General Conference in 1972 added a provision to the Social Principles of the denomination that took exception to "the practice of homosexuality" and that declared "this practice incompatible with Christian teaching."[9] The action did not identify the specific Christian teaching or church doctrine that was at issue, nor did the action specify what incompatibility with it might mean. The language of the amendment was driven by objections to, or discomfort with, practices that are part of human life. General Conference sessions after 1972 moved from deploring such practices as a social principle to declaring such practices violations of enforceable church law. This fostered a crisis of division—one of the many crises enveloping the church. As a result, the denomination is now on the brink of institutional schism.

The practices, to which General Conference delegates in 1972 objected, led the church to cast a vision of a denomination rid of people who engage in such practices. They would not be ordained, appointed, or accepted as candidates for ministry. They would not be allowed to wed in United Methodist buildings or in rituals conducted by United Methodist ministers. They would not be permitted to receive care or benefit from advocacy financed by United Methodist funds.

In short, the United Methodist Church enacted laws that effectively allow homosexual persons to participate in the life of the church as long as their practices remain unacknowledged, unrecognized, uncelebrated, unsupported, and unknown. Thus, homosexual persons are welcome only if they do not have to identify themselves for the persons they are. By doing that, however, the United Methodist Church has used a set of practices to cast a vision that drives the mission of the risen Christ, instead of relying on the mission to cast a vision that defines the practices of faithful discipleship in private piety and in public prophecy.

The MVP method could enable the church to find its purpose in the future, know that it exists by the power of the life to come, and come to life in actions that witness to the word of the risen Christ in the world. The MVP method could enable the church to designate constructive practices of discipleship. It could enable the church to become a public presence, not

---

9. *Book of Discipline of the United Methodist Church 1972*, ¶ 72 C.

just as a building on a corner lot in the city or on a campus in the suburbs, but as a voice in the streets or centers of power. It could enable the church to provide a vision for generations estranged from the faith or not yet born into it, to see signs that God's liberating justice has entered the world.

The MVP method could free the church from a reluctance and resistance to recognize that it has the authority and power to identify the sins of racism and White supremacy, to decide which sins are forgiven, and to name the sins that are retained. This is as essential to the mission of the church as are the other scriptural witnesses to the commissioning by the risen Christ.

The power of forgiveness is formidable. The words of Margaret Atwood in her work of fiction point to truth: "remember that forgiveness too is a power. To beg for it is a power, and to withhold it or bestow it is a power, perhaps the greatest."[10] And, to paraphrase the words of a preacher who is also a New Testament scholar, we are rescued from an evil age so we can live according to a new age, where we envision a world defined not by anger and hostility.[11] The capacity to judge and forgive will be exercised when the church woke.

In the Gospel readings that are often featured in the season of Advent, texts regarding John the Baptist are common. The authors of Mark and John include a text from the prophet Isaiah, and Mark adds another from the prophet Malachi, as testimony to the substance of the message from John the Baptist.[12] Among the words are phrases familiar not only from the Sunday readings in Advent but also from music, such as Handel's *Messiah*. But a familiarity with the words risks missing some of the nuances.

One is a prophetic appeal to prepare the way in the wilderness and to construct a straight (or level) highway in the desert for the Lord to arrive. It is important to remember that deserts and wilderness areas are dangerous and difficult locations that pose threats to life. They are places of searing heat and bitter cold. They present challenges to meeting the most basic human needs, including shelter and water and food. They are places where enemies prowl, including wild animals and ruthless thieves. They are places where one can easily get lost, lacking natural or other landmarks. They are hard places to survive, let alone thrive.

In difficult places, according to the prophet, people of faith are to engage in constructive work. The vision of a highway or straight road is to be fulfilled by embracing a tough mission.

---

10. Atwood, *Handmaid's Tale*, 154.
11. McCaulley, *Reading while Black*, 61, 129.
12. See Isa 40:3 and Mal 3:1 in Mark 1:2–3, and John 1:23.

What the Church Knows When It Woke

When the future appears in the promise from a prophet and in the presence of the risen Christ, the church is being called to an awakened discipleship that does not travel on smooth highways but builds them in tough terrain. When the future woke the church, its task will be a daunting discipleship that is the path of liberation. If the church woke and takes action, it is set free from bondage to forces of sin and death. It is liberated to claim the power that overcomes the world.

In the 1990 film titled *Awakenings*, Robert De Niro plays Leonard, an institutionalized and ill-functioning man, who is nonverbal and nearly catatonic. Alice Drummond plays Lucy, a woman who communicates not with her mouth but with her eyes and who is mobile enough to walk around the medical unit but limits her movements to sections of it. Their main medical providers are a nurse and a doctor, played respectively by Julie Kavner and Robin Williams.

Awakenings is based on a book[13] of the same title by Oliver Sacks. The critical turning point in the film occurs when the medical personnel allow themselves to "hear" Lucy. Hearing her does not involve listening to her utter words, for she does not speak. But they "hear" her communicate by noticing the movements of her eyes and by observing the steps she takes. As her caregivers pay attention, they realize that she is trying to reach a destination that seems too far out of her reach. She seems to long for access to a window that has a light to bless her silent darkness and for a glimpse of the horizon in the distance. But something impedes her. The light is too elusive for her to reach, and its blessings are beyond the spot where she stops when she walks. Then the medical professionals allow themselves to hear Lucy in a new way. When they hear her, they awaken to truth about her, and they make a path for her to find the light.

Lucy walks toward the window where she might see the light and the life beyond her confinement. But she stops short of it, not because she cannot physically finish the journey but because something is preventing her from going there. Eventually, the medical personnel "hear" her plea to remove an unspeakable barrier in her way. For her to reach her goal, the barrier in the system must be removed.

The medical team notices that the floor of the medical unit is built with black and white tiles in an alternating pattern. They realize that Lucy can continue her journey as far as the path goes. But the pattern stops some distance from the window. Apparently, tiles were replaced without retaining

---

13. Sacks, *Awakenings*.

the pattern. Lucy needs the disciplined pattern to finish her walk. A white space makes her path disappear. She cannot get to her goal until she can see the way.

When the medical team woke to know the truth, the staff members kneel on the floor and use black markers to eliminate the exclusively white space. Then Lucy can see the path forward and finish her journey to the light and life. She resumes her journey, and she receives the gifts of light and life. And it happens because the ones to whom she had been entrusted with the mission to care for her allowed themselves the freedom to hear her.

When we know the truth, it sets us free to remove the barriers in the way. When the church woke, it will remove the barriers that racism and White supremacy have built. When the future woke the church, it will exercise judgment and forgiveness to overcome the crisis that the church in America—and specifically Methodism in America—has too long ignored as part of its mission. Oscar Wilde, who was clearly not a Christian nor a Methodist, said, "Every saint has a past, and every sinner has a future."[14] When the church woke, it will know the truth and act in discipleship so the life to come will come to life.

---

14. Quoted in Kristof and WuDunn, *Tightrope*, 36.

POSTSCRIPT

Beyond Algernon's Flowers

The book and the film *Awakenings* have some things in common with an earlier work of science fiction. It began as a short story by Daniel Keyes titled *Flowers for Algernon*.[1] Later, Keyes wrote a novel with the same title. Thereafter, a film titled *Charly*, with Cliff Robertson in the lead role, was based on the short story and novel.

The arc of Keyes's story follows Charlie, whose life is complicated by a low IQ and other limitations. Algernon, a mouse, is a lab animal used for tests. Charlie comes to view Algernon as a friend and as a kind of comrade in research and treatment.

When an experiment appears to have a positive impact on Algernon, researchers try the treatment on Charlie. He, too, shows improvement. In fact, the procedure expands his intellectual capacity so much that he becomes part of the research team. Then, he develops observations and understandings that surpass other team members. Charlie knows more than the others in the lab around him. Because of that, he is the first to notice when Algernon begins to show evidence of decline and reversion to his former condition.

Charlie correctly concludes that the experiment on him will follow the same trajectory as the one that happened with Algernon. He woke, but his awakening is only temporary. Charlie has learned enough to know that the benefits of being awake will not last. At the end of the story, Algernon dies, and Charlie reverts to the limits that preceded his experiment. Charlie expresses hope that someone will remember to provide flowers for Algernon.

1. Keyes, *Flowers for Algernon*.

When the church woke, it is always tested by forces that could render its awakening to be temporary. The witness of Scripture, the words of prophets, the knowledge of history, and all the tasks of discipleship endure forever.

But the church has often stirred yet never quite woke. Its mission is eternal. When the church woke, it will act in every way to show trust in the Lord, who is coming to be our redeemer and our judge.

Bibliography

Ahlstrom, Sydney. *A Religious History of the American People*. New Haven: Yale University Press, 1972.
Allen, Joseph L. *Perkins School of Theology: A Centennial History*. Dallas: SMU, 2011.
"Allen Temple History." https://allentemple.org/content.cfm?id=309.
Alpert, Jonathan L. "The Origin of Slavery in the United States—The Maryland Precedent." *American Journal of Legal History* 14.3 (1970) 189–221. https://doi.org/10.2307/844413.
Anderson, Cynthia Yeldell. "AME Bishops Decry Trump Ad Linking Church to Violence and Implying Worshipers Are 'Thugs.'" *Tennessee Tribune*, September 14, 2020.
Asbury, Francis. *The Journal of Rev. Francis Asbury, Bishop of the Methodist Episcopal Church, in Three Volumes*. New York: Lane & Scott, 1852.
Asmelash, Leah. "Emory University School of Medicine Formally Apologizes after Rejecting an Applicant for His Race." *CNN*, June 20, 2021. https://www.cnn.com/2021/06/20/us/emory-university-marion-hood-trnd/index.html.
Atwood, Margaret. *The Handmaid's Tale*. New York: Knopf, 2006.
Bailey, Sarah Pulliam, and Michelle Boorstein. "'I Find It Baffling and Reprehensible': Catholic Archbishop of Washington Slams Trump's Visit to John Paul II Shrine." *Washington Post*, June 2, 2020.
Bailey, Sarah Pulliam, et al. "Trump Mocks the Faith of Others. His Own Religious Practice Remains Opaque." *Washington Post*, February 14, 2020. https://www.washingtonpost.com/religion/2020/02/14/trump-mocks-faith-others-his-own-religious-practices-remain-opaque/.
Barry, John M. *Roger Williams and the Creation of the American Soul: Church, State, and the Birth of Liberty*. New York: Viking, 2012.
Bellah, Robert, et al. *The Good Society*. New York: Knopf, 1991.
———. *Habits of the Heart*. Berkeley: University of California, 1985.
Bellware, Kim. "Calls to Declare Racism a Public Health Crisis Grow Louder." *Washington Post*, September 15, 2020.
Berg, A. Scott. *Wilson*. New York: Putnam, 2013.
Blight, David W. *Frederick Douglass: Prophet of Freedom*. New York: Simon & Schuster, 2018.
Block, Daniel. "Is Trump Our Cyrus? The Old Testament Case for Yes and No." *Christianity Today*, October 29, 2018.

The Book of Discipline of the United Methodist Church 1968. Nashville: United Methodist Publishing House, 1968.

The Book of Discipline of the United Methodist Church 2000. Nashville: United Methodist Publishing House, 2000.

The Book of Discipline of the United Methodist Church 2008. Nashville: United Methodist Publishing House, 2008.

The Book of Discipline of the United Methodist Church 2016. Nashville: United Methodist Publishing House, 2016.

Boring, M. Eugene. "The Gospel of Matthew." In *The New Interpreter's Bible Commentary*, 7:35–378. Nashville: Abingdon, 2015.

Bradford, William. *A Relation or Journal of the Beginning and Proceedings of the English Plantation Settled in New England*. London: Bellamie, 1622.

Branch, Taylor. *The King Years: Historic Moments in the Civil Rights Movement*. New York: Simon & Schuster, 2013.

A Brief Account of the Establishment of the Colony of Georgia, under Gen. James Oglethorpe, February 1, 1733. Washington: Force, 1835. https://tile.loc.gov/storage-services/public/gdcmassbookdig/briefaccountofesoogeor/briefaccountofesoogeor.pdf.

Brown, Peter. *Augustine of Hippo*. Berkeley: University of California Press, 1967.

Chalmers, David. "The Ku Klux Klan in Politics in the 1920's." *Mississippi Quarterly* 18.4 (1965) 234–47.

Coke, Thomas. *Extracts of the Journals of the Rev. Dr. Coke's Three Visits to America*. London: Wesley's Preaching Houses, 1790.

Colavito, Jason. *The Mound Builder Myth: Fake History and the Hunt for a "Lost White Race."* Norman: University of Oklahoma Press, 2020.

Cooper, Jeff. "Response to Trump Campaign Ad Featuring Bethel AME Church in Wilmington, Delaware." *Religion News Service*, September 14, 2020. https://religionnews.com/2020/09/14/response-to-trump-campaign-ad-featuring-bethel-ame-church-in-wilmington-delaware/.

Costa, Robert, et al. "Church Shooting Suspect Dylan Roof Captured amid Hate Crime Investigation." *Washington Post*, June 18, 2015. https://www.washingtonpost.com/news/morning-mix/wp/2015/06/17/white-gunman-sought-in-shooting-at-historic-charleston-african-ame-church/.

Council of Biships. "A Narrative for the Continuing United Methodist Church." United Methodist Church. https://www.unitedmethodistbishops.org/files/websites/www/a+narrative+for+the+continuing+united+methodist+church...._.pdf.

Culpepper, R. Alan. "The Gospel of Luke." In *The New Interpreter's Bible Commentary*, 8:1–420. Nashville: Abingdon, 2015.

Cuninggim, Merrimon. *Perkins Led the Way: The Story of Desegregation at Southern Methodist University*. Dallas, 1994.

Dale, Becky, and Nassos Stylianou. "Climate Change: World Now Sees Twice as Many Days over 50C." *BBC News*, September 13, 2021. https://www.bbc.com/news/science-environment-58494641.

Dias, Elizabeth. "Christianity Will Have Power." *New York Times*, August 9, 2020. https://www.nytimes.com/2020/08/09/us/evangelicals-trump-christianity.html.

Dickerson, Dennis C. "Our History." https://www.ame-church.com/our-church/our-history/.

Dillard, Coshandra. "In Downtown Dallas, a Crowd of 5,000 Watched This Black Man Get Lynched—and They Took Souvenirs." *Timeline*, October 15, 2017. https://timeline.com/allen-brooks-dallas-lynching-4fc9132ee422.
The Doctrine and Discipline of the African Methodist Episcopal Church. Philadelphia: A.M.E. Book Concern, 1940.
Doctrines and Discipline of the Methodist Church 1939. New York: Methodist Publishing House, 1939.
The Doctrines and Discipline of the Methodist Episcopal Church, South. Nashville: Methodist Episcopal Church Publishing House, 1934.
Dundon, Rian. "Why Does the Ku Klux Klan Burn Crosses? They Got the Idea from a Movie." *Timeline*, March 16, 2017. https://timeline.com/why-does-the-ku-klux-klan-burn-crosses-they-got-the-idea-from-a-movie-75a70f7ab135.
Edwards, Laurie J. "The Mound Builders: Poverty Point, Adena, Hopewell, and Mississippian Cultures." In *UXL Encyclopedia of Native American Tribes*, 1:165–81. Detroit: UXL Gale, 2012.
Edwards, O. C., Jr. *A History of Preaching.* Nashville: Abingdon, 2004.
Edwards, Owen. "How Thomas Jefferson Created His Own Bible." *Smithsonian Magazine*, January 2012.
"A Festival of Nine Lessons and Carols." https://www.kings.cam.ac.uk/pdfviewer/44242.
Flipper, Joseph Simeon, et al. "Historical Preface." In *The Doctrine and Discipline of the African Methodist Episcopal Church*, 10–17. Philadelphia: A.M.E. Book Concern, 1940.
"Fosdick Codemns Temple Tramplers; Riverside Preacher Tells of Those Who Go to Church for Unworthy Motives." *New York Times*, November 23, 1953. https://www.nytimes.com/1953/11/23/archives/fosdick-condemns-temple-tramplers-riverside-preacher-tells-of-those.html.
Francis, Pope. *Fratelli Tutti.* https://www.vatican.va/content/francesco/en/encyclicals/documents/papa-francesco_20201003_enciclica-fratelli-tutti.html.
Garcia, Nic. "Dallas County Becomes One of the Largest Areas to Declare Racism a Public Health Crisis." *Dallas Morning News*, June 17, 2020. https://www.dallasnews.com/news/2020/06/17/racism-is-a-public-health-crisis-dallas-county-commissioners-declare/.
Gillispie, Valerie. "Let's Embrace Duke's Entire History." *Duke Magazine*, July 22, 2020. https://alumni.duke.edu/magazine/articles/lets-embrace-dukes-entire-history.
Goodwin, Doris Kearns. *Team of Rivals: The Political Genius of Abraham Lincoln.* New York: Simon & Schuster, 2005.
Graham, Ruth, and Elizabeth Dias. "With Southern Baptists in Revolt, a Split Looms." *New York Times*, June 13, 2021.
Grear, Peter. "Why Vote? ALEC and the Doctrine of Exclusion." *Greater Diversity News*, May 23, 2014. https://greaterdiversity.com/why-vote-alec-and-the-doctrine-of-exclusion/.
"A Great Day for the South." *St. Louis Globe Democrat*, June 8, 1891. https://web.archive.org/web/20210125113655/https://www.newspapers.com/image/571291151/?terms=%22Lost%2Bcause%22%2Bconfederacy.
Greve, Joan E., and Julian Borger. "Top US Military General Mark Milley Apologizes for Trump Church Photo-Op." *Guardian*, June 11, 2020. https://www.theguardian.com/us-news/2020/jun/11/top-us-military-general-mark-milley-issues-public-apology-trump-church-photo-op?.

Hahn, Heather. "Bishops Encouraged to Embrace 'More Loving Way.'" *UM News*, November 3, 2021. https://www.umnews.org/en/news/bishops-urged-to-embrace-more-loving-way.

Hall, David D., ed. *Puritans in the New World: A Critical Anthology*. Princeton: Princeton University Press, 2004.

Harlan, Chico, and Stefano Petrelli. "Pope Francis's New Encyclical Is a Papal Warning about a World Going Backward." *Washington Post*, October 4, 2020. https://www.washingtonpost.com/world/europe/pope-franciss-new-encyclical-is-a-papal-warning-about-a-world-going-backward/2020/10/04/c3f89b24-026c-11eb-b92e-029676f9ebec_story.html.

Harper, Douglas. "Slavery in New York." http://slavenorth.com/newyork.htm.

Heitzenrater, Richard P. *Wesley and the People Called Methodist*. Nashville: Abingdon, 1995.

"History of Lynching in America." https://naacp.org/find-resources/history-explained/history-lynching-america.

"In U.S., Decline of Christianity Continues at Rapid Pace." https://www.pewresearch.org/religion/2019/10/17/in-u-s-decline-of-christianity-continues-at-rapid-pace/.

Jenkins, Jack. "Black Church Leaders Demand Apology for Trump Ad." *Religion News Service*, September 13, 2020. https://religionnews.com/2020/09/13/ame-church-leaders-demand-apology-for-trump-ad/.

"John C. Calhoun's Speech to the United States Senate against the Compromise of 1850, 4 March 1850." https://www.loc.gov/item/mcc.009/.

Kennedy, Mark. "Documentary Recalls When Belafonte Sat in for Carson." *News & Observer*, September 13, 2020.

Keyes, Daniel. *Flowers for Algernon*. New York: Harcourt Brace, 1966.

Kimbrough, S. T. *Charles Wesley in America: Georgia, Charleston, Boston*. Eugene, OR: Wipf & Stock, 2021.

King, Martin Luther, Jr. "Letter from Birmingham Jail." In *Why We Can't Wait*, 85–110. Boston: Beacon, 2011.

Kirchner, Lauren. "Cross Burning Is More Common Than You Think." *Pacific Standard*, May 3, 2017. https://psmag.com/news/cross-burning-is-more-common-than-you-think-72781.

Kristof, Nicholas D., and Sheryl WuDunn. *Tightrope: Americans Reaching for Hope*. New York: Knopf, 2020.

Lakey, Othal Hawthorne. "History of the CME Church." https://thecmechurch.org/history/.

Lawrence, William B. "A Question of Doctrine: Whither the United Methodist Church?" *Methodist Review* 12 (2020) 1–59.

Lawson, James M., Jr. "Black Churchmen Seek Methodist Renewal." *Christian Advocate*, March 7, 1968.

Lemire, Jonathan. "Playing Electoral Defense, Trump Claims Biden Opposes God." *Associated Press*, August 6, 2020. https://apnews.com/article/virus-outbreak-election-2020-global-trade-ap-top-news-religion-a3c57cdcf8e44755d15930b29c660e36.

Leonard, Bill J. *A Sense of the Heart: Christian Religious Experience in the United States*. Nashville: Abingdon, 2014.

Bibliography

Levitin, Adam J. "The Boy Scouts Are Abusing the Bankruptcy System." *Bloomberg Law* (blog), November 16, 2021. https://news.bloomberglaw.com/business-and-practice/the-boy-scouts-are-abusing-the-bankruptcy-system.

Luther, Martin. "The Babylonian Captivity of the Church (1520)." In *Three Treatises*, 113–260. Philadelphia: Fortress, 1978.

Madewell, Mary. "Apology 100 Years in the Making Will Start Healing of Old Wounds." *Paris News*, July 31, 2020. https://theparisnews.com/opinion/article_e58b04aa-c394-11ea-b842-e74e1f3e160e.html.

Martin, Valerie. Introduction to *The Handmaid's Tale*, by Margaret Atwood, vii–xviii. New York: Knopf, 2006.

Martinez, Krystina, and Rick Holter. "Inside a Sickening Moment in Dallas History: A Public Hanging of a Black Man." *KERA News*, April 10, 2015. https://www.keranews.org/texas-news/2015-04-10/inside-a-sickening-moment-in-dallas-history-a-public-hanging-of-a-black-man.

"Maryland Toleration Act of 1649." https://www.mtsu.edu/first-amendment/article/868/maryland-toleration-act-of-1649.

Maser, Frederick E., and George A. Singleton. "The Union American Methodist Episcopal Church." In *The History of American Methodism*, edited by Emory Stevens Bucke, 1:615–17. New York: Abingdon, 1964.

McCaulley, Esau. *Reading while Black: African American Biblical Interpretation as an Exercise in Hope*. Downers Grove: InterVarsity, 2020.

McGrath, Alister E. *Luther's Theology of the Cross*. Oxford: Blackwell, 1985.

Moss, Arthur Bruce. "Methodism in Colonial America." In *The History of American Methodism*, edited by Emory Stevens Bucke, 1:74–144. New York: Abingdon, 1964.

Nicholas, William E. *Go and Be Reconciled: Alabama Methodists Confront Racial Injustice, 1954–1974*. Montgomery: New South, 2018.

"New Words List June 2017." https://public.oed.com/updates/new-words-list-june-2017/.

O'Day, Gail R. "The Gospel of John." In *The New Interpreter's Bible Commentary*, 8:421–742. Nashville: Abingdon, 2015.

Parker, Kim, and Ruth Igielnik. "On the Cusp of Adulthood and Facing an Uncertain Future: What We Know about Gen Z So Far." *Pew Research Center: Social and Demographic Trends*, May 14, 2020. https://www.pewresearch.org/social-trends/2020/05/14/on-the-cusp-of-adulthood-and-facing-an-uncertain-future-what-we-know-about-gen-z-so-far-2/.

Patterson, Jim. "Baseball Icon Jackie Robinson's Methodist Faith." https://www.umc.org/en/content/baseball-icon-jackie-robinsons-methodist-faith.

Payne, Darwin. *One Hundred Years on the Hilltop: The Centennial History of Southern Methodist University*. Dallas, 2016.

———. "When Dallas Was the Most Racist City in America." *D Magazine*, May 22, 2017. https://www.dmagazine.com/publications/d-magazine/2017/june/when-dallas-was-the-most-racist-city-in-america/.

Perkins, Pheme. "The Gospel of Mark." In *The New Interpreter's Bible Commentary*, 7:379–556. Nashville: Abingdon, 2015.

Pollard, Edward Alfred. *Southern History of the War*. 1866. Reprint, New York: Crown, 1977.

Powell, Michael. "Following Months of Criticism, Obama Quits His Church." *New York Times*, June 1, 2008. https://www.nytimes.com/2008/06/01/us/politics/01obama.html.

Powell, William A., Jr. "Methodist Circuit Riders in America, 1766–1844." MA thesis, University of Richmond, August 1977. https://scholarship.richmond.edu/cgi/viewcontent.cgi?article=1836&context=masters-theses.

Raasch, Chuck. "When Harry Met Billy." *St. Louis Post-Dispatch*, February 28, 2018. https://www.stltoday.com/news/local/govt-and-politics/when-harry-met-billy-the-beginning-of-the-rev-grahams-presidential-relationships/article_d35fd86b-4989-54b9-a0e3-fc407ff57d67.html.

Reese, Thomas. "Five Things to Look For in Pope Francis' New Encyclical, 'Fratelli Tutti.'" *National Catholic Reporter*, October 6, 2020. https://www.ncronline.org/news/theology/signs-times/five-things-look-pope-francis-new-encyclical-fratelli-tutti.

"The Religion and Morals of the Mound Builders." *Harvard Crimson*, February 25, 1876. https://www.thecrimson.com/article/1876/2/25/the-religion-and-morals-of-the/.

"Religion and the Founding of the American Republic." https://www.loc.gov/exhibits/religion/rel06.html.

"Response to Trump Campaign Ad Featuring Bethel AME Church in Wilmington, Delaware." https://religionnews.com/2020/09/14/response-to-trump-campaign-ad-featuring-bethel-ame-church-in-wilmington-delaware/.

Richey, Russell E., et al. *The Methodist Experience in America*. 2 vols. Nashville: Abingdon, 2000, 2010.

"Risk for COVID-19 Infection, Hospitalization, and Death by Race/Ethnicity." https://www.cdc.gov/coronavirus/2019-ncov/covid-data/investigations-discovery/hospitalization-death-by-race-ethnicity.html.

Robertson, Campbell. "History of Lynchings in the South Documents Nearly 4,000 Names." *New York Times*, February 10, 2015.

Sacks, Oliver. *Awakenings*. London: Duckworth, 1973.

Sampley, J. Paul. "The Second Letter to the Corinthians." In *The New Interpreter's Bible Commentary*, 9:867–1017. Nashville: Abingdon, 2015.

Seow, Choon-Leong. "The First and Second Books of Kings." In *The New Interpreter's Bible Commentary*, 2:629–798. Nashville: Abingdon, 2015.

Shakespeare, William. *Macbeth*. London: Dent, 1935.

Smith, Samuel. "White House Hosts 100 Evangelical Leaders for State-Like Dinner: 'This Is Spiritual Warfare.'" *Christian Post*, August 28, 2018. https://www.christianpost.com/news/white-house-hosts-100-evangelical-leaders-state-like-dinner-this-is-spiritual-warfare.html.

Smith-Christopher, Daniel L. "The Book of Daniel." In *The New Interpreter's Bible Commentary*, 6:713–816. Nashville: Abingdon, 2015.

"Statistical Information." https://worldmethodistcouncil.org/statistical-information/.

"Statistics on Slavery." https://faculty.weber.edu/kmackay/statistics_on_slavery.htm.

Sudborough, Susannah. "Mass. Senate Clears Final Victim's Name from Salem Witch Trials." *Boston Globe*, May 26, 2022. https://www.boston.com/news/history/2022/05/26/massachusetts-senate-clears-victims-name-salem-witch-trials-elizabeth-johnson-jr-diana-dizoglio/.

Tharoor, Ishaan. "The U.S. and British Right Ramp Up the War on 'Wokeness.'" *Washington Post*, April 9, 2021. https://www.washingtonpost.com/world/2021/04/09/woke-wars-united-states-britain/.

"Thirteen Colonies Population." https://worldpopulationreview.com/states/thirteen-colonies.

Thomas, Cal, and Ed Dobson. *Blinded by Might: Can the Religious Right Save America?* Grand Rapids: Zondervan, 1999.

"Thomas Jefferson and the Virginia Statute for Religious Freedom." https://virginiahistory.org/learn/thomas-jefferson-and-virginia-statute-religious-freedom.

Thompson, Eddie. "Optimism: Ben Franklin and the 200-Year Endowment." *The Fundraising Executive* (blog), September 30, 2012. https://ceplan.com/franklin_endowment.

Thompson, Patricia J. "The Invisible Made Visible: A Brief Overview of African American History in the New England Conference of the United Methodist Church." http://neumc-email.brtapp.com/files/imagelibrary/e+news+photos/2020+jan+-+july/july+29+2020/the+invisible+made+visible.pdf.

The United Methodist Book of Worship. Nashville: United Methodist Publishing House, 1992.

The United Methodist Hymnal. Nashville: United Methodist Publishing House, 1989.

Vestal, Christine. "Racism Is a Public Health Crisis, Say Cities and Counties." *Pew: Stateline*, June 15, 2020. https://www.pewtrusts.org/en/research-and-analysis/blogs/stateline/2020/06/15/racism-is-a-public-health-crisis-say-cities-and-counties.

Von Loewenich, Walther. *Luther's Theology of the Cross*. Minneapolis: Augsburg, 1976.

Wall, Robert W. "The Book of Acts." In *The New Interpreter's Bible Commentary*, 9:1–292. Nashville: Abingdon, 2015.

Wallis, Jim. *America's Original Sin: Racism, White Privilege, and the Bridge to a New America*. Ada, MI: Baker, 2015.

Walsh, Joan. "49 Years Ago, Harry Belafonte Hosted the Tonight Show—and It Was Amazing." *Nation*, February 16, 2017. https://web.archive.org/web/20200314094735/https://www.thenation.com/article/archive/49-years-ago-harry-belafonte-hosted-the-tonight-show-and-it-was-amazing/.

Weems, Lovett H., Jr. *Church Leadership: Vision, Team, Culture, and Integrity*. Nashville: Abingdon, 1993.

Wesley, John. "Scriptural Christianity." In *The Works of John Wesley*, 1:159–80. Nashville: Abingdon, 1984.

———. "Thoughts upon Slavery." In *The Works of John Wesley*, edited by Thomas Jackson, 9:65–73. London: Jackson, 1872.

———. *The Works of John Wesley Published as the Bicentennial Edition of the Works of John Wesley*. 32 vols. Nashville: Abingdon, 1984.

Whitfield, Stephen J. *The Culture of the Cold War*. Baltimore: Johns Hopkins University Press, 1996.

Winston, Kimberly. "The 'Gifts' of Pentecost and Shavuot." *Religion News Service*, May 16, 2018. https://religionnews.com/2018/05/16/splainer-gifts-pentecost-shavuot/.

Winthrop, John. "A Modell of Christian Charity." In *Collections of the Massachusetts Historical Society*, 7:31–48. 3rd series. Boston: Massachusetts Historical Society, 1838. https://archive.org/details/collectionsmasso3unkngoog.

Witt, Howard. "Evidence Frays in Murder Case." *Daily Press*, April 13, 2009. https://www.chicagotribune.com/nation-world/chi-paris_murder_wittapr13-story.html.

———. "Racial Tensions in a Texas Town." *Daily Press*, November 13, 2007. https://www.chicagotribune.com/nation-world/chi-paris-storygallery-storygallery.html.

———. "Racism Bedevils Texas Town." *Daily Press*, February 25, 2009. https://www.chicagotribune.com/nation-world/chi-paris_webfeb25-story.html.

———. "To Some in Paris, Sinister Past Is Back." *Chicago Tribune*, March 12, 2007. https://www.howardwitt.com/_files/ugd/da5cb7_cf64f78218e34e7884feef3638b90575.pdf.

Woodard, Colin. "Woodrow Wilson Was Even Worse Than You Think." *TPM*, June 29, 2020. https://talkingpointsmemo.com/cafe/woodrow-wilson-was-even-worse-than-you-think.

Wright, N. T. "The Letter to the Romans." In *The New Interpreter's Bible Commentary*, 9:317–664. Nashville: Abingdon, 2015.

Zakaria, Fareed. "The Pandemic Upended the Present. But It's Given Us a Chance to Remake the Future." *Washington Post*, October 6, 2020. https://www.washingtonpost.com/opinions/2020/10/06/fareed-zakaria-lessons-post-pandemic-world/.

Zucchino, David. *Wilmington's Lie: The Murderous Coup of 1898 and the Rise of White Supremacy*. New York: Atlantic, 2020.

Index

Abele, Julian, 130
Abraham, 128
Adams, John, 54
Ahlstrom, Sydney, 134n1
Pope Alexander VI, 29, 29n6
Algernon (mouse), 182
Allen, Joseph L., 91n15, 92nn17–19, 93nn20–21
Allen, Richard, 49, 51, 52, 53, 58, 59, 60, 62, 63, 172
Alpert, Jonathan L., 36n16
Amaziah, 129, 161
Ames, Jessie Daniel, 71, 71n39, 72
Amos, 21, 129, 161
Anderson, Cynthia Yeldell, 165n17
Anderson, Isaac H., 77n6
Andrew, James O., 67
Anselm, 102n43
Arthur, Herman, 152, 153, 154
Arthur, Irving, 152, 153, 154
Asbury, Francis, 40, 41, 42, 44, 45, 46, 46n17, 47, 48, 49, 49n31, 51, 56n51, 58, 59, 60, 61, 62, 106
Asmelash, Leah, 88n4
Atwood, Margaret, 2n3, 179, 179n10
Augustine, 4, 21, 102n43
Auld, Thomas, 66

Badu, Erykah, 7
Bailey, Sarah Pulliam, 15nn4–5, 16nn6–9, 20n21
Barry, John M., 33nn9–11, 35n15
Beaman, Silvester, 166
Beckham, Barry, 7

Belafonte, Harry, 139–40, 140n19
Bellah, Robert, 19n18
Bellware, Kim, 151n19
Berg, A. Scott, 78n9
Bethune, Mary McLeod, 85
Biden, Joseph R., 165
Blackmun, Harry, 18
Blight, David W., 22n29, 66nn20–21, 68n26
Block, Daniel, 20n24
Boardman, Richard, 41, 42, 44, 45
Boorstein, Michelle, 15nn4–5, 16nn6–9
Borger, Julian, 16n10
Boring, M. Eugene, 149, 149n17
Bradford, William, 26, 26n1
Branch, Taylor, 97n32
Branscomb, John, 98n32
Brodie, Phillip, 63
Brooks, Allen, 88, 89n10, 152
Brown, Oliver, 100
Brown, Peter, 21n28
Brown, William Hand, 36n17

Calhoun, John C., 24n34, 67
Calvert, Cecil, 31, 34
Calvin, John, 131
Carmichael, Stokely, 99
Carson, Johnny, 139
Carter, Jimmy, 18, 32
Chalmers, David, 90n14
Chappelle, Dave, 120
Charile (character in *Algernon*), 182
King Charles I, 29, 34

195

King Charles II, 34
Emperor Charles V, 30
Chikwendiu, Jahi, 20n21
Christ. *See* Jesus Christ
Clephane, Elizabeth C., 102n42
Coke, Thomas, 48–49, 49nn28–29, 49n31, 51, 56n51
Colavito, Jason, 28n4
Coleman-Singleton, Sharonda, 65n19
Columbus, Christopher, 29n6
Connor, T. Eugene ("Bull"), 96, 96n26, 97
Constantine, 21, 102n44
Cook, Samuel Dubois, 130
Cooke, Harold G., 89n11
Cooper, Jeffrey, 165n17
Craddock, Lois, 92
Cromwell, 34
Culpepper, R. Alan, 125n15
Cuninggim, Merrimon, 87n2, 91, 92, 93, 93n22
Cyrus, 20

da Vaca, Cabeza, 30
Dale, Becky, 13n1
Dancy, John C., 70, 70n36
Davenport, G. M. ("Mont"), 95
David, 110, 122, 122n8
Davis, Jefferson, 68n27, 69
De Niro, Robert, 180
Dias, Elizabeth, 8n23, 20n22
Dickerson, Dennis C., 52n38
Dillard, Coshandra, 89n10
Dixon, Thomas, 90
Dixon, Thomas, Jr., 102
Dobson, Ed, 19n20, 112n41
Doctor, Depayne Middleton, 65n19
Douglas, Stephen A., 7
Douglass, Frederick, 22, 66, 68, 69
Drummond, Alice, 180
Duke family, 129, 130
Dundon, Rian, 90n12
Durham, Mary. *See* Williams, Mollie

Earl (student), 94
Early, Jubal, 68n27
Edwards, Laurie J., 28n4
Edwards, O. C., Jr., 131n26

Edwards, Owen, 53n41
Eisenhower, Dwight, 18, 18n17, 130
Elliott, John W., 91, 93, 94
Embury, Philip, 41
Equiano, Olaudah, 46n20
Esther, 21
Eutychus, 5
Ezekiel, 117

Farmer, James, 99
Few, William Preston, 129, 130, 131
Flipper, Joseph Simeon, 52n39, 58n1, 59n2
Floyd, George, 14–15, 119, 119n3, 154, 165, 177
Fosdick, Harry Emerson, 134n1, 147
Pope Francis, 154, 154n26, 155, 155nn27–29
Franklin, Aretha, 140n19
Franklin, Benjamin, 145–46
Franklin, C. I., 140n19
Franklin, Marvin A., 98n32

Garber, Paul N., 98n32
Garcia, Nic, 152n21
Garrettson, Freeborn, 48
Garvey, Marcus, 7, 7n20
Gates, Henry Louis, 140
Gillispie, Valerie, 88n5, 129, 129n25
Goodwin, Doris Kearns, 7n19
Graham, Billy, 18, 19
Graham, Ruth, 8n23
Grear, Peter, 36n16
Greve, Joan E., 16n10
Griffith, D. W., 90, 102
Grotius, 102n43

Hahn, Heather, 104nn2–3
Hall, David D., 27n3
Haman, 21
Hamilton, Alexander, 54
Handel, 179
Hannah, 110, 110n22
Hardin, Paul, Jr., 3n7
Harlan, Chico, 154n26
Harmon, Nolan B., 3n7
Harper, Douglas, 37n19
Harrell, Costen J., 98n32

Index

Hosier, Harry (slave), 49
Harvey, Cynthia Fierro, 104nn2–3
Hawkins, James A., 91, 93, 94
Heck, Barbara, 41
Heck, Paul, 41
Heermann, Johann, 101n41
Heitzenrater, Richard P., 39n21, 39n23, 42n1, 43n9, 44n13, 46nn20–21, 131n27, 163n13, 164, 164n16, 173n2
King Henry VI, 160
Hodge, Bachman Gladstone, 96
Hodges, John, 152
Hodges, William, 152
Holsey, Lucius, 77
Holter, Rick, 88n8
Hoover, Herbert, 20n25
Hoover, Theressa, 136n6
Hosier, Harry, 46, 49
Huffington, Roy, 146n4
Hughes, Bob, 96, 97
Hurd, Cynthia, 65n19

Igielnik, Ruth, 135n3
Isaiah, 138, 179

Jackson, Susie, 65n19
Jairus, 125
Jefferson, Thomas, 53, 54
Jenkins, Jack, 165n18
King Jeroboam, 129, 161
Jesus Christ, 4, 5, 27, 84, 101, 106, 107, 108, 109, 110, 111, 113, 115, 116, 117, 120, 125, 127, 128, 131, 132, 138, 139, 141, 145, 146, 148, 149, 156, 157, 157n35, 158, 159, 160, 161, 163, 164, 167, 168, 169, 174
Pope John Paul II, 16
John the Baptist, 148, 179
Jones, Absalom, 52, 53
Joseph (husband of Mary), 5

Kavner, Julie, 180
Kelly, Leontine T. C., 83n22
Kennedy, John F., 18, 18n14, 114, 130
Kennedy, Mark, 140n19
Keyes, Daniel, 182, 182n1

Keysor, Charles W., 136n4
King, James, 63
King, John, 41
King, Martin Luther, Jr., 3, 4, 4nn10–14, 130, 140n19
Kirchner, Lauren, 90n12
Kristof, Nicholas D., 181m14

Lakey, Othal Hawthorne, 77nn4–5, 77n7
Lance, Ethel, 65n19
Lane, Isaac, 77
Lawrence, William B., 134n1
Lawson, James, 99, 99n35
Lazarus, 5
Lee, Robert E., 68n27
Lee, Umphrey, 91, 93
Leland, John, 54
Lemire, Jonathan, 20n23
Leonard (character in *Awakenings*), 180
Leonard, Bill J., 65n17
Levitin, Adam J., 176n7
Lincoln, Abraham, 7
Lucy (character in *Awakenings*), 180, 181
Luther, Martin, 1, 1n1, 30, 119, 131
Lyle, Ethel Hedgeman, 64n13
Lyles, James V., 91, 93, 94

Macbeth, 144
Madewell, Mary, 153n25
Madison, James, 54, 55
Malachi, 110, 179
Martin, 2n3
Martin, Paul E., 92, 93
Martinez, Krystina, 88n8
Mary (mother of Jesus), 5, 25
Maser, Frederick E., 60n6, 61n9
Mason, George, 54
Mason, James, 24n34
Mather, Cotton, 2
Mayfield, Earle Bradford, 90
McCaulley, Esau, 29n5, 179n11
McGrath, Alister E., 102n43
Miles, C. Austin, 157n39
Milley, General, 17n10
Milner-White, Eric, 159

Moore, Arthur J., 98n32
Moses, 109, 110, 128
Moss, Arthur Bruce, 46n18
Mouzon, Edwin, 89, 89n11

Nicholas, William E., 3n9, 96n25, 96nn27–29, 97nn30–31

Obama, Barack, 18
O'Day, Gail R., 117, 127nn18–19, 149, 149n14, 156n31
Oglethorpe, James, 38, 39, 40n24
O'Kelly, James, 60n4
Otterbein, Philip William, 39, 40, 50

Palmer, Phoebe, 2
Parker, Kim, 135n3
Parks, Rosa, 96, 100
Patterson, Jim, 100n37
Paul, 1, 4, 5, 23, 101, 148, 149, 158, 167–68
Payne, Darwin, 87n2, 88n7, 89n9
Pence, Mike, 165
Penn, William, 31, 34, 35
Perkins, Joe, 91, 92, 93
Perkins, Lois, 91, 92, 93
Perkins, Pheme, 141n26
Petrelli, Stefano, 154n26
Philip, 29
Pilate, 117
Pilmore, Joseph, 41, 42, 44, 45
Pinckney, Charles, 54
Pinckney, Clementa, 65n19
Plessy, Homer A., 69
Poitier, Sidney, 140n19
Pollard, Edward Alfred, 68, 68nn27–30, 69nn31–32
Powell, Michael, 18n15
Powell, William A., Jr., 44n10
Proctor, Samuel DeWitt, 130, 131
Purcell, Clare, 98n32

Quinn, William Paul, 63–64, 64n13

Raasch, Chuck, 18n16
Reese, Thomas, 154n26
Richey, Russell E., 2n6, 42n1, 42n6
Rickey, Branch, 100

Riley, Negail R., 91, 93, 94
Robertson, Cliff, 182
Robinson, Jackie, 100
Rolph, James, 71n39
Roof, Dylann, 65n19
Ruckle, Paul, 41
Rush, Christopher, 62n10
Rutland, John, 96, 97

Sacks, Oliver, 180, 180n13
Salama, Vivian, 14n2
Sampley, J. Paul, 168, 168n22
Sanders, Tywanza, 65n19
Sarah, 110
Scott, Derrick, III, 103n1
Scott, Orange, 65, 67, 67n23
Selecman, Charles C., 89, 90
Shakespeare, 144n1
Short, Roy H., 98n32
Shuttlesworth, Fred, 96
Simmons, Daniel, 65n19
Singleton, George A., 60n6, 61n9
Smith, A. Frank, 92
Smith, Al, 20n25
Smith, Henry, 152
Smith, Samuel, 19n20
Smith-Christopher, Daniel L., 157n33
Solomon, 122, 122n8, 124
Spencer, Peter, 60
Spencer, Rob, 153
Spong, John Shelby, 147
Steimle, Edmund, 137
Stephen, 157
Storey, Peter, 22
Strawbridge, Elizabeth, 40, 41
Strawbridge, Robert, 40, 41, 42
Stylianou, Nassos, 13n1
Sudborough, Susannah, 2n4
Sunderland, La Roy, 65, 67

Taylor, Prince Albert, 98
Tharoor, Ishaan, 7n22
Thomas, 113
Thomas, Cal, 19n20, 112n41
Thomas, James S., 98
Thompson, Eddie, 146n4
Thompson, Myra, 65n19
Thompson, Patricia J., 78n8

Thompson, Sally, 2
Titus, 143
Tomochichi (chief of the Creeks), 39, 39n21
Truman, Harry, 18, 19
Trump, Donald J., 20, 165
Tutu, Desmond, 22

Varick, James, 62–63
Vasey, Thomas, 48
Vesey, Denmark, 65, 66
Vestal, Christine, 151n19
von Loewenich, Walther, 102n43

Wall, Robert W., 163, 163n12
Wallace, George Corley, 97
Walsh, Joan, 139n18
Walters, Melinda, 153
Walton-Roberts, Janese, 154
Warwick, Dionne, 140n19
Washington, George, 54
Watkins, William T., 98n32
Watts, Isaac, 101n41
Webb, Thomas, 41, 42
Webster, Mary, 2, 2n3
Weems, Lovett H., Jr., 104, 104n5
Wesley, Charles, 38, 39n21, 40n24, 101n41, 160n7
Wesley, John, 2, 2n5, 22–23, 22nn30–31, 23n33, 38, 39, 40, 40n24, 42, 42n6, 43, 43n8, 45, 46–47, 47n22, 48, 49, 56, 59, 91, 106, 119, 121n5, 131, 161, 163n14, 164, 171, 173n2
Whatcoat, Richard, 48, 51
Whitfield, Stephen J., 18n17
Wilde, Oscar, 181
Willard, Frances, 2
Williams, A. Cecil, 91, 93
Williams, Cecil, 91n16, 92, 94
Williams, Mollie, 61, 61n8
Williams, Peter, 61, 62
Williams, Robert, 41
Williams, Robin, 180
Williams, Roger, 33–34, 35
Wilson, Woodrow, 78
Winston, Kimberly, 138n12
Winthrop, John, 27, 27n3, 32, 33
Witt, Howard, 152n22, 153nn23–24
Woodard, Colin, 78n9
Wright, N. T., 6, 6n18
Wright, Richard, 42
WuDunn, Sheryl, 181m14

Zakaria, Fareed, 166, 166n20
Zucchino, David, 69n34, 70nn35–36

www.ingramcontent.com/pod-product-compliance
Lightning Source LLC
Chambersburg PA
CBHW021728220426
43662CB00008B/756